22113515

TEACHING TECHNOLOGIES IN LIBRARIES
A Practical Guide

TEACHING TECHNOLOGIES IN LIBRARIES
A Practical Guide

Linda Brew MacDonald
Mara R. Saule
Margaret W. Gordon
Craig A. Robertson

G.K. Hall & Co.   Boston, Massachusetts

First published 1990
by G.K. Hall & Co.
70 Lincoln Street
Boston, Massachusetts 02111

10 9 8 7 6 5 4 3 2 1

Library of Congress Cataloging-in-Publication Data

Teaching technologies in libraries: a practical guide \ Linda Brew
    MacDonald . . . [et al.].
        p. cm.
    Includes index.
    ISBN 0-8161-1906-6 (hc). – ISBN 0-8161-1907-4 (pbk).
    1. Library orientation – Technological innovations.
    2. Information technology – Study and teaching.
    3. Data base searching – Study and teaching.
    I. MacDonald, Linda Brew.
    Z711.2.T44   1990
    025.5'6 – dc20   90-43579
                                                                        CIP

The paper used in this publication meets the minimum requirements of
American National Standard for Information Sciences – Permanence of Paper
for Printed Library Materials. ANSI Z39.48-1984. ∞™
MANUFACTURED IN THE UNITED STATES OF AMERICA

To Nancy B. Crane, Head of Reference,
Bailey/Howe Library, University of Vermont
from MG, LM, CR, and MS

Contents

Introduction

Linda Brew MacDonald
Mara R. Saule
Margaret W. Gordon
Craig A. Robertson

In 1980 reference and instruction librarians taught patrons how to use the library and find information by using well-worn, familiar printed reference sources. After all, the library *was* largely printed sources: books, journals, and pamphlets, with an occasional film or audio tape. Computerized information sources were used by the newly established online services librarian for special patrons with special questions. Of course, there were rumblings, particularly in special libraries, that patrons could do their own searching of computerized databases without librarian intermediaries; however, this "end-user searching" seemed most appropriate for business people with unlimited budgets looking for stock market information.

Our instructional approach in 1980 was straightforward: we loaded our book trucks with representative bibliographies, indexes, and abstracts, listed those sources on pathfinders, and taught our patrons to use reference materials in one-hour stand-up sessions or one-to-one at the reference desk. Instructional technology was limited to an overhead projector and, in some cases, a slide carousel, videotape, or audiotape.

As we enter the 1990s, the situation has changed dramatically. End-user searching of remote online and local CD-ROM databases has become commonplace. According to the 1989 Cuadra Associates *Directory of Online Databases*, the number of databases, both online and CD-ROM, has grown from 400 in 1979 to over 4,000 in 1989. Most of these databases are being marketed directly to the end user rather than to the librarian or special database searcher. In fact, the term *end-user searching* is becoming redundant. Like printed literature searching, computerized literature searching is done by both librarians and patrons on the same databases and systems. Many patrons don't even need to come to the library to find information. They can search the library's local online catalog, remote online databases, and even networked CD-ROM databases from their home or office microcomputers.

Where does all this new information technology leave the instruction librarian? Our trusty overhead projector alone won't do to teach dynamic, interactive computerized database searching, especially to users who may not physically come into the library at all. Furthermore, the information sources themselves are no longer constructed by predictable, linear patterns: for the 4,000 computerized databases currently available, there are over 600 different searching modes and user interfaces. And lastly, electronic media has not yet supplanted other publication media; users must be more informed about the range of information sources available to them, and be able to choose the most appropriate source for a particular information need.

Clearly, our approaches and techniques for user instruction must change in the face of new access to information. We must rethink what we teach and how we teach it, focusing on the best way to achieve "information literacy" in our patrons. One way we can do this is to call upon the very technologies that we teach to be used as teaching media.

USING TECHNOLOGY TO TEACH TECHNOLOGY

Teaching Technologies in Libraries, then, is about using technology to teach technology. Faced with the same confluence of information technologies that confronts librarians everywhere today, we have had to design and implement various instruction programs in order to deal effectively with the challenges of teaching many and diverse library users about electronic information sources. In other words, we have had firsthand experience with the computerized technologies discussed in the following chapters.

This book is designed for librarians who, like us, must use alternative methods of instruction to deal with the task of teaching complex skills and concepts to many learners. It is intended as a basic guide, offering general and practical information rather than comprehensive technical discussions. The kinds of technologies covered by *Teaching Technologies in Libraries* include those that would be commonly available to most librarians in an automated setting: help screens, online tutorial services, compact discs, slide shows and videotapes, computer-assisted instruction (CAI), and expert systems. More esoteric or embryonic technologies, such as true artificial intelligence and interactive video, are briefly reviewed but not discussed in detail.

Following an introductory overview of the current issues and theories concerning teaching about technology in libraries, we provide guidelines for selecting media for library instruction. Six chapters follow, each focused on one of the media we have used. We begin with the technologies that come to the library as finished products, over which we have the least creative influence: the help screens, optical discs, and online tutorial services. Next, we discuss the media that we not only can use in instruction but can also produce ourselves: video, CAI, and expert systems. We asked five librarians to contribute brief essays on the special characteristics of their users in relation to teaching and learning library technologies; chapter 9 is a lively combination of the observations of public, school, academic, medical, and business librarians on this topic. Finally, in chapter 10, we offer a glimpse of future technologies.

Teaching Technologies in Libraries is the result of our experiences and research. It is intended to answer some of the questions that librarians have asked following talks and presentations we have given: "How do you keep up with the demand for instruction on CD-ROM products?" "How did you write your CAI?" "Do you have to be a computer programmer to understand an expert system?" As a result, we have stated opinions, evaluated programs, and given advice. We hope that by using *Teaching Technologies in Libraries* as a guide, other libraries will be able to implement successful instructional programs for, and with, technology.

1

Teaching for Library Technologies

Mara R. Saule

Picture a patron entering a computer-rich library to look for information, to look for an answer to a question. First, she is met by a bank of 16 or so online catalog terminals located near the familiar, but no longer updated, card catalog. In addition to reflecting the library's own holdings, the online catalog provides access to indexing and abstracting databases, such as MEDLINE and ERIC, and serves as a gateway to other libraries' online catalogs. Near the bank of online catalog terminals the patron is faced with 20 more computers, each offering a different CD-ROM database. Close by, two microcomputers advertise access to over 100 online databases through BRS/After Dark and Knowledge Index. A sign above the reference desk points to the microcomputer lab, where a patron can use computers to do word processing but cannot search for bibliographic information. Finally, beyond the green haze of CRTs, she sees rows and rows of printed bibliographies, indexes, and abstracts. Not unlike Alice in Wonderland trying to get home, this patron needs help. She needs to be shown how to maneuver through the maze of information sources in order to find the best answer to her question.

Of course, reference and instruction librarians have always taught patrons how to find answers to questions; in today's increasingly computerized libraries, however, teaching patrons how to use information technologies becomes a new and different challenge. Even though we often view new technologies simply as electronic tools for information retrieval, computerized information sources are not just more tools in the range of reference sources available. In fact, David King and Betsy Baker point to the dangers of viewing technology in purely technical terms: "The consequences of this perspective on information technology are evident in all corners of library practice and thought: it fosters the notion that information, like data bits, is comprised of discrete units with the characteristics of physical commodities; it fosters the notion that information seeking, like electronic processing, is a set of procedures which can be formalized, followed, and taught as step-by-step sequences; it fosters the notion that tools, especially electronic ones, solve information problems and satisfy information needs. Some library users share these notions" (King and Baker, 85). Computerized information sources differ significantly from printed reference tools in their structure and use; viewing these differences as cosmetic rather than substantive results in a dangerously narrow view of the way in which we use and teach powerful information technologies.

Not only do automated information retrieval systems work differently than printed sources, but patrons and librarians react to computers and computerized information differently than they do to printed materials. Placing an InfoTrac microcomputer in a library's reference area elicits quite different reactions than the addition of another printed title: people are both attracted to the computer and confused by it. They may be afraid to touch it, or they may fearlessly start pounding on the keys and pushing the buttons. As more and more computers and computerized information systems are added to the library's collection, this confusion will grow.

The systems and the way that people search the systems demand a new approach to library instruction.

COMPUTERS AND NOT COMPUTERS

The major differences between computerized reference sources and the traditional printed ones are fairly obvious. Searching for information via microcomputer offers faster retrieval of a greater range of materials using more dynamic and varied search modes. The searcher can go "deeper" into the bibliographic record to find what she needs, free from the constraints of linear, controlled vocabulary searching in printed indexes and abstracts. She can combine terms, limit which fields she chooses to search, search a range of years at once. Not the least of the advantages to computerized literature searching is the ability to print off results once a search has been completed: patrons can work effectively in the library without paper and pencil.

We know the benefits of computerized information retrieval. We also know that there are problems with computerized databases, problems that didn't concern us when there were only printed sources for answering reference questions. Of course, one of the most persistent and time-consuming problems with microcomputers is hardware support and compatibility; librarians have added screwdrivers and cans of antistatic spray to their repertoire of reference support tools. Hardware maintenance, however, usually concerns librarians rather than users. For the user, computerized information sources present the more significant problems: Which computer or database will answer which question? And, once a database is identified, what search strategies and procedures will retrieve the needed information? Furthermore, if the computer does not answer the patron's question, where else can she go to find answers?

While computers may look alike, they offer different answers for different questions. It is difficult for patrons to discern easily what any given computer will do for them when all computers look the same. At the University of Vermont, we may point patrons to four different computers to answer one question: to WILSONDISC for a preliminary list of references; then to BRS/After Dark or Knowledge Index for updated or retrospective information; to LUIS, the online catalog, to determine which items the university owns; and finally, if we do not own what the patron needs, to the public access OCLC station to find out which library does own the item. Each computer, however, presents the same beige box with the same dark, featureless screen. Understandably, our patron may be confused about which computer will satisfy her information need.

Unlike computer terminals, printed reference sources each tell a different story just by the look of their covers. Printed reference sources, like the card catalog, give the patron more visual clues to the size and nature of the database contained within their covers than the computer screen. The patron can see the number of volumes, read the years covered by each volume on the spine, open the printed index and understand the structure of the entries. Patrons can also see that one index is separate from another, that index titles imply different subject coverage. The flat computer screen does nothing to help orient a patron to the structure and workings of the database it searches. Of course, the nature and content of printed indexes are not always self-evident and can confuse searchers as well, but at least their appearance and structure fit into a familiar "book and page" context. The benefit of having a single computerized database – including thesaurus and indexing terms, journal list, citations, abstracts, and occasionally full text of articles – is negated if the searcher cannot orient herself to the scope and structure of the database itself.

In a 1989 *American Libraries* article, Anne Lipow discusses the confusion in spatial and content orientation that the computer engenders and addresses other differences between online and card catalogs as well. Although the focus of her article is online catalogs, many of her points can also be applied to the comparison of other computerized information systems to their print counterparts.

Not only do online catalogs and other computer-based systems offer no sense of the size or nature of the database being searched, but the screen-by-screen display makes it difficult to understand how the database is constructed or to know how to revise a search when the result is disappointing. "By contrast, the card catalog user can understand the organization of the entire database by opening and examining one drawer" (Lipow, 864). Similarly, printed indexes and abstracts can be flipped through, scanned, dog-eared, and marked up, all of which help the user form a clear mental model of how the index works; in fact, this understanding can be directly generalized to all indexes. Because most computerized information retrieval systems have unique search software and user interfaces, it is more difficult to generalize what is learned from one system to another.

The system user, and often the librarian, may not be able to understand why and how the computer is doing what it is doing. Because the computer is doing the searching for us, we have no sense of the steps involved in that search. If a search produces no results, it is difficult for the searcher to know if there are, in fact, no corresponding sources for her inquiry, or if the search strategy was at fault, or even if the system itself is flawed. While sophisticated system error messages and help screens may alleviate some of this disorientation, the physical computer provides no indication of how the data is put together. The opaque nature of the search system makes indexing errors in an online catalog, or any online system, also difficult to detect and even more difficult to correct.

Lipow discusses yet another difference between printed and computerized sources: choice of record display in online catalogs may cause problems and confusion for the searcher. Because searchers often can specify which fields to display and print, or which preformatted record displays to choose (e.g., short, medium, or long formats), they may miss information that might be important if they miss a display option. Specifying display options often requires an understanding of the structure of the bibliographic record–in some cases the full Machine-Readable Cataloging (MARC) record–as well as an understanding of what the terms "field" and "record" mean and imply. Furthermore, the searcher must know how to name elements in the bibliographic record in order to retrieve the best answers. She must understand what is really meant by a subject in terms of Library of Congress Subject Headings (LCSH) or *Medical Subject Headings (MeSH)*, author, corporate author, etc. Forms of entry can be confusing for the seasoned librarian, much less for the novice library user.

Printed sources, on the other hand, immediately reveal their record structure to a user when she scans a page of entries. Of course some printed indexes, such as citation indexes, are not fully transparent in structure; nonetheless, for the naive user, the printed version still can often be easier to search than the computerized version. A feeling for the controlled indexing vocabulary used by a printed index can also be discerned by scanning the subject headings and entries.

Finally, the searcher needs to know how to type, and to type accurately, in order to search an automated information retrieval system successfully. Not only will a patron's search be slowed if she doesn't know how to type, but computerized information sources are also unforgiving of spelling and typographical errors; a "close" spelling simply will not work. Because error messages in automated systems generally do not specify the cause of the error, the user may not realize that the reason the system replied "no entries found" to her search request was a simple typing error.

The differences between print sources and computerized information sources highlight the need for approaching these with a different instructional manner. When end-user searching first became available, many reference librarians felt that widespread use of automated systems would mean less need for bibliographic instruction. The opposite has proved true: "nearly every automated reference tool differs from every other, standardization of format and search\ languages is almost nonexistent, and the nature of automated access entails a merciless propensity to yield no search results, regardless of the brilliance of the search strategy, if there is the slightest spelling or logical error" (Miller and Gratch, 397). Electronic information systems, then, have demanded new approaches to instruction. Approaches that we employed to teach printed reference sources cannot always be applied successfully to teaching automated sources. Automated and printed sources are too fundamentally different.

Just as the content, structure, and presentation of the sources differ, user reactions to printed and electronic sources differ as well.

PEOPLE AND COMPUTERS

Our hypothetical patron may react to the high-tech library in several ways. Depending on her age, her educational background, her previous experience with computers and other automated systems, and her emotional state at the time of entering the library, she may view the computers she encounters as simple mechanical tools, as mysterious answer machines, or as fearsome monsters to be avoided at all costs. Studies indicate that simply because she's a woman she may have more difficulty with, and be less receptive to, technology; if she is a student majoring in one of the humanities disciplines, the likelihood that she will not embrace computer technology is compounded (Sullivan, Borgman, and Wippern, 39).

Tom Bosser has outlined several different principles of classification that can be used for grouping users in order to predict their reactions to new computer systems. Some of the principles deal with the user's education and training. First of all, the more educated the user, and the greater her general knowledge, including knowledge of mathematics and foreign languages, the more likely she is to succeed in computer use. Also, she is more likely to react positively to a particular computer system if she has had previous training in computer use, and if she has some understanding of the way in which the individual system she will search operates. Clearly, the more familiar the user is with any one system, and the greater the number of different systems that the user has searched, the more likely it is that the searcher will not hesitate to learn a new system.

Another set of Bosser's principles deals with the particular task for which the searcher is using the computerized system. If the user has a clear understanding of the purpose for which the computer is being used, she will be able to focus on searching concepts and protocols more effectively. If she is under great time pressure to complete the search, however, she will be more anxious about learning and understanding the system and, consequently, less efficient in her search. Both the understanding of the purpose of the search and the time pressure to complete the task affect the searcher's motivation to learn the system. Other factors, such as rewards for learning the system and completing the task (for example, grades or performance evaluations), also affect the searcher's motivation for learning. Finally, the user's anticipated application of the searching skills to future tasks and projects will influence how she reacts to a new computer system (Bosser, 107).

David King and Betsy Baker also discuss the significance of the amount of time and effort that a user is willing to spend on learning a new system. Although librarians expect users to commit enough time to learn the system in order to become proficient in searching, users often expect to spend only a limited amount of time learning the system in order to answer a particular searching question. Both these expectations may be unrealistic. "In fact, many library users, perhaps most of them, hold different values than librarians and have their own purposes for using the library" (King and Baker, 92). When librarians teach users, they must balance their own high expectations with the users' immediate needs and understand that the amount of time any given user is willing to spend learning a system will vary from user to user.

On the whole, the way in which a user reacts to an individual computer system may depend on how the user views computers generally. King and Baker cite Sherry Turkle's *The Second Self* in categorizing types of human-computer relationships. Turkle identifies two ways in which users view computers. One type of user sees the computer as a tool to be mastered and controlled; the computer is simply a machine to be manipulated for the user's purposes. King and Baker observe that librarians and users familiar with automated library systems fall into this group (King and Baker, 87). Another kind of user, usually an inexperienced user or one who has had unsatisfactory initial experiences with automated systems, anthropomorphizes the computer, ascribing human characteristics to the machine. This user relinquishes control of the interaction to the computer, not understanding the computer's responses. King and Baker speculate on the effects these attitudes may have on the search:

> The psychological relationship between human and machine influences how choices about technology are made and how effectively the technology is used. Some of those who anthropomorphize the system, or who feel the interaction involves loss of control over the search process, may have a negative response or may find their interaction unproductive. Some of those who envision the system as simply a tool to be controlled, who find the pseudohuman dialogue and repetitious menus of the system cumbersome or annoying, may respond with impatience or exaggerate the limitations of the technology. For many, the result may be a rejection of the new technology out of hand or perhaps in preference for more familiar tools like the card catalog and printed indexes. (King and Baker, 88).

In other words, a user's basic attitudes toward computers can affect whether she will use a computer for her information searching at all.

Turkle's two categories of users, those who view the computer as simply another machine and those who endow the computer with mysterious or human characteristics, represent two extremes of computer-users' attitudes. In teaching computerized systems, the instruction librarian must instill confidence about a patron's searching capabilities and must dispel some of the fears that a user might have about computers and computerized information.

AGE MAKES A DIFFERENCE

When considering how different types of users might react to a computerized information retrieval system, we must also consider the age and developmental level of the searcher. Theories of adult learning, called "andragogical theories" or "andragogy," emphasize the importance of considering the unique needs of adult learners: "In light of the U.S. adult population's increasing size and leisure time, the importance of understanding this population's learning processes takes on special significance for librarians, instruction librarians in particular" (Frick, 71). Adult learners, those over the age of 25, are dominant in public and special library settings, and are becoming an increasing factor in academic libraries. *Literature discussing the characteristics of adult learners, like the number of adult learners themselves, is growing.

In terms of teaching adults to use computerized systems, Stephen Bostock and Roger Seifert outline some salient points: "There are four main features of this kind of adult education which distinguish it from education at school and college, and also from other types of adult learning and adult training. These are its voluntary nature; the equality of the tutor and of the students; the absence of narrow utilitarian motives in terms of careers, training and certification; and the variety of students' age, experience, motivation and ability" (Bostock and Seifert, 19). The truly voluntary nature of adult education affects how enthusiastically adult students may embrace learning computer technology; on the other hand, the variety in background and ability may temper this enthusiasm.

Bostock and Seifert outline the best approaches for teaching adult learners: "We believe that the general lessons to be learnt from experience so far are, firstly, that adult educators are the best people to teach adults about computers, rather than computer scientists, company trainers, or software manufacturers. Secondly, teaching should be done in a classroom (away from the workplace) with tutor and enough computers for significant hands-on time for students. Thirdly, the curriculum must be developed by negotiation with the students, and possibly with their organisation, but it should include elements of principles of hardware and software structure and operation, relevant applications software, and wider social and work implications". (Bostock and Seifert, 149). Given the distinct needs of adult learners, librarians should make special consideration of these needs and characteristics when designing instructional programs. Independent, yet thoughtful and sensitive, adult learners can be both a challenge and a joy to instruction librarians.

THE MANY FACES OF COMPUTER USERS

Of course, as librarians, we don't need to be trained in psychology in order to understand how users–young or old–tend to react to computers in our libraries. We can see users run up to an online catalog terminal, type in a periodical article subject search, and leave frustrated despite our attempts to redirect the search to another database. We can see searchers haphazardly pounding on the computer keyboard if the search takes a little longer than usual, or if the printer doesn't work. We can also see groups of searchers teaching and supporting each other, coming to the reference desk elated with the ease and success of their searches.

At the 1988 Association of College and Research Libraries' Bibliographic Instruction Section annual program in New Orleans, Randall Hensley clearly outlined some of the behavior types that we see in users as they interact with computerized reference systems.

Popularity/Euphoria

Most users absolutely adore being able to search for information via a microcomputer rather than paging through issue after issue of a printed index. They will stand in line to use the WILSONDISC version of *Readers' Guide to Periodical Literature* instead of looking through the familiar green printed volumes. Much of this euphoria, of course, is a result of the convenience of being able to print citations; however, once users realize that they are searching a range of years and can combine different search concepts, these features become appealing as well. Increasingly, patrons have come to expect computerized versions of printed sources to be available and, in some cases, are frustrated when they are told that no automated counterpart for an important source exists.

Impatience

Although users may prefer searching the computerized version of an information source, they are also impatient when it doesn't work as quickly or as efficiently as they expect. "Users become addicted to fast response time; become impatient with slow response time, break-downs, extended explanations or the need for too elaborate commands, too extensive printed commands, or the need for a return to traditional sources such as printed versions of the CD-ROM product" (Hensley). Impatient searchers may start randomly pounding on the keyboard, or may turn the computer on and off repeatedly. Furthermore, because computer searchers are used to fast response on the computer, they may become irritated at the librarian who cannot drop everything to correct the problem or they may give up on the computer search entirely.

Cooperation

Computer users much prefer asking other users for help rather than asking a librarian. This is true of printed source use as well as for computerized information searching. As Hensley pointed out, "camaraderie is rampant in computer areas." Unfortunately, this reliance on other searchers over librarians may result in the perpetuation of misinformation or inefficient searching procedures.

Oracle Transformation

As observed earlier, all computers look the same; because of this, searchers often come to feel that any one computer should have all of the answers. In systems that offer databases having distinct, subject-related names, such as Agricola or PsycLit, patrons may eventually come to understand that not all computers, or all databases, offer the same information. In broad-based systems such as InfoTrac, however, the patron may believe that the computer offers all information on all topics just because it has some information on many topics. In this case, librarians' efforts to redirect a searcher to more appropriate printed or computerized sources may be frustrated.

Memory Loss of Traditional Knowledge

Not only do patrons view "one computer as all computers," but they forget searching skills they have learned from using printed indexes and abstracts that could be applied to computerized sources as well (for example, controlled vocabularies, citation formats, the hierarchical structure of terms, and so on). As Hensley observed, when patrons begin searching computerized databases, they lose previous knowledge about printed sources at "an astonishing and thorough rate."

Pigeon/Stimulus-Response

While librarians may understand the need for users of computerized information sources to have a conceptual understanding of the structure of information and of the nature of database content, searchers only want to know which buttons to push in order to get an answer. When a searcher presses a computer key, something happens; she usually gets an immediate payoff. Even though the answer she gets may not be complete, or just right for her question, she is happy. The value of understanding the structure and scope of the database is lost.

The Computer Knows

Finally, the interactivity of the computer along with the immediacy of the responses may lead the searcher to believe that the computer "knows" more than any other kind of reference source, including the reference librarian himself. It is not only Turkle's anthropomorphizing computer user who may be deceived by the implied power of the technology. Computerized information sources give the impression that they can "think," that they can "intelligently" interpret and answer questions.

Many users, of course, do not initially embrace computerized reference sources. Some patrons gingerly sidestep the WILSONDISC or InfoTrac stations, fearful that a librarian or other library user will direct them to the computers. In most cases, however, once these patrons experience firsthand the advantages of computerized literature searching, they are pleased and excited about its potential to make their research easier. In fact, Christine Borgman observes that sometimes the patrons most resistant to new information technologies, particularly those in the humanities, become the greatest advocates of computer use once they have overcome their hesitations (Borgman, 32).

IMPLICATIONS FOR INSTRUCTION

What can we learn from these stereotypes of users and user behaviors? First of all, because most patrons are attracted by new information technologies we can use this appeal to refresh relationships with patrons: library technology is a good public relations tool. And, if a patron feels positively about the library and its research tools, she is more likely to be open to learning from a librarian.

We can also use searchers' inclinations to learn from each other to help teach searching procedures and concepts. We can encourage students to learn in groups, particularly in pairs. David Towbridge discovered that students working in pairs at the computer were more engaged in the search process, displayed more interactivity with the computer program, and made 30 percent fewer incorrect responses to program questions than individuals or even than students working in triads (Towbridge, 50).

Most searcher behaviors at the computer, however, do not have positive implications for formal instruction. Searchers who are impatient, who view the computer as all-knowing but only want to learn which keys should be pushed in order to get an immediate answer to a question, and who question the librarian's authority over the computer, will not be eager to attend formal training sessions, fill out lengthy searching workbooks, or even listen to extended one-on-one explanations. It is a library cliché based on extensive experience that no one reads printed instructions, so that the value of charts and other signs is also questionable. Nonetheless, most users of computerized information systems will need some sort of guidance in system use.

Learning styles between searchers also can vary, so that not all teaching approaches will work for all students, at all developmental or cognitive levels. As we have seen, adults may demand different instructional methods from younger learners, and among themselves adults may reflect different learning styles as well. Sonia Bodi defines the various components of different learning styles: "*Learning styles* is a broad term that includes the cognitive, affective, and physiological. Our cognitive style is how we perceive and process information. Our affective style is how we feel about and value learning experiences. Our physiological style involves the environment for effective learning, as well as the time of day we learn best, the lighting and noise level we require, and the position our bodies need to be in to facilitate learning. The characteristics of style reflect genetic coding, personality development, motivation, and environmental adaptation" (Bodi, 114-15).

Good teaching takes into account diversity in learning styles and adjusts instructional goals and methodologies in view of individual student differences. The instructional approaches outlined in this book need to be considered at all times in terms of the characteristics of the particular population and individuals to be taught.

COSTS OF TEACHING TECHNOLOGY

While we may recognize the need for teaching users how a particular information technology works, there are compelling reasons not to do much special training for library technologies. First of all, time on some systems is not a cost factor. While BRS and DIALOG end-user online systems still charge per minute of searching time or per citation viewed or printed off, CD-ROM and other optical systems are made available through annual subscription. Unlike BRS/After Dark and Knowledge Index, the more often CD-ROM systems are searched, the more cost-effective they become. In some respects, then, the speed and efficiency of the search doesn't matter; searchers can spend as much time as they need learning and "playing with" the system without concern for time or citation charges.

Secondly, computer searchers are often smarter than we think and, in fact, are getting progressively computer literate. We may feel that users should attend workshops, complete tutorials, or fill out searching workbooks, but system users will pick up most of the simple searching techniques they need on their own or from peer interactions. While these spontaneous methods of learning may not teach users the fine points of searching, searchers will in most cases discover what they need in order to do a successful basic search.

Systems are also becoming increasingly easy to use, and system vendors are recognizing the need for more accurate, thorough, and clear printed and online system documentation. System designers are responding to the call by librarians and other computer and information professionals to design search software that addresses the needs of a variety of searchers, from the novice to the expert. Future applications of artificial intelligence, expert systems, and hypertext portend even smoother user-computer interactions. The user interface is becoming more "friendly."

Because users are becoming more comfortable with computers in general, and because the search software in most systems is becoming easier to use, searchers often resist formal instruction. They generally want as little instruction as possible in order to get an answer to their research questions. Unless instruction is required in order to search a system, users are not inclined to attend workshops or other training sessions.

The final and most compelling reasons for not training patrons in the use of information technologies are the various cost components involved in training. Library staff time in designing and executing instructional materials and sessions, as well as ongoing administrative costs, can make special training programs for computerized information systems too costly. Total costs for training can include fees for a training course, such as for videos bought from the database producer; cost of librarian time during planning and actual training; cost of locally developed training materials; and cost of evaluation and review. Variables such as the life cycle of the search system being taught, the turnover rate of new searchers in the library, and, because casual system users tend to forget what they have learned, the frequency of system use by searchers can affect how often systems need to be taught or retaught and thus increase costs of instruction (Bosser, 15).

IMPORTANCE OF TEACHING TECHNOLOGY

Even though the costs of teaching technologies may be high and, on the surface, the benefits of training may be questionable, designing pedagogically sound instructional programs for library technology is nonetheless extremely important for both the library and the library user. Left to their own devices, users "tend to learn the newer electronic tools as they have learned manual tools in the past: superficially, inadequately, from peers and by trial and error" (King and Baker, 98). As a result, patrons perform inefficient searches that seem complete and satisfactory but can be, in fact, deceiving. And, even though "artificial intelligence and generalized 'front ends' may alleviate some of the technical problems of end-user searching, instruction librarians have an ongoing responsibility to educate their patrons in the deficiencies, as well as the capabilities, of the new information technologies" (Shill, 446). King and Baker issue a strong mandate for instruction in technology: "Considering the many problems [of information technology], particularly since so many of them emanate from the approaches taken in design and implementation of the technology by the library itself, formal education opportunities for the user should not be viewed as simply a nice gesture by the library, but as an obligation" (King and Baker, 98). The reasons in support of a special effort to teach library technologies far outweigh the costs of such instruction.

Even though the monetary costs of searching computerized information systems may be less significant than in the early days of end-user online searching, patron searches should nonetheless be as quick and efficient as possible. While the searcher may be temporarily gratified by the speed of a superficial search, she will ultimately realize the inappropriate and incomplete nature of the search results. There is also a danger that, once learned, inefficient search techniques are difficult to "unlearn." Furthermore, as the popularity of computerized literature searching grows, patrons will need to do their searching quickly if only to resolve queuing and scheduling problems that may arise.

While searchers may be smarter than we think, systems that claim to be "user friendly" can test the mettle of even the most computer-literate searcher. As systems become more "user friendly," database structure and the system operations become more opaque to the searcher. King and Baker point out how dangerous some user-friendly systems can be in terms of the user's understanding of what she and the system are doing. Searchers lose contact with the search process; they can't see what the system did or how it works; and thus the user-friendly system encourages users to relinquish control of their search. User-friendly systems force searchers into a linear pattern of searching, a pattern that does not correspond to the ways that information is really constructed and retrieved. "The system protocols and responses are either accepted on blind faith, or the system is abandoned by the user for meaningful information seeking. For those users who select the former course,. . .they may obtain less than they would have through the use of other tools and may believe in the completeness of their searches even more" (King and Baker, 90). Librarians, then, should not use the fact that systems are being touted as "user friendly" as a reason to decide against formal instruction for library technologies.

Furthermore, neither printed or online system documentation nor help screens are as useful as the system vendors may imply. In most cases, vendor-supplied documentation is not enough to make the searcher self-sufficient, and librarians should not rely on this documentation to fulfill the instructional needs of their patrons.

Whether the system is friendly or hostile, one of the dangers of end-user searching is, of course, that searchers will not seek out other types of information sources to answer their questions, that they will view information seeking as a narrow rather than broad-based process. Teaching users to search computerized information sources, however, can provide an opportunity for overall bibliographic instruction that will combat this narrow view. The inherent appeal of computerized literature searching can be used to attract users to bibliographic instruction; the structure and search mechanisms of computerized databases can be used to teach search strategies that can be applied to print as well as to the variety of computerized information sources. In particular, because CD-ROM retrieval systems offer a choice of search modes (such as controlled vocabulary browsing, simple keyword searching, and implicit and full Boolean searching) they can be especially useful for teaching approaches to print, online, and optical disc-based systems.

The meaning and implications of the term "information literacy" are currently being broadly debated in the library community. End-user searching instruction not only can help to make a library user a more proficient searcher but can also be used to create a more information-literate patron with information retrieval skills that can be applied throughout the patron's life. Computerized information systems can be used to demonstrate the process of research, writing, publication, indexing, and access to scholarly and creative materials. The outcome of end-user searching training, then, "should be a thorough grounding in information organization/retrieval concepts and print/online searching skills appropriate for life-long learning in varied work and living environments during an era of constant, rapid change" (Shill, 449). Furthermore, Howard Shill points out that in adopting the goal of information literacy, the library not only provides a context for lifelong information competence in its patrons but also enhances its perceived importance in the community it serves (Shill, 449). Focusing on information literacy can benefit the patron and the library.

The possibilities for computerized information systems as instructional tools go beyond using them to teach search strategy. They can be used to foster creative and intuitive thinking about the research process. We must recognize "the great contrast between interactive, online searching and the conventional research process. Rather than merely compiling a bibliography, end-users are able to explore new leads and generate new ideas from citation printouts" (Shill, 436). Middlebury College in Vermont recently experimented in its writing center with the WILSONDISC demonstration disc, which contains six months of 16 different databases on one disc, to teach this broader view of the research process. Tutors in the writing center searched one subject through several of the databases on the demo disc to show students writing research papers how databases can be both separate and yet overlapping. A search on the subject "aeronautics," for example, retrieves citations not only from the expected *Applied Science and Technology Index*, but also finds interesting and unexpected citations from *Art Index*, *Business Periodicals Index*, and *Humanities Index*. By showing the interconnectedness of databases, students also get an understanding of the interdisciplinary nature of some areas of study. We see similar possibilities for cross-database, cross-system searching as the networking capabilities of other systems become more refined.

TEACHING THE BIG PICTURE

Remember our patron in the library's overly abundant computer wonderland: presuming that she does, indeed, need some sort of help or instruction in order to find the answer to her question, what kind of instruction should librarians provide? On the one hand, we can teach this patron searching *skills* that are based on an analysis of a system's particular functions. We can teach her what keys to press in a specific system to achieve a desired result. Or, on the other hand, we can teach *concepts*, the general principles of database construction, selection, searching, and evaluation of results. We can, in other words, give her a conceptual framework for understanding any database, any computerized information retrieval system.

Librarians, and computer system educators in general, are recognizing the importance of teaching concepts over skills. As Bosser observed about computer training, "more general knowledge is more valuable in the long run (provided it finds applications). It makes transfer to other tasks easier" (Bosser, 16). Teaching concepts such as information structure and research strategy will help searchers approach new retrieval systems with confidence. As a library adds more computerized information sources, each one with a different user interface, different search software, and different system protocols, the user will be able to anticipate what the system is searching and how the system works. Without such a larger context, new automated reference sources become "*library* tools rather than *information-seeking* tools. Users may grasp the mechanics without understanding the process. Even more disturbing, they may be forced to redefine their personal information goals to meet the inadequacies or requirements (actual or perceived) of the technology" (King and Baker, 86).

Furthermore, King and Baker cite recent research indicating not only that searchers who have been trained according to conceptual models perform better searches than those trained only in searching procedures, but also that they are able to perform more complex tasks with the system and have fewer misunderstandings about the system's capabilities (King and Baker, 87). If the goal of user instruction is to make students able to repeat the same kind of searching patterns in one system, then a skills approach would be more effective. If the goal of instruction, however, is for students to be able to generalize their knowledge to a variety of information systems, then a conceptual approach is preferred (Lippincott, 183).

SETTING THE CONTEXT

In order to understand how automated information retrieval systems work, a searcher needs to understand several key concepts in database structure and search software design.

First of all, the system user needs to know what is meant by the term *database*. Like other computer-related terminology, the word is used so frequently and in different ways (as a noun, adjective, and verb) that searchers may not have a clear picture of what a database really is. Lippincott notes eight different points that need to be explained to the user about databases: (1) the simple definition of *database* as an organized collection of items; (2) that there are a wide variety of different types of databases; (3) that these databases cover different, both broad and narrow subject areas; (4) that different databases may provide access to different types of materials (periodical articles, dissertations, audio-visual materials, and so on); (5) that databases have limitations in ranges of dates covered; (6) what the relationship of the computerized database is to any printed counterparts; (7) how useful a database may be for a particular situation; and (8) that individual databases are part of a larger information system (Lippincott, 186-87).

A searcher also needs to know how a database is constructed. The basic unit of the database, in most cases a bibliographic record, needs to be explained. Searchers should have a clear picture of what a typical record structure looks like; this involves understanding the concept of "fields" in a record. Lippincott encourages the searcher to view fields as access points, as the elements that make up a bibliographic record and that can be specified in a search (Lippincott, 187). Fields can also be used to teach controlled vocabulary versus free text searching as well as field delimiting in searching.

The structure of a database from its most basic element to the whole should be graphically explained to the searcher. Individual phrases, words, and even parts of words (searched by truncation) together make up a field; many fields, each with its own label or name, make up a record; many records, each with the same kinds of fields, make up a database; and, many databases, usually searched with the same software, make up one system such as BRS or DIALOG. By teaching the structure of a database the searcher can begin to understand the various searching, displaying, and printing options open to her. While the individual commands for truncation ($ or ? or : or *) or field delimiting will vary from database to database or system to system, the capability to do particular functions should be available in almost any information retrieval system that a patron may encounter.

IMPORTANCE OF SEARCH STRATEGY

In order to get the information that a searcher needs out of the database that she is searching, she needs to construct a solid, predictable search strategy that will work with any information medium. Whether the searcher is using the printed, CD-ROM, or online version of *Psychological Abstracts*, for example, she needs to have an understanding of what strategies will lead to the best search results.

Preliminary to constructing a formal search strategy, the searcher needs to consider her research question and to analyze its components. Asking a question in a way that is most likely to elicit the best answer is a difficult skill whether the patron is asking the reference librarian or the reference computer. Searchers must be encouraged to spend time thinking about their questions, identifying key terms and relationships in the question, and listing synonyms or related words for these key terms. It is at the question formulation stage that patrons can be encouraged to use printed thesauri, if available, to help generate related terms and to find descriptors that will enhance search relevance. Often a search planner or other search strategy sheet will be helpful in formulating the search question.

Part of question analysis for a specific search is consideration of the language and structure of the discipline from which the information is derived. For example, the structure and nomenclature of the study of literature varies from that of the study of anthropology, or the study of psychology, or the study of linguistics, even though each discipline deals with the study of human behavior and expression. Searchers, and particularly student searchers, should be aware that the terms of discourse in any given discipline will be reflected in the structure of the databases generated from that discipline.

Central to both question analysis and search strategy formulation is the concept of sets. Sets are commonly defined as groups of like items; in the case of computerized literature searching, these sets may be synonymous or related terms, or they may be variant spellings and forms of the same term. Once a searcher has grouped like terms, those groups can be assigned numbers or letters and then manipulated using Boolean operators.

It is difficult to avoid the term *Boolean operator* when teaching or discussing computerized literature searching. Central to teaching set manipulation is teaching Boolean connectors, or operators, that can be used to broaden or narrow search results. Searchers, therefore, need to understand how the operators *and*, *or*, and *not* can be used in a search. Even if the system being searched uses implicit Boolean searching such as WILSONDISC's Wilsearch mode, the searcher still needs to have an understanding of how the software is manipulating sets. Venn diagrams have traditionally been used to teach set theory and, thus, to teach using sets in formulating search strategy; the most successful means of showing how sets intersect and relate is through the use of graphics, whether with Venn diagrams or another model.

Although most indexing and abstracting retrieval systems allow for the numbering and manipulation of sets, online catalogs and other simple retrieval systems generally do not permit the creation of separately named sets. In these systems, such as the popular NOTIS automated library system, set numbers cannot be referred to and manipulated; instead, the searcher must use nesting to achieve the same effect. Therefore, any discussion of sets must also include some reference to nesting as a tool for expressing a search statement.

In addition to discussing the use of larger searching techniques, we can give our prospective searchers tips, or searching advice, about the relative merits of different search strategies. While not essential to the conceptual understanding of systems, searchers can be taught which strategies will be more accurate, which strategies the computer will be able to process more quickly, and which strategies will be most successful in most systems. For example, a list of searching tips could include the following: a caveat about truncation (it tends to slow most systems down); encouragement to use field delimiting, including searching by descriptor, to make a search quicker and more accurate; calling up an online thesaurus in order to find the correct form of entry; and, of course, asking for help if the search isn't progressing satisfactorily.

Constructing an effective search strategy, using the concepts of question analysis, sets, and Boolean logic, is the single most important searching skill that an end user can master. In order to construct an effective strategy, the searcher needs a solid conceptual understanding of how databases are structured and how a search is formulated and executed. In addition, an important part of a search strategy is choosing between various information sources, both in print and on computer. The searcher needs to know the range of sources available, their relative strengths in terms of particular questions, and the benefits and limitations of their format (for example, print, online, or optical disc). In addition, the searcher must have some understanding of the nomenclature and structure of the discipline from which the database used is generated. Providing guidelines for determining which technology for which information need is an important part of the overall search strategy process.

PUSHING THE RIGHT BUTTONS

Of course, a successful search is based not just on the searcher's conceptual understanding of information retrieval systems. She must also know the procedures involved in operating a specific system. Five of the most commonly used end-user retrieval systems – SilverPlatter, WILSONDISC and WILSONLINE, BRS/After Dark, Knowledge Index, and InfoTrac – all use different search software. The commands to begin searching, to execute a search, to combine and truncate terms, to view answers, to print results, and to get help differ with each system. It is difficult for a librarian who may search these systems several times a day to keep the different command structures straight. For patrons, the task is nearly impossible without some help.

The specific features that a searcher should be shown for each system she will use include logging on and off the system, including system security features; keyboard mechanics, such as how function keys operate and which key sends a command to the system; and input and output procedures, such as beginning and executing a search, truncation symbols, and displaying and printing protocols (Lippincott, 189).

WHAT TO DO WITH RESULTS

Getting a nice list of relevant citations to books and articles about a particular topic is certainly satisfying for both searcher and librarian alike. The list of citations itself, however, does not provide indications of how trustworthy, complete, or valuable the information in the cited documents will be for the searcher. It is important to teach patrons how to evaluate the citations that they have retrieved. For example, searchers should be able to distinguish between journals and magazines and to understand the differences in content, audience, and focus between the two types of periodicals. The number of pages that an article comprises is an important indication of its usefulness for certain purposes. Finally, the language used in article titles also provides clues to the potential value of the article itself: the searcher should examine whether the language is technical, nontechnical, or colloquial in order to see whether the level of article is appropriate for the information need. As libraries and patrons increasingly depend on interlibrary loan systems for document delivery, it is especially important for searchers to assess the potential value of individual citations before initiating an interlibrary loan request. This kind of evaluation also depends on a conceptual and practical understanding of the structure and language of published literature.

Once the searcher has identified which citations are useful to pursue, she should then be told how to locate the materials found through the use of any given system. The scope of a library's collections and how it is reflected in a system is important. For example, a library probably owns every item reflected in its online catalog. It may own most of the references found in the WILSONDISC *Readers' Guide*; the library's holdings can then be verified in the online catalog. Items retrieved from a *BIOSIS* or *COMPENDEX* search, however, may not likely be owned by the library. In the case of items not owned, the patron should be shown interlibrary loan procedures.

If the searcher has been trained to understand how systems work conceptually, then coping with the variety in command languages will be easier for her. The use of individual command charts and signs next to each system can prompt her for the appropriate system-specific command. A command comparison or conversion chart given to her and discussed at an instructional session can help her to understand the variety of command options used to elicit standard system responses. In any case, the focus of database searching instruction should not be on the particulars of system use, but instead on the concepts driving information retrieval systems in general.

FEELING GOOD ABOUT SEARCHING

Equally as important to a successful search session as a conceptual framework for the search process is the confidence of the searcher. When our searcher enters the computerized library, she should look forward to her interactions with the library's computerized systems, rather than feel confused and overwhelmed; she should feel like the odds are in favor of her finding the answer to her question. The feeling of confidence in the library and its services is particularly important in face of the rapidly changing technological mix in libraries. The library that the patron enters today may look entirely different tomorrow. Marchionini and Nitecki summarize the instructional mandates for librarians and address the need for searcher confidence:

> In the midst of these [technological] changes, the focus of the academic librarian should be to provide settings and tones that induce comfort and a sense of human control over systems; guidance on what resources most effectively meet various information retrieval needs; basic instruction in search techniques; and assurance that the entire process is not difficult and is evolving toward more efficient, effective, and easy-to-use systems. Such demands may not allow for the most thorough examination of every nuance of use of online systems, but should be met with greater flexibility and attitude conditioning to cope with and welcome inevitable change. (Marchionini and Nitecki, 108)

STAFF TRAINING IMPLICATIONS

While it is important to teach library users the concepts and skills involved in computerized information retrieval, it is no less important to teach staff the same kinds of skills. The motivation for staff to learn computerized literature searching may differ from patron motivations; however, their reactions to new technologies, and to the changes in their work patterns that the new technology may bring, can parallel user reactions. Sheila Creth, Anne Lipow, and others have written a great deal about the challenges and importance of staff training for technologies. In many libraries, staff training is dealt with separately from user training; nonetheless, it is important for librarians involved in implementing new end-user technologies to remember the needs of staff learning these technologies as well.

Library automation, specifically the automating of library catalogs and circulation systems, was originally in the domain of the technical services departments of the library. Logically, catalogers automated the catalog, circulation staff automated the circulation function, and acquisitions librarians automated serials and acquisitions systems. Public services staff were often the last to be consulted during implementation or trained after systems were brought up.

With the widespread use of automated reference systems and the growth of online public access catalogs (OPACs), however, the involvement of public services personnel in library automation has increased. It has become clear that, in an automated setting, the work of separate library units affects the work of other library units. The OPAC, used primarily by the public and by public services staff, reflects the integration of the work of different library units into one unified database. Unfortunately, reference librarians and other public services staff members often are not included in formal system training, especially if the training is primarily directed to technical services staff. If a library has an OPAC, however, librarians who deal primarily with the public and not with the MARC record should be trained in the behind-the-scenes construction of the OPAC records. And just as public services librarians should be trained in technical aspects of database construction, so should technical services staff be shown how the public may view and interpret OPAC screens. It is not just OPACs and library systems that require attention to staff training; reference systems designed for the end user, such as CD-ROM databases, also demand that staff be adequately trained in their use before the public is exposed to the systems.

Feeling that public services librarians are often the ones least involved in catalog design, Anne Lipow has outlined six points that public services staff should understand about how automated catalogs function; these points also apply to what staff should know about other computerized information retrieval systems. Public services staff should understand (1) how records get into the database; (2) how the records are structured; (3) what causes the order of record display during a search; (4) how a searcher's choice of search strategy affects retrieval; (5) what types of errors can be corrected and how to correct them; and (6) which errors result from faulty inputting as opposed to system-produced flaws (Lipow, 864). It is interesting to note that, except for the last point, Lipow is asking that public services staff have the same system understanding that we would ideally hope of end users: a conceptual and practical understanding of why and how a system works.

Brian Lantz suggests that automation trainers use two levels of instruction: one for professional librarians and another for nonprofessional technical staff. Both staff and professionals need to understand the appropriateness of any given technology for carrying out a particular task; to master the skills needed to use a technology; to learn computer skills that will assist them in achieving career advancement; and to have a ready forum for the exchange of information and ideas on the applications of technology. In addition, professional librarians should have an understanding of the range of technologies available and of the use of computers in teaching and in collection development (Lantz, 51-52).

It is important, then, for staff to be comfortable in searching automated reference systems, including the OPAC, if the user is also to be proficient and comfortable with those same systems. While staff may need to understand how the OPAC or another database works on a more technical level than the general end user, the approaches to training can be the same.

HOW TO TEACH TECHNOLOGY

Because of the inherent differences between computerized and printed reference sources and between the ways users react to these sources, teaching electronic information sources becomes a new and different instructional challenge. Computerized information systems have caused us to re-evaluate how we teach library and research skills. With automated information sources, we must "unlearn old concepts and adopt new ones, and must train users to do the same" (Lipow, 863).

Traditional methods of bibliographic instruction (BI) may not necessarily work for teaching computerized literature searching, particularly if the intent of the instruction is to convey concepts and create mental models of information systems rather than just teaching skills. The heart of most BI programs, at least in academic libraries, has been the one-hour instructional session; in this one class period, the librarian generally distributes a bibliography of sources pertinent to the course or to a class project, offers a search strategy, and discuss the scope and uses of individual reference sources. Most instruction librarians, however, have found one hour inadequate for teaching both print and computerized sources. It is not just that the added computerized sources take too much time to cover; because the two sources are fundamentally different, the librarian, in trying to teach both, may fail to convey essential conceptual frameworks and mental models (King and Baker, 98). It is particularly difficult to address the varying levels of knowledge, experience, and attitudes of different students in the one-hour session. Furthermore, course-integrated instruction reaches only a very small percentage of automated reference system users. Remote users of local online systems – those dialing into the catalog or other locally mounted databases from offices, dorms, or homes – may not have the opportunity to attend course-integrated sessions.

Some libraries are trying to add a one- or two-credit course to the required undergraduate curriculum in order to cover adequately the many dimensions of research, both print and computer-based. A course that spans the semester gives the student and library instructor time to teach concepts as well as searching skills, and also to discuss the entire realm of information sources and research processes. In most institutions, however, a course such as this may be difficult to implement: the size of the teaching staff needed to support the course will be great; passing the course proposal through college curriculum committees may be time consuming; and instructional facilities for the course may not be adequate.

Other forms of BI are equally as time consuming and labor intensive. Of course, the reference desk one-on-one interaction is sufficient to show the searcher very minimal searching skills; however, concepts and mental models cannot be conveyed in such a hurried setting. Voluntary separate workshops in database searching are sparsely attended and do not address the importance of learning over time. While workbooks can be valuable for the motivated learner, they cannot accurately reflect the interactive nature of database searching.

USING TECHNOLOGY TO TEACH TECHNOLOGY

Using teaching technologies, such as help screens, online tutorials, videotapes, CAI, expert systems, and artificial intelligence, to instruct library users in computerized literature searching can overcome some of the problems presented by traditional instructional methods. If it is well done, instructional technology provides the searcher with many of the same attractions as the searching technology itself: it is available at all times; it is fast; its pace is user-controlled; it is interactive; it can give immediate positive reinforcement for correct responses; it can address the needs of a variety of users; it can be turned off or left if the learner has had enough.

For the librarian, using technology as a teaching aid can save time and money. Once the initial costs of designing and implementing the teaching modules has been borne, instructional technology can free the reference librarian from giving lengthy, repetitive searching instructions. In most cases, computer-based instructional packages can be easily updated to reflect changes in software or systems. Technological media can also be used to teach concepts in a way that printed instructional sheets or workbooks cannot: it is interactive and, depending on the software or medium being used, can build conceptual frameworks and create mental models slowly.

Staff training can also be facilitated through instructional media: the same media that can be used to teach patrons can also be used to teach staff. The use of CAI, videotapes, and expert systems to cover the basics of system use can free supervisors and staff trainers to concentrate on the finer points of system operation or on individual searching needs. Instructional technologies can also make new staff training more consistent and smooth, allowing the staff member to learn systems as he or she has time without scheduling pressures.

Technology-aided instruction, in all of its manifestations, is appealing to both the searcher and the instructor but is not, just like the information technologies that it teaches, an end or an answer in itself. It is simply one component in an overall instructional program. The most important aspect of the library instruction curriculum is the content of the instructional sessions. Marchionini and Nitecki explain their views on how library systems should be taught: "instructional modules that address topics users need help with should be provided in short, intensive units and in a variety of media that allow self-directed study. It is not the medium that makes a difference, but the instructional content. Providing a variety of media may help attract a wider range of users to the system" (Marchionini and Nitecki, 108). Instructional technologies can provide intense, module-based instruction that is both attractive to users and pedagogically sound.

The following chapters discuss various teaching technologies, highlighting their particular strengths and unique applications in libraries. As you read through the book, think about the patron trying to find answers in today's highly automated library, in *your* library. What are the instructional technologies that will help her the most? Which technologies are most feasible in your institution? How will you present these technologies to your patrons? What is the mix of instructional approaches that will work best for your patrons and for your staff?

Works Cited

Bodi, Sonia. "Teaching Effectiveness and Bibliographic Instruction: The Relevance of Learning Styles." *College and Research Libraries* 51, no. 2 (March 1990): 113-19.

Borgman, Christine L. "Psychological Research in Human-Computer Interaction." *Annual Review of Information Science and Technology* 19 (1984): 33-64.

Bosser, Tom. *Learning in Man-Computer Interaction: A Review of the Literature.* New York: Springer-Verlag, 1987.

Bostock, Stephen J., and Roger V. Seifert. *Micro Computers in Adult Education*. London: Croom Helm, 1986.

Frick, Elizabeth. "Theories of Learning and Their Impact on OPAC Instruction." *Research Strategies* 7, no. 2 (Spring 1989): 67-78.

Gratch, Bonnie G. "Rethinking Instructional Assumptions in an Age of Computerized Information Access." *Research Strategies* 6 (Winter 1988): 4-7.

Hensley, Randall. "CD-ROM Users and Technology-Induced Behavior." Presented at the American Library Association's Association of College and Research Libraries' Bibliographic Instruction Section Annual Program. New Orleans, June 1988.

King, David, and Betsy Baker. "Human Aspects of Library Technology: Implications for Academic Library User Education." In *Bibliographic Instruction: The Second Generation*, edited by Constance A. Mellon, 85-107. Littleton, Colo.: Libraries Unlimited, 1987.

Lantz, Brian. "Staff Training for Information Technology." *British Journal of Academic Librarianship* 2, no. 1 (Spring 1987): 44-64.

Lipow, Anne Grodzins. "The Online Catalog: Exceeding Our Grasp." *American Libraries* 20, no. 9 (October 1989): 862-65.

Lippincott, Joan K. "End-User Instruction: Emphasis on Concepts." In *Conceptual Frameworks for Bibliographic Instruction*, edited by Mary Reichel and Mary Ann Ramey, 183-91. Littleton, Colo.: Libraries Unlimited, 1987.

Marchionini, Gary, and Danuta A. Nitecki. "Managing Change: Supporting Users of Automated Systems." *College & Research Libraries* 48 (March 1987): 104-9.

Miller, William, and Bonnie Gratch. "Making Connections: Computerized Reference Services and People." *Library Trends* 34, no. 4 (Spring 1989): 387-401.

Schill, Harold B. "Bibliograpbic Instruction: Planning for the Electronic Information Environment." *College & Research Libraries* 48, no. 5, (September 1987): 433-53.

Sullivan, Michael V., Christine L. Borgman, and Dorothy Wippern. "End-Users, Mediated Searches, and Front-End Assistance Programs on Dialog: A Comparison of Learning, Performance, and Satisfaction."

Journal of the American Society for Information Science 41, no. 1 (January 1990): 27-42.

Towbridge, David. "An Investigation of Groups Working at the Computer." In *Applications of Cognitive Psychology, Problem Solving, Education, and Computing*, edited by William P. Banks, et al. Hillsdale, N.J.: Lawrence Erlbaum Associates, 1987.

Turkle, Sherry. *The Second Self: Computers and the Human Spirit.* New York: Simon and Shuster, 1984.

For Further Reading

Allen, Robert B. "Cognitive Factors in Human Interaction with Computers." *Behaviour and Information Technology* 1, no. 3 (1982): 257-78.

Baker, Betsy. "A Conceptual Framework for Teaching Online Catalog Use." *Journal of Academic Librarianship* 2 (May 1986): 90-96.

Borgman, Christine L. "Psychological Factors in Online Catalog Use, or Why Users Fail." In *Training Users of Online Public Access Catalogs*, edited by Marsha H. McClintock, 23-34. Washington, D.C.: Council on Library Resources, 1983.

Creith, Sheila. *Effective On-the-Job Training: Developing Library Human Resources.* Chicago: American Library Association, 1986.

Danziger, James N., and Kenneth L. Kraemer. *People and Computers: The Impacts of Computing on End Users in Organizations.* New York: Columbia University Press, 1986.

Kirkland, Janice, issue ed. *The Human Response to Library Automation*, special issue of *Library Trends* 37, no. 4 (Spring 1989): 385-542.

Mehlmann, Marilyn. *When People Use Computers.* Englewood Cliffs, N.J.: Prentice-Hall, 1981.

Roszak, Theodore. *The Cult of Information.* New York: Random House, 1986.

Rudd, Joel, and Mary Jo Rudd. "Coping with Information Load: User Strategies and Implications for Librarians." *College & Research Libraries* 47 (July 1986): 315-22.

2

Deciding among the Options

Linda Brew MacDonald

As the challenging questions posed at the end of chapter 1 indicate, there is a wide range of instructional technologies to consider. Because all of the technologies examined in detail in the following chapters have strengths and weaknesses, you need a reasonable, coherent system by which to evaluate them for use in a training program. Some decisions will seem self-evident. You would use online tutorial services, for example, only in a library that provides access to some form of online end-user search service. Computer-assisted instruction (CAI) may not be practical without sufficient workstations to make it easy for students to use the program, unless you circulate diskettes. What criteria can you use to evaluate technologies, and why is it vital to select media carefully?

WHY CHOOSE CAREFULLY?

Since the goal of library instruction is learning, it may seem that the basic criterion for choosing among various media options is obvious: which medium has been shown to be most effective as a teaching tool? After more than 30 years of research in library instruction and education in general, the conclusion of many authorities is that *no* medium can be identified as the best.

In the third edition of the *Handbook of Research on Teaching*, educators Richard Clark and Gavriel Salomon analyze the research completed and theories developed between 1970 and 1985 concerning media in teaching. Their summary includes the following statements (Clark and Salomon, 474):

"1. Past research on media has shown quite clearly that no medium enhances learning more than any other medium regardless of learning task, learner traits, symbolic elements, curriculum content, or setting."

"2. Any new technology is likely to teach better than its predecessors because it generally provides better prepared instructional materials and its novelty engages learners."

Several valid bases for differentiating among media are proposed, however, including cost efficiency and appeal to students. New media, especially computers, can be powerful agents in developing innovative instruction programs.

Similar conclusions have been reached in the more specialized field of library instruction. "Overall, there is no conclusive evidence that one mode of instruction is superior to another in providing instruction, although attitudes toward nontraditional methods are reported to be superior. Taken as a whole, the evidence suggests that differences in learning are more likely due to interactions among individual characteristics, subject matter, and media. A pragmatic approach would be to provide a variety of media and allow the learner to choose which to use" (Marchionini and Nitecki, 106).

Even if you decide to develop a variety of approaches, you will place some in higher priority than others. Since you are considering the automated and computer-based technologies, you can depend on their documented appeal to some learners. Because the teaching technologies require expensive equipment and considerable development time, you will want to choose the most cost- and work-efficient media for your purposes. By making these decisions carefully you can avoid the pitfall of poor media selection: an expensive, unsuccessful, and abandoned project.

Larry Hardesty and Frances Gatz comment on the importance of selecting media carefully. "In the development and use of mediated library instruction, the selection of media is critical. Too often poor selection has not allowed media to be used to their full potential. And further, the choice is made solely on the basis of great press reviews, success in other situations, or multisensory capabilities. All of these factors may be irrelevant to the specific learning task at hand" (Hardesty and Gatz, 16).

STEPS IN CHOOSING MEDIA

Clearly, then, teaching technologies must be chosen carefully to avoid wasting library resources while compounding users' frustrations. The process of reaching an effective decision can be divided into the following steps.

Identify Problem

Successful media selection begins with attention to a particular learning demand. You are considering developing or modifying an instruction program in response to a need. This need may have become obvious after the installation of a CD-ROM index in the reference area; suddenly the reference librarians are besieged with requests for help in using the product, and are complaining to you that they cannot face explaining the basics of the search software to one more new user. Or the transaction log for your online public access catalog may reveal that your users are having difficulty with subject searching. They seem to enter the same unsuccessful terms repeatedly, then abandon the search completely without trying to modify their strategy.

Your first step should be to think about the need for instruction and write a simple statement expressing it. For example, the public catalog problem could be expressed, "Public catalog users do not understand how to prepare for and execute subject searches." This exercise focuses your attention on the specific problem. You may want to teach subject searching in the context of author and title searching, since they are all important means of finding information through the catalog. You will want to feature subject searching in your instruction effort, however, because the problem statement pinpoints it as the main issue. With this in mind, you might design a CAI module, handout, or other material that discusses subject searching first. If you begin with author and title searching, many users will never reach the most important section.

State Goals and Skills

Having identified and stated the problem, you need to write a similar simple statement expressing the goal of your instruction. What outcome do you want your teaching program to have? How will the knowledge and behavior of your students or users change? Using the public access catalog problem again, your goal statement might be, "Users will be able to search the public access catalog by subject." You can then continue the process of analyzing the problem and devising a solution by listing the skills your learners need to acquire in order to meet that goal. A sample list of skills for this problem might read:

1. User will be able to operate the catalog terminal correctly.

2. User will understand the software protocols for entering a subject search statement.

3. User will know that subject headings must conform to Library of Congress (or other) controlled language.

4. User will be able to use Library of Congress (or other) thesaurus to locate appropriate subject term(s) for topic.

5. User will be able to conduct search through various levels of information presented by catalog to reach item records.

6. User will recognize and correctly interpret catalog information including location, call number, circulation status.

7. User will be able to employ added subject headings on relevant item records to expand search if desired.

Formulating and writing these brief statements will help keep your attention focussed on the problem you first identified. As your project develops, you may need to change all of these guidelines, eliminating some statements and adding others. Hardesty and Gatz comment, "A characteristic problem in developing task descriptions for library skills is that these skills are difficult to define; they often appear to be more intuitive than conducive to description because of the complexity and variety of approaches that may be used for a particular library task" (Hardesty and Gatz, 12). Analyzing library instruction in this way may not be easy, but it is a vital step in selecting the best medium for your program.

Determine Learner Characteristics

Now turn your attention to your learners or students. Gathering as much information as possible about their characteristics is part of the process of selecting the best instruction medium. You may get this information directly from the learners, from your own knowledge of their background, or from other sources like classroom instructors or workshop coordinators. Briefly note or summarize the answers to such questions as the following:

1. What is the educational level? The answer will vary from a narrow range to a broad spectrum. For example, you may be teaching a class of high school sophomores, or designing instruction for all undergraduates at a small college, or planning materials for use in a public library that serves every educational level. Several authors have commented on the importance of evaluating learners' intellectual development in relation to instruction (Hardesty, 29; Golen and Keller, 78). High school students and lower-level undergraduates are likely to perceive concepts in black and white: they think every question has one right answer. Instruction

designed for these students must accommodate their level of understanding. Graduate students or professionals in a special library would be able to understand the complexity of information resources and the importance of evaluating materials because they have advanced beyond "either-or" thinking.

2. What common background do learners have? Your learners may have some common background such as interest in a subject area, employment at the same institution, use of English as a second language, or other situation that will affect planning for library instruction.

3. Is there a preferred learning style? Some students learn better by reading, some by viewing videotapes, some by listening to an instructor. Learners also vary in their independence. We are all familiar with those who prefer to be given a handout or workbook so that they can proceed on their own, and with others who want a librarian to explain and demonstrate every aspect of using a resource. Dorothy Bowen has assessed the learning styles of African students using standardized tests. She determined that overhead projectors, demonstrations, hands-on experiences, small groups, and cooperative assignments were effective approaches to bibliographic instruction for these students (Bowen, 410-13).

4. What are learners' attitudes toward automated sources? Even though microcomputers have become common equipment in some schools, offices, and libraries, many students and other library users are unfamiliar with them. Lack of basic knowledge about computerized resources can lead to anxiety, distrust, fear of embarrassment, and other negative attitudes that will have a strong impact on your training program. Many people are resistant to change; they may view the replacement of the card catalog with public access terminals as threatening. On the other hand, students and others who have a great deal of experience with some aspects of computer use, such as basic programming, spreadsheets, or word processing, may bring an overconfident, "know-it-all" outlook that can be equally problematic for instruction. Elizabeth Bramm Dunn says, "An additional complicating factor is that the level of students' understanding of and comfort with automated sources is likely to be far more variable than with print sources" (Dunn, 220). In any group of learners, some students may be experienced and confident with technologies that others resist and distrust.

5. What about motivation? Are your learners self-selected or required to participate in the instruction program? Lack of interest in subject matter is a powerful barrier to learning (Golen and Keller, 78). You may want to use the jazzier possibilities of some media to compensate for deficiencies in motivation.

6. Can you adopt the learner's perspective? As a final exercise, pretend that you are a learner. Temporarily erase your library expertise and approach the problem or task as a novice. If you are designing training for a public access catalog, try various reasonable strategies at the terminal and see what results you get. Sandy Ward, at Stanford University, comments, "The ability to put yourself in the position of your students is very important....Sometimes my preconceived notions of what I should teach change dramatically after ten minutes of hands-on student oriented research on the assignment" (Mensching 1988, 137).

Review Resources

By this point, you may have developed a strong interest in one or more teaching media. What resources are available to support development of your possible choices? Writing CAI programs, exploring artificial intelligence, and working with other teaching technologies demand expertise, equipment, money, and time. Before committing your instruction program to any of these media, you need to investigate and list the resources available to you. Remember that although you should begin with in-house resources, you should look beyond them as needed. Money may be requested from grants, departments, school districts, and many other sources. Equipment may be shared, borrowed, or rented for certain phases of project development. Above all, human knowledge and experience with automated resources are accessible through networks, online bulletin boards, conferences, and professional literature.

Expertise

Working with videotape or computer-based forms of library instruction demands various degrees of expertise with a variety of equipment, software, concepts, and processes. Before settling on a medium for your teaching program, consider the skills you already have and those you must gain in order to carry out the project. For example, writing a CAI package to explain subject searching to public catalog users requires that you understand the basics of computer operation, since you will have to use a microcomputer to create the program. You will need enough knowledge of software in general to evaluate the programs available for writing CAI; once you have selected a program, you will have to become thoroughly familiar with it. You will also need to know the basics of systematic instruction planning, to make your lessons accomplish their tasks.

There are many ways to acquire the necessary knowledge. Books, journal articles, and computer manuals will provide the background in microcomputers, but the best teacher is always experience. Library literature is full of articles offering guidelines and reports on selecting software and using CAI, online tutorial services, artificial intelligence, and other media for instruction. Contact other librarians, computer center staff, computer sales personnel, teachers, and any other specialists whose advice you need to consult. "Human resources are of particular concern. Not only does the librarian need to locate those individuals who can contribute to the solution of the problem, but in many cases librarians must work closely with them in utilizing their particular talents" (Hardesty and Gatz, 19). In one case, a puzzling technical problem was solved by consulting a media equipment representative and the campus electrician.

Equipment

What equipment do you have for developing automated instruction materials? Is there a video production lab on campus or in the school? Do you have an office microcomputer and will it be available for the long hours you need to develop an artificial intelligence program? Is that microcomputer powerful enough to run the software you would like to use?

Investigate and list the equipment you have at hand and what you will need for any technology in which you are strongly interested. Be specific. Having a microcomputer is not enough; you must be sure it has the required amount of memory, graphics capabilities, and compatability with other systems for many applications. To demonstrate CD-ROM or online searching, for example, you may want a liquid crystal display (LCD) unit. Does your microcomputer have the graphics capacity and a suitable connection to be able to communicate with the LCD pad? Will the equipment be available as needed for instruction use? You may have access to a very powerful microcomputer that must be shared with several other users; it would be frustrating to try to schedule it for demonstrating CD-ROM products to numerous classes.

With ingenuity and cooperation, you should be able to locate equipment for developing and providing the teaching technologies appropriate to your need. Video cameras may be rented or signed out, existing computers upgraded or enhanced. In addition, equipment and expertise go hand in hand. Once you locate the necessary hardware, you will probably find someone who knows how to use it.

Time

Creating good library instruction materials in any medium takes time–time to research, compare, create, and evaluate. Automated or computer-based media consume great amounts of time, and it must be time of a special quality. The processes involved in working with microcomputers are so complex that many librarians need long, uninterrupted blocks of time to become immersed in the project. How many libraries can offer such a release from the pressures of reference desk schedules, classes, meetings, sudden demands for online searches, and all the other components of a typical day?

James Harrington outlines the time requirements for a typical project in automated instruction. He decided to write a CAI program to use in combination with a vendor-produced videotape to teach end users how to search BRS/After Dark online. The CAI package, called LearnToSearch, consists of two main parts; the first lesson is a tutorial on the basics of computer searching, and the second is a simulation of an After Dark search. Harrington spent two weeks researching CAI design and reviewing software programs and two weeks writing the text. He coded the program in Turbo Pascal, which took four weeks. LearnToSearch includes quizzes and is programmed to provide feedback to incorrect and correct answers. The search simulation was written in four days. The LearnToSearch CAI program took Harrington nine weeks to research and produce; his report does not specify what percentage of his work time was devoted to the project (Harrington, 152-54).

You should estimate the amount of time you will need and how to secure the best lengths of work time you can. Perhaps you can plan to use a semester break or slow period, or you can modify your schedule to concentrate on the project.

Money

Elizabeth Bramm Dunn summarizes this issue very clearly: "One of the areas in which automation has its greatest impact is the pocketbook. Ten years ago the instruction librarian needed a place to teach, some chalk, an overhead projector, a supply of blank transparency sheets, a typewriter, and access to a photocopier. Now we need all of these tools plus enough personal computers for database management, word processing, online searching, CAI presentations, and desk-top publishing; special software to enhance graphics capabilities and create tutorials; and a liquid crystal display screen, or an even more sophisticated and expensive alternative, to permit demonstration of online searching" (Dunn, 222).

She points out the expensive nature of all this up-to-date equipment, and remarks that librarians must employ creative approaches to obtain funding for it. You will need to list the costs for all elements of hardware, software, and peripherals needed for the project you are considering. What funding sources are available to finance costs? Can you propose a grant for any portion of the expenses? Can the costs be shared with other departments, districts, or libraries? Can any of the needed equipment be borrowed, rented, or purchased in planned phases?

Compare Media Features

At this point in the selection process, you may want to compare certain aspects of several media in which you are interested. Larry Hardesty mentions a number of important characteristics, including "such factors as flexibility, durability, ability of the designer, cost effectiveness, convenience, and availability of the various media" (Hardesty, 34).

Comparing these and other media features may be easier if the information is represented graphically, such as plotted on a diagram or entered into a flow chart. Robert Diamond uses a simple graph to compare cost and flexibility of a number of audiovisual media, including film strips, audio cassettes, and video cassettes (Diamond, 50-52). Figure 2-1 shows a similar graph comparing video, onscreen help, CAI, artificial intelligence, online tutorial services, and optical discs on the bases of development effort required and ability to customize for a specific library. It becomes evident that a trade-off exists between the low development effort required by vendor-produced materials like optical discs, videos, and off-the-shelf CAI, and their impersonality. These media can be tailored to a specific library only by adding other materials like handouts, exercises, or lecture/demonstrations. Artificial intelligence and homegrown CAI, on the other hand, can be highly individualized to meet an institution's needs, but only at the cost of great effort in their development.

If you had considered writing a CAI package to help users learn to search the public catalog by subject, this representation of two important factors might help you decide whether to continue with that plan or to examine alternatives. For example, you might postpone the CAI project until you could allocate time for it, relying for the short term on onscreen help messages with the addition of simple printed handouts placed at the terminals.

Figure 2-1. Instruction Media Comparison Graph

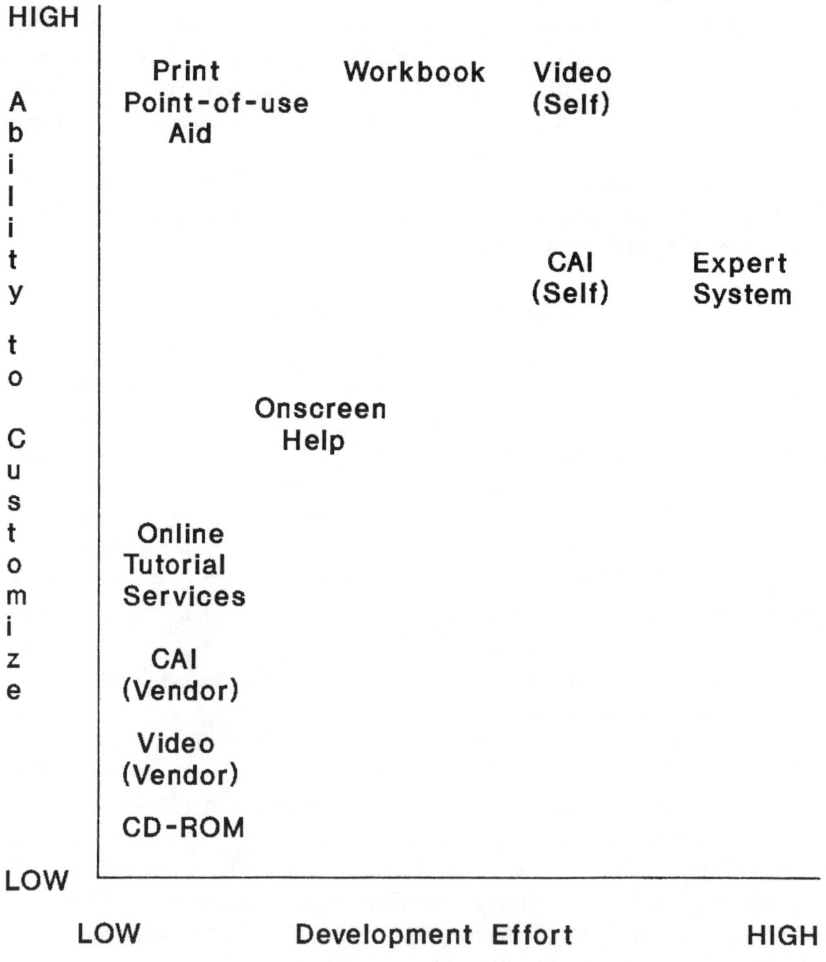

```
HIGH  |
      |
A     |    Print        Workbook    Video
b     |    Point-of-use             (Self)
i     |    Aid
l     |
i     |
t     |                             CAI        Expert
y     |                             (Self)     System
      |
t     |
o     |
      |         Onscreen
C     |           Help
u     |
s     |
t     |    Online
o     |    Tutorial
m     |    Services
i     |
z     |    CAI
e     |   (Vendor)
      |
      |    Video
      |   (Vendor)
      |
      |    CD-ROM
      |
LOW   |_____

      LOW          Development Effort          HIGH
```

You may want to sketch several charts, graphs, or lists of similar factors in deciding which medium is best for your purpose. No single selection will be ideal, but gathering this information and evaluating it methodically will help you choose the most effective method of teaching.

Consider Media in Context

Fortunately, teaching technologies do not exist in a vacuum. You will be adding one or more automated instruction tools to an existing program of library instruction. What traditional methods can you use to complement the strengths and weaknesses of artficial intelligence, online tutorial services, or optical disc products?

These technologies should not be seen as replacements for lectures, classes, or tours when those methods are most appropriate. Reference interviews and one-on-one assistance are very important as balancing elements in any teaching program that is heavily automated. For example, consider the problems faced by a student who is anxious about using computers and has an assignment that requires searching online. If the training relies heavily on CAI, there is an added burden of stress on that learner as she struggles to interpret an unfamiliar keyboard. Edward Kaslauskas and Jacqueline McCrady, discussing the advantages and disadvantages of courses or workshops, comment, "On the positive side, this training approach allows the opportunity to have an 'expert' on hand to provide assistance. The instructor can provide more than just cognitive learning – the instructor can assist in affective learning, that is, in developing correct attitudes towards microcomputers and in eliminating computer-phobia" (Kaslauskas and McCrady, 93). One of the most common reasons for failure and rejection of instructional technologies is the attempt to substitute them for human contact (Gayeski, 12).

Select Media

By following the process outlined above, you may have arrived at several decisions concerning which media will be best for your instruction program. There is really no single point of choice, but rather a number of considerations that may lead to a range of possibilities.

To summarize the process in relation to our sample problem concerning the public catalog, you may have decided on both immediate and long-range actions. For the present, you can use existing microcomputers, word processing software, and a printer to create single-page printed handouts that include sample searches. These will be placed at the terminals. You can review the catalog's help screens for subject searching and, if they meet your criteria for clarity and sense, refer users to them in the handouts. If the help screens are not clear, you can investigate whether they can be changed. You may also plan to acquire new software to write your own simple CAI during the next period when you anticipate having the time that project demands. Because your learner assessment indicates a high level of anxiety about computers, you would like to have a part-time person work as a counselor or tutor helping users with their searches; perhaps you will offer several brief demonstrations at advertised times during the day.

DECISION CYCLES

Choosing media for library instruction is not a straight-line, start-to-finish process. A well-defined beginning, with problem identification, may not necessarily presage a clear ending. Testing and evaluating your results, and changing approaches as necessary, may lead back cyclically to a need to gather more information, restate goals and skills, and reconsider the media choice.

Test and Evaluate the Product

As soon as you have a rough draft of your CAI, video, or other automated instruction product, begin testing it. Show it to your colleagues and ask for their reactions and advice. Ask users to try the program and give you their opinions. It is much easier to accept criticism and corrections when your work is in the draft stage than when you have, in your own mind, put the finishing touches on it. You need not design formal surveys or checklists, but should note the users' comments and suggestions for your own use.

Sharing your project with others in this way may reap the added benefit of generating colleagues' interest and participation. Although one dedicated person may develop a mediated instruction project unaided, many such projects are abandoned when their creator leaves the library or becomes absorbed in other tasks. When a group is involved in the process, it is more likely that someone will take responsibility for keeping the system active and up to date. As noted above, the library must invest time, money, and equipment in teaching technologies; group work can help to protect this investment (Widman and Nourse, 52).

Change and Revise as Needed

Based on the results of your first evaluations, revise the product. Even after you have reached a final version and put it into use, build in some form of review or reconsideration of its place in your instruction program. One simple, objective means of evaluating the success of instruction is to tabulate the number of times a specific question is asked before and after the media-based and other materials are in place (Lubans, 34). If users continue to request help with subject searching at the same rate after you provide handouts, personal assistance, and CAI, you should pay attention. If the questions are at the same basic entry level, you should try to find out why your teaching materials are not meeting your objectives. On the other hand, if the questions are more complex, your entry-level instruction is having an effect.

At the University of Vermont, the head of reference appoints a three-person ad hoc task force each summer to examine the operation of our Automated Reference Center. Training and teaching materials are one of the task force's concerns. Workbooks, CAI, workshop outlines, student assistant training methods, handouts, and posters are all reviewed and critiqued. This process helps keep our materials, procedures, and services current, timely, and effective.

MEDIA SELECTION IN INSTRUCTIONAL DESIGN

Choosing the most effective medium for library instruction is one part of the greater process of instructional design. Educators have created a complex and multifaceted literature dealing with this topic; research is complicated, however, by the fact that authorities cannot agree on a general definition of the term *instructional design*. Nonetheless, a clear, readable collection of brief articles that will provide a basis for understanding the theory, following the process, and identifying current research on this topic may be found in *The International Encyclopedia of Education*. The subject is subdivided into essays on media attributes, media selection, perceptual factors, systems approach, and task analysis. The article on media selection, by E. U. Heidt, reviews six types of selection models, lists six groups of selection factors, identifies contexts, and discusses recent research.

In the more specialized area of library instruction, there are two approaches that should be examined in more detail: instructional development and learning control-centered design.

Instructional Development

Instructional development, also known as the "systems approach to instructional design," or "systematic instruction," refers to a well-organized approach to designing instruction. Models, such as flow charts and other diagrams, are a distinctive feature of instructional development. It has been described as "a goal-oriented, problem-solving process involving such techniques as the development of specific objectives, the analysis of learners and tasks, preliminary trials, formative and summative evaluation, and continued revision" (Hardesty and Gatz, 4).

Hardesty identifies ten main steps in instructional development:

1. Needs assessment

2. Solution selection

3. Analysis of task and content

4. Development of instructional objectives

41

5. Selection and sequencing of instructional strategies

6. Selection of media

7. Development and location of necessary resources

8. Tryout and evaluation

9. Revision/recycle

10. Social aspects

Our steps for selecting media are generally based on this process, with some simplifications. Instructional development offers excellent guidelines for employing the newest technologies in library instruction, as evidenced by several recent articles and reports. Judith Pask has used a modified systems approach to developing CAI in an academic library. She describes seven steps: needs assessment, objectives, program language selection, hardware selection, writing the program, evaluation, and revision (Pask, 6-11). Brian Nielsen and Betsy Baker summarize a similar model program that they used to determine effective methods for teaching online catalog use at Northwestern University (Nielsen and Baker, 571-85). And David Clow and Clive Cochrane report on using instructional development to design both user education and staff training programs at Queens University in Belfast, Ireland (Clow and Cochrane, 17-25).

Learning Control-Centered Design

Marilla Svinicki and Barbara Schwartz have proposed an additional facet to the instruction design process. They have developed a system for categorizing teaching methods based on the "standpoint of who or what determines the sequence of events as the students learn" (Svinicki and Schwartz, 7). This factor is called the "degree of control over learning," which can be plotted along a continuum ranging from direct to semidirect to indirect instruction (see figure 2-2).

Videotapes, point-of-use aids, and demonstrations are examples of direct instruction. With these media, the librarian or instructor determines what information is presented and how. There is little opportunity for learners to influence or respond to the medium, whether human or automated. The purpose is efficient delivery of information, but there is no mechanism for feedback.

Figure 2-2. Continuum for Categorizing Instructional Methods

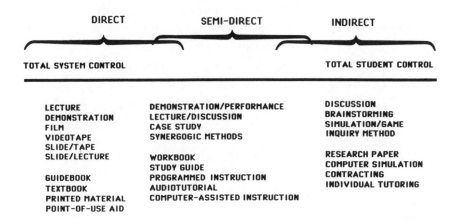

Reprinted from Designing Instruction for Library Users, p. 7, by courtesy of Marcel Dekker, Inc.

Semidirect instruction includes methods that are basically guided by the instructor but are influenced by learners as well. CAI that contains quizzes and branching to provide responses to correct and incorrect answers is a semidirect medium, since the learner exercises some control over the progress of the program. Optical disc exercises and workbooks are other semidirect instruction methods.

Learners have the greatest degree of control over indirect methods like individual tutoring, artificial intelligence, and free use of online tutorial services. Goals and objectives are determined by the student, and the instructor serves as a resource, supplying information as requested. Indirect media encourage students to be responsible for their own learning, which may make them more independent library users; however, these methods are also time consuming and may be very expensive to provide.

Svinicki and Schwartz illustrate their theories with eight case studies. One case outlines an approach to teaching graduate students how to search BRS/After Dark so that they may conduct literature reviews on dissertation topics. Their analysis of goals and objectives, learner characteristics, and resources is effectively graphed with the degree of control over learning variables in figure 2-3.

The direct method for this class is a lecture to describe the advantages of online searching and to introduce Boolean logic. Demonstration, discussion, and exercise worksheets completed in groups in class are semidirect means of teaching search strategy development. The students then are responsible for preparing and carrying out their own searches; printed point-of-use directions are available at the terminals. These activities involve a combination of semidirect and indirect instruction. Finally, the students meet in a second class session to review and discuss search results, modify their strategies, and continue the research process.

Figure 2-3. Case Study Analysis

Constraint		Teaching Options
Objectives	Describe advantages - Basic	Direct
	Identify key concepts - Intermediate	Semi-direct
	List synonyms - Intermediate	Semi-direct
	Use boolean logic - Basic and intermediate	Direct and semi-direct
	Choose data bases - Advanced	Indirect
	Use terminal and execute search - Intermediate	Semi-direct
	Refine search statement - Advanced	Indirect
Students	Graduate students	
	Sophisticated learners	
	Familiar with library but not on-line or BRS After Dark	Semi-direct or indirect
	Highly motivated	
Situation	Small class	
	No time limits	Anything
	No class restrictions	

Reprinted from Designing Instruction for Library Users, p. 173, by courtesy of Marcel Dekker, Inc.

While following the essential principles of basic instruction design, learning control-centered analysis adds an important factor to your choice of media. Where do the methods featured in your teaching program fit on the continuum? If most of your media are grouped at one end, perhaps you are not serving the full range of learning styles and situations equally effectively.

CASE STUDIES

Many librarians who have installed online catalogs, CD-ROM products, and other automated resources, and who have developed instruction programs for them, have contributed journal articles and essays to the professional literature. Their reports offer useful information about the guidelines they followed to choose teaching media.

Wayne State University

Patricia Lynn and Karen Bacsanyi have written a detailed description of how librarians at the Purdy/Kresge Library at Wayne University selected methods to teach end users how to search CD-ROM systems. The optical disc products SilverPlatter PsycLIT, DIALOG ERIC (Education Resources Information Center), Compact Disclosure, and WILSONDISC Social Sciences Index were installed in September 1987. Their report states or implies most of the instructional design steps outlined in this chapter.

Two problems were identified: the powerful search and retrieval methods of CD-ROM products made them seem complicated to novices, and as a result, demands on the reference staff for assistance and instruction were much greater than anticipated. Consequently, the librarians' goal was to teach end users the basic skills required to search CD-ROM systems; their skills statements can be inferred, although they are not given in detail. Understanding Boolean search strategies, limiting a search, using the FIND, SHOW, and PRINT options, and coping with an online or print thesaurus could be included in a list of skills their users needed to learn.

Several different groups of learners were identified: 30,000 undergraduate and graduate students, faculty, staff, many Detroit area residents, and students from other local institutions. "These users ranged from those who had never touched a computer keyboard, to library science students practicing DIALOG Command search strategies, to business faculty downloading company reports for analytic purposes" (Lynn and Bacsanyi, 18). Their instruction had to accommodate the widest possible range of backgrounds and skill levels.

Several statements give an idea of Wayne State's resources and constraints. The library had made heavy investments in computer and communication technology and planned to continue this level of commitment through its next five-year plan. The Purdy/Kresge Library also had in place a variety of computer-based systems when the CD-ROM products were introduced, including an online catalog, mediated search service, and InfoTrac. Librarians could expect adequate funds and had access to an existing pool of automation expertise and computer equipment. On the negative side, the instructors had to learn to use the CD-ROM products during the fall semester, so time for material development was a problem.

The report does not contain a review of media features, but the librarians presumably carried out this step as part of their decision to offer five teaching methods: instruction leaflets, individual instruction on demand and by appointment, scheduled group sessions, and course-integrated training sessions. Selected characteristics of these methods are discussed in terms of the perceived results of each form of instruction. Printed materials were time consuming to produce, and users were reluctant to read them. Individual instruction was the users' and librarians' ideal method but proved extremely demanding for staff to provide either on demand or by appointment. Scheduled group sessions attracted few learners, but those who did attend valued them. Class presentations in subject areas were difficult to perform without a classroom, microcomputer, and projection unit for that purpose, but student comments were positive.

Wayne State librarians did an excellent job of evaluating their instruction program; they designed and administered a four-page survey on users' "institutional affiliation, area of study, library attendance, computer experience, evaluation of the system used, search results, and instructional methods recommended" (Lynn and Bacsanyi, 19). Results were enlightening, although the sample was small (84 completed). Instruction methods in order of preference were individual instruction on demand, CAI, scheduled training sessions, workbooks, peer instruction, instruction within subject classes, and instruction within a formal library program.

Lynn and Bacsanyi indicate possible revisions in the program, based on the first year's experience teaching end users on CD-ROM products. "While the library presently offers CD-ROM users access to printed instructions, individualized instruction, and class sessions, it may be necessary to go beyond the traditional forms of bibliographic instruction and begin offering computer assisted instruction. More ambitious instruction programs would ensure that users comprehend the power of CD-ROM technology and learn to perform advanced searches" (Lynn and Bacsanyi, 22). Purdy/Kresge Library has the resources to add a successful CAI component to the CD-ROM training materials; a single CAI could teach concepts basic to all of the systems and provide sample searches for each product. Librarians identified transfer of learning among the different software programs as a serious problem. Workbooks also deserve consideration, since they were moderately well rated on the user survey and are adapted for use with classes.

Rochester Institute of Technology

Librarians at the Rochester Institute of Technology faced a more complex set of issues and developed an innovative response that blends traditional and technology-based bibliographic instruction methods. Loretta Caren of the Wallace Memorial Library has reported on their work in a recent article in *Library Trends* (Caren, 366-73).

The librarians found that, while successful bibliographic instruction relied heavily on faculty support, the necessary cooperation was missing with respect to new technologies because faculty members were unaware of the new resources or had used them only for special purposes. Although RIT students were described as computer literate, faculty members were often unaware of the effects that electronic information systems were having on the library.

The teaching goal, then, was "to familiarize faculty with the full array of electronic information retrieval services available to them and their students through the library" (Caren, 366). Instruction focused not on skills such as online searching but on concepts, background, and overviews. Objectives could be stated generally: faculty members would understand "the difference between the library's own online catalog, online searching, CD-ROM searching, or the OCLC database terminals often available for patron use" and would be better prepared to assess their appropriateness for student research assignments (Caren, 367).

Learner characteristics were more narrowly defined than at Wayne State University. Academic faculty members could be expected to possess various degrees of familiarity with traditional library resources and functions; all would be subject specialists, with detailed knowledge of research in their own areas. They would also be likely to be aware of the fast pace of technology implementation in general and highly motivated to increase their knowledge of possible benefits to their students and themselves.

Resources for instruction development can be inferred from Caren's report. RIT has had an online catalog and online search services for nearly ten years. CD-ROM products have recently been introduced, and the collection of resources in that medium is growing. The library "has quickly espoused the capabilities of new information retrieval technologies" and is "utilizing the campus VAX network to extend remote access to library systems and electronic reference services" (Caren, 368). The librarians had access to a sophisticated array of equipment and expertise, both within the library and in the campus community. Their bibliographic instruction laboratory was equipped with slide projector, overhead projector, and a phone line; a PC workstation, modem, CD-ROM drive, and liquid crystal projection unit were available in the reference area. The financial climate seems positive, since at the time of writing, a building expansion with a microcomputer lab was planned. The report does not mention how long it took to design and create the instruction program.

As at Wayne State, the librarians' analysis of media features can best be reconstructed from the resulting program. To increase their faculty's comprehension of library technologies, RIT instructors developed a seminar called "Library Connections," with four modules covering a historical review, local connections, bibliographic connections, and document delivery and future connections. The seminar format is a familiar and appealing one for most members of an academic faculty, and the entire session was planned to take one and one-half to two hours, a reasonable time for them to schedule.

The first element of the seminar is a slide presentation and lecture on history by the assistant director for information services, a former art librarian. "Historical photos of the library's successive generations of catalogs and services are intermingled with humorous, artistic, or graphic slides to depict otherwise subtle or abstract ideas. This introduction sets the stage for the seminar as a lively and exciting journey and puts the forthcoming 'connections' into perspective" (Caren, 369). Here is an effective use of a common bibliographic instruction technology, familiar to the faculty and therefore nonthreatening.

Local connections are the theme of the second module of the seminar. The general instruction librarian uses the microcomputer, modem, and liquid crystal projection unit to demonstrate connecting to the online catalog through the campus VAX network, as faculty could do from home or office. Searching the catalog and using RIT's electronic reference service, "twenty-four hour maximum turn-around time on straightforward reference questions via electronic mail," are also shown and discussed. Going beyond the campus, local connections include dial-up access to a regional linkage project that joins four local colleges and a public library for catalog searching. The RIT instructors have streamlined their online demonstration with autolog-on programs, and have also downloaded sample searches to floppy disks so that the seminar is not dependent on flawless telecommunications and systems operation. "One staff member is also 'at the keyboard' while another is speaking, a separation of labor that works well to keep the demonstration running smoothly both visually and orally" (Caren, 369).

The third module, which compares online and CD-ROM searching, is presented by the online services coordinator and the head of reference or a subject bibliographer appropriate to the particular interests of the faculty attending. Autolog-ons and backup searches safeguard the online portion of the demonstrations. "This is a major module of the seminar and the first two modules are kept brief to make sure that this segment gets a full share of time" (Caren, 370).

The fourth and final module concerns interlibrary loan systems and other document delivery connections, and future connections. Either the head of reference or the director of the library conducts this segment, which combines lecture and discussion. The list of future connections is impressive, including conversion to a new online catalog in 1989, change in networking to OCLC with public access at the reference desk, addition of CD-ROM products, onsite loading of databases, document delivery by telefacsimile, and downloading of SDI searches directly to faculty workstations. "This module encourages faculty input – suggestions and reactions which form an important dialogue – and builds bridges for future interaction" (Caren, 370). It also uses a familiar forum style to wrap up the seminar.

The modular seminar approach has several advantages as a method for solving the broad instruction problem identified by the RIT librarians. It combines high technology with traditional forms of teaching, including lecture, discussion, and printed materials. Handouts summarize the major electronic library services, list available databases in their various forms, and provide brief instructions for use of the public catalog and CD-ROM products. The seminar format conserves time and promotes staff involvement by employing the talents of many librarians, both in preparation and presentation of instruction. The original approach was general, but proved easily modified to meet the need for subject-specific seminars by focusing the sample searches and databases in the desired area. Finally, this approach is flexible. New technologies can be covered by adding new modules to the existing seminar as required.

RIT librarians have not neglected the steps of evaluation and revision, although no formal survey is reported. Proof of the seminars' success came when "an overwhelming response necessitated adding four additional seminars, reaching over seventy faculty" (Caren, 371). Attendee comments were positive, and the faculty requested more general seminars and specialized versions. In fact, the seminars have been moved to a larger lecture room to meet the demand.

The instructors shared their seminar with library staff while it was still in the draft stage and revised their text, pace, and delivery in response to comments and criticisms. Changes planned for the future include offering the seminar to students, involving more library staff, and broadening the scope of the presentations. New equipment will be needed, since the present microcomputer workstation used for demonstrations comes from the reference area.

The RIT instructors have completed all of the basic instructional design steps in creating their modular seminar for faculty. Their approach meets a difficult teaching problem gracefully by capitalizing on the resources available, supporting their own conclusion that "meeting the demands of a new and complex technological approach to information storage and retrieval has caused revamping of the approach to instruction in a dynamic and responsive manner and has raised the visibility and peer recognition of librarians within the campus community" (Caren, 373).

RESOURCES FOR LEARNING AND SHARING

Whether you work in a small library, perhaps as the only professional with sole responsibility for instruction, or in a large institution where many instructors contribute to the teaching effort, you will want to be aware of others' work with media and to share your own experiences and conclusions. There are many ways to stay in touch with your colleagues.

Professional Literature

The case studies reviewed above are good examples of the wealth of information you can find in library journals. The issue of technology in libraries is a "hot" topic, and articles cover the complete range of related issues, from reviews of specific software programs to theoretical arguments about the effectiveness of various teaching media. Print or online searches of *Library Literature, Library and Information Science Abstracts, Education Index,* and *ERIC* will lead to writing focused on the interests and needs of librarians. At present, the literature seems dominated by academic and special librarians, since the first wave of technology has occurred in their institutions. You should contribute to the literature if possible, especially if you work in a school or public library.

Workshops and Conferences

Attending a state, regional, or national conference or workshop provides several benefits. First, you will hear papers and presentations on the latest experiments and issues in media and library instruction. Second, you will be able to meet and talk informally with many librarians who have gathered to learn about the same topics that interest you. And third, you can see and test the newest hardware and software products at the vendors' exhibits. Some of the conferences likely to contain information about teaching and technologies are National Online, Computers in Libraries, Online, Databases in the Schools, and the meetings of the American Library Association subdivisions that specialize in related areas, such as the Library and Information Technology Association, the Association of College and Research Libraries Bibliographic Instruction group, and the Reference and Adult Services Division Machine Assisted Reference Services group. State and regional meetings, which may be more practicable to attend, are also excellent sources of information.

Electronic Mail Networks

Even if you live in the most remote location, your computer, modem, and telephone line can put you in touch with librarians around the world if you join an electronic message network. These networks commonly provide several services: you can maintain a "mailbox" and send files to or receive them from other individuals on the system. ALANET is the network most familiar to many librarians. On some networks, you can join special interest groups and start electronic conversations with colleagues at many libraries. BITNET, used by many colleges and universities, has PACS-L, an interest group focusing on issues and problems related to public access computer use; BI-L, for a broad discussion of instruction topics; and several others. Ask a question about a project you are considering, such as "What are the best programs for developing CAI?" and you may find many responses in your "mailbox" the next day.

Library Orientation/Instruction Exchange

The resources described above are primarily ways to get information about media and instruction. Where do you turn if you want to read other librarians' workbooks or point-of-use materials, or borrow videotapes or CAI to examine? Eastern Michigan University's Library Orientation/Instruction Exchange, commonly known as LOEX, provides this important service. David Gregory summarizes LOEX's contributions:

> Since 1972, LOEX has served as a central exchange for library orientation and bibliographic instruction programs and materials in the United States and Canada. Initially funded by the Council on Library Resources, LOEX is now a self-supporting agency that offers a variety of services to its institutional members for an annual fee of $50.00.

> The agency's quarterly newsletter, *LOEX News*, contains lists of materials available for purchase or loan, bibliographies, announcements of meetings and conferences relating to bibliographic instruction (BI), reports on current activities at regional and state clearinghouses, and a "Letters" column that facilitates direct exchange of information and materials among readers. In addition to its newsletter, LOEX maintains a Speakers Database, a BI Information and Referral Database (containing information on activities and programs at over 830 academic libraries in the U.S.) and—most important—a collection of some 38,000 sample instructional materials, from which members may borrow at no additional cost. LOEX also hosts an annual meeting on bibliographic instruction. (Gregory, 12)

According to the LOEX guidelines, "any and all types of training or instructional materials are appropriate for the LOEX collection." The following automated media are specifically mentioned: audio or video, computer-assisted or computer-directed instruction packages, and hypermedia. Examining the work of other librarians can be very helpful in the process of designing your own instruction materials, and you may be able to conserve time by using sections of the borrowed teaching tools, if you credit the developers properly. Most librarians, however, need highly individualized handouts, CAI, and videos.

Carolyn Kirkendall commented on this problem in 1981: "Past experience from the central vantage point of the LOEX exchange indicates that, in the majority of cases, the quality and content of audiovisuals produced both commercially and in-house are usually not acceptable for use by others. The expense and time priorities involved in adapting existing programs for local use are often too extensive to justify, and much work needs to be done to develop some sort of apparatus to test and compare the effectiveness of audiovisual teaching aids" (Kirkendall, 110). In the last ten years, quality of both vendor and in-house audiovisuals has improved as better equipment has become available, and the whole spectrum of microcomputer-based media has been introduced. Borrowed materials are still more likely to be useful as models or examples, however, than as replacements for your own work.

LOEX Surveys

In April 1987, LOEX conducted a survey of 1,826 academic libraries in the United States to assess several variables related to their bibliographic instruction programs. One of the goals of this survey was to compare the 1987 results with data on the same issues cumulated in 1979. Although the survey was restricted to academic libraries, some of its results may indicate trends within library instruction in general.

According to Teresa Mensching, "course-related and orientation lectures, point-of-use programs (print and nonprint), conducted tours, and individualized instruction (either at the reference desk or by appointment) were the most widely used methods of instruction for both time periods" (Mensching 1989, 8). Audiotape or videotape tours, nonprint point-of-use programs, CAI, and slide/tape tours were less frequently used. "The largest reported increases in use were for point-of-use programs (such as videotaped instructions at the OPAC terminals or printed guides accompanying the CD-ROM indexes) and individualized instruction. Also showing an increase were the number of libraries reporting use of CAI programs to teach library research skills, and the number reporting use of videotape or audiotape for library tours and general orientations" (Mensching 1989, 8-9; see figure 2-4).

The 27 percent increase in point-of-use programs of all kinds and the similar 28 percent jump in individualized instruction may reflect the introduction of complex technologies into academic libraries. Note that Mensching, the former director of LOEX, refers specifically to OPAC terminals and CD-ROM indexes, which must have been mentioned by librarians responding to the survey. In closing, we may also want to take note of the highest figures in the table. Lectures, point-of-use programs by librarians, conducted tours, and individualized instruction outstrip every other reported method by wide margins, and every one of these methods features the most essential and most popular form of instruction – a librarian. The teaching technologies are important and their use will continue to grow during the next ten years, but for the foreseeable future they will complement and not replace our own vital work.

Figure 2-4. LOEX Survey of Instructional Methods

Methods	1987 Respondents		1979 Respondents		% Change
	no.	%	no.	%	
Credit course	238	29	347	42	-13
Term paper clinics	144	17	173	21	- 4
Lectures	788	94	790	95	- 1
CAI	122	15	18	2	+13
Point-of-use programs	804	96	575	69	+27
By librarian	788	95	—	—	—
Print	473	57	—	—	—
Nonprint	100	12	—	—	—
Tours:					
Conducted	714	86	670	81	+ 5
Tape	151	18	87	10	+ 8
Videotape	90	11	—	—	—
Audiotape	61	7	—	—	—
Slide/tape	149	18	139	17	+ 1
Printed self guides	270	32	263	32	—
Individualized instruction	792	95	558	67	+28

Copyright Mountain Publishing, Inc.; reprinted with permission.

Works Cited

Bowen, Dorothy. "Learning Style Based Bibliographic Instruction." *International Library Review* 20 (1988): 405-13.

Caren, Loretta. "New Bibliographic Instruction for New Technology: 'Library Connections' Seminar at the Rochester Institute of Technology." *Library Trends* 37 (Winter 1989): 366-73.

Clark, Richard, and Gavriel Salomon. "Media in Teaching." In *Handbook of Research on Teaching*, edited by Merlin C. Wittrock, 464-75. New York: Macmillan, 1985.

Clow, David, and Clive Cochrane. "User Education and Staff Training in a Continuing Education Programme." *Education for Information* 4 (1986): 17-25.

Diamond, Richard. "Piecing Together the Media Selection Jigsaw." *Audiovisual Instruction* (January 1977): 50-52.

Dunn, Elizabeth Bramm. "The Challenges of Automation and the Library Instruction Program: Content, Management, and Budget." *North Carolina Libraries* 46 (Winter 1988): 219-22.

Gayeski, Diane. "Why Information Technologies Fail." *Educational Technology* 29 (February 1989): 9-15.

Golen, Steve, and Thomas Keller. "Communication Barriers in Microcomputer-based Courses." *Collegiate Microcomputer* 6 (February 1988): 77-79.

Gregory, David. "LOEX: An Important Training Resource for NOTIS Libraries." *NOTISes* no. 43 (June 1989): 12-14.

Hardesty, Larry. "Use of Media in Library Use Instruction." Paper presented at the Annual Conference of the American Library Association, Dallas, Texas, June 25, 1984. ED 261 688.

Hardesty, Larry, and Frances Gatz. "Application of Instructional Development to Mediated Library Instruction." *Drexel Library Quarterly* 16 (1981): 3-22.

Harrington, James. "Computer-Assisted Instruction for End-Users: Our Pandora's Box." *Library Software Review* 8 (May-June 1989): 152-54.

Kaslauskas, Edward, and Jacqueline McCrady. "Microcomputer Training Approaches: Review and Evaluation Criteria." *Microcomputers for Information Management* 2 (April 1985): 91-101.

Kirkendall, Carolyn. "Information Exchanges for Library Instruction: Disseminating the Media." *Drexel Library Quarterly* 16 (1981): 103-15.

Lubans, John. "Mediated Instruction: An Overview with Emphasis on Evaluation." *Drexel Library Quarterly* 16 (1981): 27-40.

Lynn, Patricia, and Karen Bacsanyi. "CD-ROMs: Instructional Methods and User Reactions." *Reference Services Review* 17 (Summer 1989): 17-25.

Marchionini, Gary, and Danuta Nitecki. "Managing Change: Supporting Users of Automated Systems." *College & Research Libraries* (March 1987): 104-8.

Mensching, Teresa. "Trends in Bibliographic Instruction in the 1980's: A Comparison of Data from Two Surveys." *Research Strategies* 7 (Winter 1989): 4-13.

-----., Teresa. "Resistance, Empathy, and Technical Expertise." *Research Strategies* 6 (Summer 1988): 136-39.

Nielsen, Brian, and Betsy Baker. "Educating the Online Catalog User: A Model Evaluation Study." *Library Trends* 35 (1987): 571-85.

Pask, Judith. "Computer-Assisted Instruction for Basic Library Skills." *Library Software Review* 7 (1988): 6-11.

Svinicki, Marilla, and Barbara Schwartz. *Designing Instruction for Library Users: A Practical Guide*. New York: Dekker, 1988.

Widman, Rudy, and Jimmie Anne Nourse. "Delivering Hi-Tech Library Instruction: A Hands-On Approach." *Laserdisk Professional* 2 (November 1989): 50-54.

3

Type H for Help:
Onscreen Help as a Teaching Tool

Mara R. Saule

A patron sits down in front of a microcomputer workstation in order to search a computerized index to journal articles. She has never searched the system before, and she's a little apprehensive about computers in general. She looks at the computer screen, trying to assimilate the information in front of her. Although there is a librarian nearby, she's hesitant about bothering him, so she decides to try to figure out the system on her own. At the bottom of the screen in front of her she reads "Type H for Help." When she types H, she sees a screen full of dense text; or she sees a brief line of explanation full of computer or library jargon; or she sees a menu of further help options and is uncertain which option to choose. Not surprisingly, the patron gives up on the help screens and tries to get back to the beginning of the search program by pressing keys that only make the computer beep wildly. Frustrated and impatient, the patron leaves the machine and, quite likely, leaves the library.

In the ideal online or optical disc search system, help screens, like search training in general, would be unnecessary. The search software and user interface would be so "user intimate" that the searcher could enter a search request in her natural language patterns, the software would "understand" what she meant and wanted from the system, and the results would be presented without further interaction with the searcher. Any errors in the search statement would be interpreted and corrected transparently by the system. While developments in natural language processing and artificial intelligence hold future promise of such a system, in all practicality a smooth, "invisible" interface between the searcher and the system is still far away.

Most online and optical disc search systems include onscreen helps, either in the form of onscreen prompts at the top or bottom of a screen or as separately invoked help screens that appear when the searcher enters a help command or when a problem in searching arises. Lesley Trenner observes that "good online 'help' can make the user-computer interface more friendly which will, in turn, encourage and support users and facilitate their searching. 'Help' can be particularly important for novices or infrequent searchers, especially with the increasing trend towards end-user searching and the widely publicized wish by online hosts to attack the end-user market" (Trenner, 119). Most searchers, however, don't use the prompts and help screens that are available to them, preferring instead to "hunt and peck" their way to success or to ask for help from a fellow searcher or librarian.

Unfortunately, it is the poor design of many onscreen help systems that causes searchers to give up on the system-provided help. Often the inadequacies of the system's search software and its user interface are reflected in the help facility as well, creating together what Joseph Matthews and Joan Frye Williams have called a "user vicious system." Matthews and Williams's "UFI–User Friendly Index" rates information retrieval system "user friendliness" from -4 to +4:

+4 *The User Intimate System*, in which the system knows exactly what the user wants, corrects errors automatically, "learns" from user pattern and adjusts itself accordingly. The "total effect is almost sensuous."

+3 *The User Friendly System* is not as intuitive as the User Intimate System; nonetheless, User Friendly System searchers "have actually been known to smile or whistle a tune while working."

+2 *The User Cordial System* has "old world charm . . . treats users with grace and consideration." Users feel "somewhat at home."

+1 *The User Polite System* is courteous but not always useful, "only a first step in a long journey."

0 *The User Oriented System* includes most online systems. The user must first be trained or oriented to use the system.

-1 *The User Crabby System* is user indifferent, has some inconsistencies, and is irritating when used.

-2 The User Ornery System includes systems that are "too stubborn to recognize that the sun is shining and it's a nice day outside."

-3 *The User Hostile System* is a system that is "typically designed and programmed by a committee, often in a large university."

-4 *The User Vicious System* takes "great delight in inflicting cruel and unusual punishment on anyone foolish enough to attempt to use them" (Matthews and Williams).

A system's help facility can affect user response to the whole system, thereby affecting its overall usefulness as a search tool – as well as its ranking on this scale.

Although the help facilities on many online and optical disc search systems cannot be locally adjusted, librarians can assist searchers to use these help systems more efficiently. Also, many system vendors are eager to receive suggestions from users on help screen design and functionality. In most cases, help systems for online public access catalogs (OPACs) and other locally mounted databases can be rewritten and redesigned by the users themselves, without vendor intervention. This chapter discusses the ideal functionality of onscreen help and the various types of onscreen help available for online and optical disc systems, as well as present guidelines for designing the most useful screens locally.

SYSTEMS AND SEARCHERS

It is generally acknowledged that a user's first encounter with a system is the most critical (Hildreth 1982, 160); furthermore, users are unmotivated to invest much time in learning a new system. In order to make the first encounter with a system as smooth and productive as possible, an information retrieval system should address the kinds of questions a user might have about a system. These questions include:

What have I done wrong? (Why have I received this error message?)
Am I doing the right thing?
Where am I and what can I do next?
How do I do something (e.g., logout, display results)?
How do I get some information (e.g., on databases, on cost)?
Why has the system failed? (Trenner, 119).

A system can address these concerns by providing several different types of guidance to its users: general information about a system's files, commands, or operational status; online documentation that supplements hard copy documentation; specific search or session status information; error management; and instructional facilities, including prompts, help displays and online tutorials (Galitz, 52; Hildreth 1982, 161). Hildreth proposes two techniques for providing system guidance: unrequested help in the form of suggestive prompts and constructive error messages; and optional help in the form of a multifaceted help facility (Hildreth 1982, 161-62).

While technically part of the system's search software and not part of a separate help facility, system prompts and error management play an important role in the searcher's need for help: if the system-supplied prompts and error management system are sophisticated and clear, the user will not need to invoke a separate help facility.

SYSTEM PROMPTS

System prompts include instructional information, in the form of messages, questions, or commands, that helps to guide users step by step through a search. These prompts, such as "Press ENTER to begin search" and "F4 to print," may appear at the bottom of each query screen and/or at the top of the screen. Word-processing programs often provide prompts that define the roles of control characters and function keys in the particular system. In some systems, prompting can be turned on or off at will by the searcher, thus aiding the inexperienced searcher yet cutting down on the amount of unnecessary information on a screen for the experienced user. Ideally, prompting should be selective on the part of the user (Galitz, 53).

ERROR MANAGEMENT

Error management systems are invoked when the user enters an unrecognizable command in the form of a false search key, a misspelling, or a keyboard error such as inappropriate shift key use. Galitz identifies three aspects to error management: prevention, detection, and correction. Toward better error prevention, a system should be able to accept common misspellings and errors in commands and requests: "Person-to-person communication does not require perfection. Person-to-computer communication should impose no more rigor" (Galitz, 48). Furthermore, once an error is made, the system should immediately detect all errors, highlight the error, and position the cursor at the point of the error (Galitz, 47). Finally, constructive error messages with clear indications of corrective actions should be immediately available to the searcher after an error has been made and identified (Galitz, 49). While Galitz's guidelines for a sophisticated error management system may be desirable, they are generally unrealized in the bibliographic systems used in most libraries. Hildreth has outlined "second generation" OPAC features that include "automatically displayed guidance for reformulation/refinement of search" (Hildreth 1989, 117). In the future, artificial intelligence interfaces may aid in error prevention; however, in today's systems other user aids must fill the gap.

ONLINE DOCUMENTATION

Another type of system help that can be separate from the online help facility is formal online system documentation. System vendors will often provide an online version of the system's operational details and user manual instead of, or in addition to, the traditional printed manual. This documentation is intended to be printed off and used as though it were originally provided in printed form; the system, then, is merely a vehicle through which printed documentation is delivered. In some cases, online documentation can be searched using keyword and Boolean operators, thus providing on-the-spot problem resolution. There are several advantages to online documentation over hard-copy manuals: online documentation is available when needed, it can be rapidly accessed, and it is difficult to misplace (Galitz, 53). Online documentation, however, is not as interactive as system prompts, error management, or help screens. Even if it can be searched by topic, it must be separately invoked and does not reflect the specific context of the searcher's problem or question.

ONLINE TUTORIALS

Online tutorials are often considered part of the overall help function of an information retrieval system. Tutorials are intended to train users to search a particular system by providing system background and information in addition to online exercises and sample searches. A tutorial will often lead a searcher, step by step, through a typical search, which includes a demonstration of the variety of searching techniques available. Like online documentation or user manuals, online tutorials are separately invoked functions of the system, independent of a particular search session on the system. (See chapter 5 for a detailed discussion of vendor-supplied online tutorials.)

VARIETIES OF ONLINE HELP

The heart of an online help facility, of course, is the network of help screens that addresses particular searching problems or questions that a user may have during the searching process. Charles Hildreth outlines three different types of help. *General help* is requested by typing HELP or ? and gives a general description of the help facility in addition to a glossary of the individual topics covered by the help screens. General help is often the first step in getting more specific help on a searching problem. *Explicit specific help* covers a particular help topic, such as Boolean operators or author searching, but is not specific to the context of the current search session. For example, in DIALOG's search system, the user can specify the kind of help she needs by entering HELP followed by a help topic, such as HELP BOOLEAN. Of course in this case, the searcher must first recognize the type of help he or she needs and be able to ask for the help topic by name. Finally, *implicit specific help*, also called "context-sensitive help" or "point-of-need help," responds directly to a searcher's difficulty. "When this feature is employed, a simple, unqualified help command is entered, and the system responds with help appropriate to the user's last command and/or the immediate context" (Hidreth, *Online*, 162). In some cases, a help command is not needed; when the system displays an error message, such as "no entries found," it will present the searcher with an unsolicited help screen giving suggestions about why the search did not work and what alternative might be used to correct the search statement.

Most help that is available in online systems is a combination of command and menu driven. The searcher enters a help command, such as "H," "HELP," or "HELP BOOLEAN," and the system responds with a menu of further help selections, or with a particular help screen. In some systems, a menu of help options is always visible and available at the bottom of the search screen. Still other systems rely on function keys to access help screens; SilverPlatter's CD-ROM products provide a plastic template to place over the function key pad indicating that F1 provides help. It is interesting to note that, in systems that use function keys for commands, the help function key is usually F1 (CD-ROM search systems produced by SilverPlatter, UMI, and Wilson all share this convention). As mentioned earlier, unrequested help can appear without the use of a command or a menu selection. Windowing can be especially effective for "pop up" unrequested help screens; with windows, the searcher can still see the original search query and results while reading the help screen window. Expanded error messages can also lead to context-sensitive help screens.

The way the help screens are presented may reflect the way in which the user interacts with the system in general. Some systems are based on a question-and-answer mode of interaction; in these systems, the user may ask for help in the form of a question. A system based on menu selection will generally include a help menu item; similarly, command-driven systems will incorporate help commands. Some computers, such as Apple computers, operate by the direct manipulation of icons; in these systems, the user can "point and click" on the help icon (Galitz, 27-29).

As Trenner has pointed out, there is a great variety in the content, structure, availability, and style of user assistance features. When help is available, how help is accessed, what help topics are available, how much help is available, and how helpful the information provided is can all vary from system to system (Trenner, 121). Similarly, different users reflect different levels of searching expertise and require different levels of help: the first-time system user, depending on his or her previous experience and comfort with computers, will need more system help than the veteran user, who may need only occasional reminders on how to perform a new or less-used function. Of course, between the pure novice and the expert user is the infrequent searcher who will need to "relearn how to use the system, quickly, conveniently, and on demand, while at the terminal" (Hildreth 1982, 159). A truly effective help facility will match the different types of help available with the needs of the particular user searching the system at any given time.

FUNCTIONAL SPECIFICATIONS OF HELP

Whether the variety of help available is general, context-sensitive, or implicit, any help facility should include certain features and follow certain standards in order to be most effective for the searcher. It is important that a help facility be *comprehensive,* including information on how to get help, on the structure and nature of the database being searched, on the syntax and parameters of available commands, on how to undo the effect of a command, and on how to extricate oneself from a situation; be *consistent* in the means of seeking help and in the presentation of information; be *appropriate* to the individual user and to the situation of the moment; and be *timely* for the user as he or she is constructing the command, executing the command, and between commands (Beech, 50).

Specifically, a help facility should meet the following guidelines (as discussed by Beech, 56; Galitz, 54-55; Hildreth 1982, 165; Trenner, 123-25):

1. Online help should be available at all times, at every point in the search interaction, whether through menu or command.

2. Help should be easily accessible. The command for invoking help should be easy to remember and easy to use. It should be easy both to enter and to exit the help facility.

3. Help should provide a multilevel structure that is clear to the system user. The help facility should proceed from very general to very specific and detailed explanations. Its hierarchy should include an introductory display that explains the help structure, logical sections of help reflecting the system's structure, a table of contents for the help sections, and good cross-referencing within sections.

4. The help structure should be easily browsed.

5. Help should accommodate different levels of user and include a choice between brief and detailed explanations. Users should be able to "switch off" onscreen prompts or unrequested verbose help.

6. Help should be specific to the situation. When specific help is not explicitly requested, the system should automatically provide help appropriate to the context of the interaction.

7. Help should be well written: concise and easy to read, avoiding dense presentation of text and scrolling. Help should also avoid computer or library-related jargon.

8. Help should employ carefully chosen examples that reflect searches that a user might be likely to perform.

9. Help should be well presented, employing highlighting, screen headings, and bulleted outlines.

10. Help should retain the context of the search in progress, and provide an easy way for the user to return to his or her search if the search is no longer displayed on the screen. It should not disrupt processing of the command.

Help screens should also reflect the system metaphor, or mental model of the system, which has been presented to the user through the individual record and screen displays. A system metaphor provides users with an organizing framework for the system, such as a filing cabinet or a card catalog or, in the case of Apple computers, a desktop. "People have a natural tendency to try to build some kind of mental model of the way a system works. If the system itself doesn't give users some organizing clues, they are going to make their own model, and it's probably going to be the wrong one . . . Without a metaphor to use as a road map, they get lost . . .because they have incorrect expectations about what the system is going to do" (Borgman, 141). A help facility can support the system metaphor or model presented by any given automated system by reflecting the structure and terminology of that metaphor in its screens.

SCREEN LAYOUT AND TEXT GUIDELINES

In addition to the above general guidelines for help screen functionality, particular attention needs to be paid to screen layout and text presentation as they apply to each individual help screen and to the links between screens. In general, help screens should be consistent, brief, and compatible with each other, grouping related information together and following a predictable visual scheme (Matthews, 556).

First of all, it is important that the user have a search context for the information that is being presented on the help screen. "Since the user sees only one screen at a time, he needs to know which screen it is and where it falls in the search process. Searching is a sequential process; as the user steps from one phase to another, the system should help the user to change his viewpoint whenever necessary" (Norman, 118). Each screen, then, should identify or repeat the user's input, or what the help screen is for. To help keep the search context, there also should be clear screen-to-screen linkages, through verbal linkages such as repeated terminology or through spatial linkages such as windowing. The use of mnemonics and arrows can also facilitate linkages between screens (Norman, 122).

For consistency, the organization and display of text and data should be standardized across help screens. In particular, the screen should be divided into three segments (top, middle, and bottom) with each segment reserved for specific functions. For example, the top of the screen usually shows how the user got to the present screen; the middle of the screen presents the current information, and the bottom of the screen is typically reserved for the display of options available to the user (Matthews, 560). Dashed lines or other graphic delineations may be used to segment the screen.

Most importantly, crucial instructions for system operation should not be buried in the middle of a section; people remember items displayed at the beginning or end of a range (Borgman, 138). In order to facilitate the user's identifying and remembering the important help information, only information essential to the user's needs should be displayed. Borgman has observed that "the average user can comprehend seven (plus or minus two) chunks of information" at a time (Borgman, 138). Information such as terminal address or time and date should not be displayed; it only detracts from the truly necessary information. In all, no more than 30 percent of available character space should be used; 15 percent is recommended (Matthews, 559).

Matthews has outlined eight general text guidelines for the presentation of help screen information:

1. Data should be arranged logically, by function,

2. Text should be a mix of upper- and lowercase letters,

3. Each sentence should end with a period,

4. There should be little or no hyphenation of the text,

5. Text should be left-justified,

6. Text width should be no more than 55-60 characters,

7. Important pieces of text should be highlighted,

8. Paragraphs should be no longer than four lines each, separated by a blank line (Matthews, 557).

In addition to general text layout guidelines, specific sentence and stylistic conventions should also be observed:

1. Sentences should be short, simple and clear,

2. Instructions should be stated in the affirmative, focusing on what to do rather than on what not to do,

3. Instructions should be in the active voice, rather than the passive voice (for example, "Press **Enter** to begin searching" rather than "**Enter** should be pressed to begin searching"),

4. Instructions should be in terms that indicate what particular physical action the user will do (for example, "Type line number" rather than "Select line number"),

5. Word order should follow the temporal sequence of events, corresponding to the sequence of activities (for example, "Press **Enter** to begin searching" rather than "To begin searching, press **Enter**"),

6. Language should be nonauthoritarian, nonthreatening, and nonpunishing,

7. Examples and word choice should be nonanthropomorphic,

8. Wording and terminology should be consistent,

9. Library and computer jargon should be avoided when possible (Matthews, 559; Galitz, 82).

Galitz has provided a list of computer terminology that should be avoided and has listed some possible substitutions (Galitz, 86).

Avoid	*Use*
Abend	End, Cancel, Stop
Abort	End, Cancel, Stop
Access	Get, Ready, Display
Available	Ready
Boot	Start, Run
Execute	Complete
Hit	Press, Depress
Implement	Do, Use, Put Into
Invalid	Not Correct, Not Good, Not Valid

Key	Type, Enter
Kill	End, Cancel
Output	Report, List, Display
Return	Key Enter, Transmit
Terminate	End, Exit

A similar list of library-related terms could also be constructed. Terms such as "bibliographic record," "Boolean operator," "logical connector," "truncation," "subject heading," and "controlled vocabulary" can all be confusing even to veteran library users and system searchers. While it is often difficult to think of synonyms for these terms, effort should be made to explain library-related concepts in lay terminology.

Whether a librarian is designing help screens herself, or simply evaluating the effectiveness of an optical or online system's help facility, both the general text guidelines and the specific stylistic conventions should help in assessing the potential success of help screens.

SPECIAL DISPLAY FEATURES

Most mainframe-based online systems are limited in the number of special display features that they can support; system designers can be limited to flat graphic devices such as dotted lines, arrows, asterisks, boldface, and highlighting to help emphasize points and draw attention. Microcomputer-based systems, particularly those using optical technologies, can employ more creative and dynamic visual and auditory effects: windows, pop-up menus, color, beeps and other sounds, and even voice simulation can be used to enhance the sense of the help screen text. Although such display techniques can help a user to focus on and retain important information, the guidelines of simplicity, consistency, and appropriateness should always be considered. Indiscriminate use of graphics, color, and sound can be confusing and distracting.

Windowing and the use of color are two display features that are becoming increasingly common in help screen facilities. Windowing can be especially effective for providing access to multiple sources of information, such as help screens (see figure 3-1). Windows can also be used for reminding searchers of how to do a particular system operation and for monitoring the progress of a search (Galitz, 97). Windows are generally of two types: tiled and overlapping. Tiled windows do not overlap and their contents are always visible. Consequently, the number of tiled windows that can be displayed on a screen at any time is limited. Tiled windows are less confusing to view and, therefore, can be used most successfully with novice searchers and single task activities. Overlapping windows may be placed on top of one another, obscuring the contents of underlying windows. Overlapping windows are effective for expert users who can keep track of obscured information as the windows overlap and for switching between multiple tasks in one operation (Galitz, 99). As with any special display feature, windows can be overused; no more than six or seven windows should be displayed at one time (Galitz, 99). Also, it should be clear to the searcher how to remove the windows and how to get back to the search or to the original task.

Figure 3-1. ABI/INFORM Help Window Screen

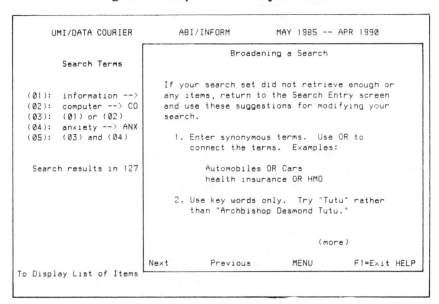

Color is another visual feature that can be particularly effective in help facilities. Color can be used to differentiate and to relate different fields of a display and to call attention to important pieces of information (Galitz, 204). It can hold a searcher's attention and increase his or her retention of the displayed information: "Color motivates. It gets attention. If applied with its limitations and requirements in mind, color can be a powerful manipulator of our attention, memory and understanding" (Durrett, 53). Color can also be used to input and manipulate data in a more intuitive way, so that searchers are "taking cues from colors rather than having to study the text on the screen" (Cribbs, 113). Because of the potential power of color in displaying information, color monitors are becoming standard for some mainframe and microcomputer-based systems, although the cost of such monitors is still a concern. As in the use of windowing, the use of color can also be overdone. Use of too many different colors can be distracting and, for some searchers, visually fatiguing. Some people have color viewing deficiencies and may miss important information if color is used too exclusively for conveying that information (Galitz, 205).

The use of sounds and voice simulation can also enhance understanding of system operation. In library systems, of course, excessive use of sound can be distracting to others working in the library. Beeps and buzzes, however, can alert searchers to errors and can signal the need for invoking a help screen or asking for some other form of help. Although auditory cues can help searchers to catch mistakes, they can also be interpreted as punitive machine reactions: other searchers will immediately know that someone has made an error. In some cases, the computer or terminal will not cease beeping until an error has been corrected. Needless to say, this can cause some embarrassment and disorientation for the erring searcher!

In general, visual and auditory special effects can be powerful reinforcements to information presented on help screens. The potential for indiscriminate use is also great; as display technology is developed and refined, however, even more creative uses of windowing, color, and sound can be expected.

HELP FEATURES AND THE USER

Although many of the above features of help facilities cannot be controlled by the librarian, understanding a system's help facility can aid a librarian in directing a system user to the most effective way of getting help on a particular system. Therefore, even a librarian who understands how a computerized library or information retrieval system works should still become familiar with that system's help facility. At the very least, the librarian should be able to recognize what a system's help screens look like in order to tell if a patron is in the help facility and, therefore, needs help. Ideally, the librarian can use help screens to teach system operations to the patron. In any case, librarians should be critical of help screens and pass their observations along to system designers and vendors.

ISSUES AND OPTIONS FOR DIFFERENT TECHNOLOGIES AND DATABASES

While the criteria for the most effective design and functionality of help screens remain constant across different technologies and different kinds of databases, the content, design options, and implementation issues for help facilities will vary. Users of different kinds of information retrieval systems vary as well, thus requiring different kinds of help. Online and optically based catalogs; locally mounted and remote online bibliographic databases; locally owned bibliographic optical disc databases; and full-text, numeric, and nonbibliographic databases present different concerns for system users, librarians, and help facility designers alike.

Library Catalogs: Online and Optical Disc

Library catalogs, whether online or optical disc, are the most common computerized library information retrieval systems that a user will encounter. The purpose of library catalogs, of course, is to facilitate access to a library's or institution's holdings. The database is self-limiting in scope: it contains records only for materials that a library or library system owns. While the range of materials reflected in the database may be wide, including materials such as sound recordings, films, and museum holdings in addition to book and journal titles, the database generally does not include references to journal articles. The database records themselves are fairly brief, without abstracts; some fields that a patron can search, however, may be in the Machine-Readable Cataloging (MARC) record and not reflected on the public bibliographic screen. Although some larger institutions are mounting indexing and abstracting databases, such as MEDLINE and ERIC along with the online catalog, the online catalog database usually remains a separate entity.

Although most users of online or optically based catalogs are searching the library's holdings from within the library, the needs of remote catalog users are also significant. Remote users do not have access to direct librarian help in searching the system, or to printed search aids such as signs or handbooks. Consequently, help screens take on a much more significant role for these users; help screens may be their aids to searching or to understanding a library's collections. Librarians and local help screen designers should make special consideration of remote users' needs in searching the automated catalog.

In view of the unique content and user base of library catalogs, help screens for library catalogs need to include special information that help facilities for other kinds of systems do not need to address. In addition to providing information that will help a user search the automated catalog itself, library-specific information is also very important: information on library hours, the nature of the particular library's collections, and special notices of services or events can be of interest to users of local library catalogs. The help facility should also include information about access to library holdings such as charge status and items ordered but not yet received.

Because of the great amount of local information and database customization that libraries can include in local automated catalogs, help and news screens can also be locally designed. Therefore, a library is not stuck with help screens that a system vendor has provided, but can redesign help screens to reflect local needs. The NOTIS automated library system allows for great flexibility in help and other information screens. For example, help and news screens in the University of Vermont's LUIS online catalog describe library locations and their collections. The news screen even provides whimsical information to entertain system users (such as a listing of obscure holidays or festivals). Remote users of the LUIS catalog are given special instructions on a series of introductory screens.

Although online and optically based library catalogs share the same types of users and database contents, their technologies are significantly different. Online, or mainframe-based, catalogs can store greater amounts of information and can be updated more quickly than optical disc catalogs, but can employ only a limited number of dynamic display techniques. Optical disc systems, on the other hand, because they are microcomputer-based, can take advantage of windowing and cutting-edge visual display and auditory cueing techniques to enhance help facilities. Unfortunately, their help screens cannot be adapted for local needs as easily as help screens in online systems.

Locally Mounted Online Bibliographic Databases

While most automated library catalogs do not include references to journal articles, increasing numbers of libraries are acquiring tapes of bibliographic indexing and abstracting databases and mounting them through the online catalog. Local online databases, such as ERIC and MEDLINE, can be searched by library patrons using the same user interface as for the library catalog; unlike the online catalog itself, however, vendor tapes are usually not keyed to the library's own holdings (although there is much development in this direction). In other words, there is room for confusion about what a library owns or does not own, as well as about what types of holdings the different databases within the catalog reflect (for example, journal articles with abstracts versus journal titles). If several local online databases have been loaded, then searchers must also distinguish between the contents of each database.

Furthermore, vendor tapes and online catalogs may use different indexing schemes. At Vanderbilt University, for example, patrons can search the ACORN online catalog to find university library holdings as well as search the ACORN-PLUS system, which provides access to MEDLINE and three Wilson databases (General Science Index, Social Sciences Index, and Humanities Index). At the 1989 NOTIS User's Group Meeting in Chicago,

Vanderbilt librarians reported that patrons are confused about the three different subject indexing schemes (ACORN's *Library of Congress Subject Headings* [LCSH], *Medical Subject Headings* [MeSH], and Wilson headings) and are having trouble determining which database to use for a given research question.

Because of the increased scope of catalogs that have been expanded to include many different databases, clear screen layout has become a particular concern for system designers. Carnegie Mellon University recently incorporated five Information Access Corporation (IAC) databases into its online catalog, including Magazine Index and National Newspaper Index. In planning the integration of these databases into Carnegie Mellon's existing online catalog, the design goal was "to try to eliminate the need for printed documentation or other help sources by making the system internally self-documenting as far as possible" (Evans, 113). Carnegie Mellon found that choosing "exactly the correct, unambiguous, meaning-laden terms and keeping use of these terms consistent throughout the system" was the most challenging aspects of designing screens that were clear and concise and addressed the needs of a variety of users (Evans, 114).

Loyola University encountered the same difficulties in finding clear and descriptive terminology for field labels that held the same meaning for all users. Through the implementation of their NOTIS-based INDY system, public services staff at Loyola found that users were confused by the elements in bibliographic citations to journals; terms such as *source* or *indexed in* were not self-evident to most searchers. Because several Wilson databases are available through INDY, searchers at Loyola, like those at Vanderbilt, have had difficulty identifying which database they were searching at any given time (Bakowski, 40).

Help screens can either allay or add to the confusion generated by accessing both vendor databases and the local automated catalog with the same search interface. As with the automated catalog, help screens for locally mounted vendor databases can usually be adjusted to local needs. Help screens for such integrated systems are particularly important and must clearly inform the user about the differences between databases and collections. Error messages and onscreen prompts must also be clearly related to the particular databases being searched. Vanderbilt found that patrons often thought they were searching ACORN when they were really searching MEDLINE or the Wilson system. If a patron is using subject headings that are inappropriate for the database she is searching, the system should alert her to this problem and redirect the search. Help screens should not only refer to the particular database being searched but also address problems in distinguishing between databases.

The introductory screen for systems offering multiple databases becomes particularly important in helping the searcher identify the scope and contents of the various separate databases being offered. The first screen a system user sees when she begins her search should include a brief, explicit listing of the databases included in the local online system with a concise, phrase-length description of the subject contents of the individual databases. Searchers should also be informed of the default database. On the actual citation screens, field labels and choice of fields displayed should reflect the average searcher's information needs and understanding of bibliographic terminology. All screens should display prominently what database the patron is searching.

Remote or "invisible" users of online catalogs can become especially confused by multiple databases and may, thus, be the library's true "lost" users. George Machovec observes that remote users of Arizona State University's CARL system present the most challenging telephone questions about the CARL databases to public services staff (Machovec, 169). When designing help and other screens for local online systems, special consideration should be made for those users who are not in-house and cannot receive on-the-spot searching help.

Remote Online Bibliographic Databases

Remote online retrieval systems, such as BRS, DIALOG, and Wilsonline, have been used in libraries by librarians since the late 1960s. Because most librarian searchers had been specially trained to search these systems, often by the vendors themselves, help screens could be fairly simple, serving as reminders of search options rather than training tools. Furthermore, librarians understood the jargon and structure of bibliographic retrieval, so that help screens could rely on knowledge of terminology such as *Boolean operators* or *truncation*. With the advent of large-scale end user searching in the late 1970s, however, patrons without special training or knowledge of information retrieval were beginning to search these same databases. Help screens for the end-user, consequently, needed to be easier to use yet more extensive and sophisticated than those used by librarians.

End-user online systems such as BRS/After Dark, DIALOG's Knowledge Index, and Dow Jones News Retrieval must employ help facilities that are easy to access, easy to understand, and easy to leave (such as that in figure 3-2). The databases that vendors offer are varied and complicated, and the user base is diverse and remote. Printed documentation is minimal, and in many cases librarians cannot devote much time to assisting end-user searchers, especially during the night and weekend hours that systems are available. The onus of end-user assistance, then, often falls to the help screens.

Figure 3-2. DIALOG Knowledge Index HELP HELP Screen

```
? help help

HELP HELP


KNOWLEDGE INDEX has an online HELP feature designed to provide a brief
explanation of the many options on the KNOWLEDGE INDEX system.  Simply
enter the word HELP followed by the term for which you are seeking
an explanation.

The online HELP feature of KNOWLEDGE INDEX contains the following
options:
                        ---
General
    HELP KI             HELP COMMANDS
    HELP HELP           HELP SECTIONS
                        ---
Commands
    HELP BEGIN          HELP COST           HELP KEEP
    HELP FIND           HELP EXPAND         HELP ORDER
    HELP DISPLAY        HELP PAGE           HELP LOGOFF
    HELP TYPE           HELP RECAP          HELP AU
    HELP JN .           HELP PY             HELP UD
    HELP LIMIT          HELP KWIC           HELP HILIGHT
                        ---
Sections
    HELP AGRI           HELP ECON           HELP MAGA
    HELP ARTS           HELP EDUC           HELP MATH
    HELP BOOK           HELP ENGI           HELP MEDI
    HELP BUSI           HELP FOOD           HELP NEWS
    HELP CHEM           HELP GOVE           HELP PSYC
    HELP COMP           HELP HIST           HELP REFR
    HELP CORP           HELP LEGA           HELP RELI
    HELP DRUG           HELP LITS           HELP SOCS
                        ---
System Information
    HELP HOURS          HELP RATES
    HELP BILLING        HELP TELECOM
    HELP TERMINAL       HELP SERVICE
    HELP ERICCOD        HELP NTISCOD
    HELP MAIL           HELP DIALNET
```

While help screens for remote online databases cannot be individually adjusted for the needs of each institution accessing the database systems, librarians can critically evaluate the success of these help screens. By referring to the functionality, screen design, and text guidelines outlined earlier in this chapter, librarians can judge the effectiveness of remote online database help screens and provide concrete suggestions for revision to database vendors and designers.

Optical Disc Databases

The storage capabilities, fixed cost, transportability, and interactive features of optical disc technology make it one of the most popular and successful media for presenting bibliographic information. Patrons at public, academic, and special libraries are seeing printed indexes and abstracts increasingly become available on compact disc via microcomputer; in some libraries, printed index subscriptions are being dropped so that patrons may have no choice but to search the CD-ROM version of an index or abstract. As CD-ROM databases become integrated into the range of reference sources available to library users, librarians need to consider how best to instruct patrons in their use. In chapter 4 of this book, Linda Brew MacDonald addresses the special instructional challenges presented by CD-ROM databases and presents innovative ways to teach CD-ROM searching. In view of librarian and searcher time constraints, however, help screens and onscreen prompts may still be the most common way for CD-ROM users to get oriented to the system (next to the "hunt and peck" method of learning, of course).

Because of the dynamic nature of the technology, help screens for optically based retrieval systems can employ a wide range of visual and auditory cues. Since optical disc systems are often used in conjunction with local automated catalogs (to verify holdings) and with online end-user systems (to update search results), optical disc help screens should address the scope and limitations of the database being searched. Help screens on optical disc as well as online systems should acknowledge that patrons in today's libraries use a variety of computerized information retrieval systems and should point to choices in information retrieval. While optical discs may be evolving into the storage and retrieval medium of choice, the content of the discs, such as the help screens, cannot be easily changed by the individual library using the database. As with remote online systems, however, librarians can be critical of help screen design and provide suggestions to optical disc vendors.

Full Text, Numeric, and Other Nonbibliographic Databases

As patrons gain more exposure to different information storage and retrieval technologies, publishers and librarians are looking at using these technologies to store information other than bibliographic records. In order to facilitate access to the full articles referenced by bibliographic databases, some companies are developing full-text retrieval systems. University Microfilms, Inc. (UMI), in particular, publishes full texts of business and engineering publications on CD-ROM; both BRS and DIALOG provide similar access to several magazine and newspaper databases. The kind of help screens necessary to support full-text databases vary from those that are most useful for standard bibliographic databases. Because searching the complete text of thousands of articles in one search statement poses unique searching problems (for example, the occurrence of many "false hits," the particular need to delimit searches by sentence or paragraph, and so on), help screens must address these particular searching idiosyncrasies.

Libraries, particularly university and research libraries, are beginning to support nontext databases as well. Datafiles containing raw numeric data, such as can be found in census or Inter-University Consortium for Political and Social Research (ICPSR) files, can be mounted on the same system as local online catalogs and searched using relational database management software through the online catalog interface. While the availability of such research data is exciting for scholars and scientists, it is also confusing for undergraduate users who are already faced with deciding between many computerized information sources. Help screens for the numeric databases themselves should address the sophisticated researcher, who will not rely on them as the sole means of learning or using the database or system. For undergraduate system users, however, help screens in the online catalog must explain these databases in more general terms to prevent the user's getting lost among all the database choices.

Whether the technology involved is magnetically or optically based, and whether the database is local or remote, bibliographic or numeric, the guidelines for screen content and layout still apply. Help screens should be concise, accurate, appropriate, and complete. In all cases, the screen designer should carefully consider the individual characteristics of system users and the unique characteristics of the databases themselves. Help screens should not be generic.

Furthermore, help screens can serve to help orient library patrons to the uses and limitations of all these databases and technologies. In addition to providing help in individual system use, by following the guidelines detailed by Matthews, Hildreth, Trenner, and others, help facilities can assist users in deciding between systems. Help screens should broaden their scope beyond the particular database or system involved to the range of databases and systems available. Although this kind of internal self-referencing in help screens will need to be written locally and is dependent on the systems available in any given institution, help screens can go a long way toward aiding patrons in understanding the range of databases available.

GUIDELINES FOR LOCALLY DEVELOPED HELP SCREENS

As stated earlier, most optical disc and remote online database systems do not have help facilities that can be locally revised by the individual library using the system; librarians must work with system developers and vendors in order to create effective help facilities that are generic to the system but not customized for the library. On the other hand, help and information screens for local online systems, such as online catalogs and locally mounted vendor databases, generally can be revised to fit local library and institutional needs. Although revising or recreating help screens can be a time-consuming endeavor, a complete, accurate, and appropriate help facility can save librarians' and users' time in searching and in system instruction.

Most online library systems include a help facility with the search and user interface software. These system help screens, however, reflect varying levels of writing clarity and style, content completeness and accuracy, and local information. Each library, then, can make changes to the help screens to reflect local tastes and information. Screen revisions are generally of two types: factual corrections and minor editing of local inaccuracies, and complete revision of individual help screens or of the entire help screen complex. In order to facilitate both the correction and revision of the help facility, librarians, local systems personnel, and system users can work together following logical and progressive steps in help screen redesign.

Be Aware of System Limitations

System limitations, such as screen number, line, and character restrictions, will affect how many and what kinds of revisions can be made on help and information screens. In some systems, help screens cannot be changed significantly, in which case your job will be to provide customized system instruction using other media. In other systems, only a certain number of screens can be used for the help facility or for the information screens; if twenty screens have been set aside for the help facility, that number cannot be increased. Conversely, if less than the requisite number of screens will be used, you will need to determine if the "blank" screens will cause any system problems or odd screen messages. The screens themselves are also limited by the number of lines and characters they can support. While most screens are 25 lines long by 80 characters wide, this can vary from system to system. For example, in the NOTIS system, the bottom four lines of any screen are devoted to system messages and prompts, and must be left stable. In other systems, the top lines are reserved for status and terminal information. Other system limitations or requirements may involve the wording of commands; while help screens can be changed, how commands are phrased and entered may not be flexible.

Create a Committee

Most librarians already serve on a variety of library or institutional committees and may not welcome the proposal to create yet another new committee. For help screen revision, however, the suggestions of a wide range of librarians and users will greatly enhance the overall effectiveness of the help facility. The screen design committee should be relatively small – no more than five to seven people – and include representation from many areas of the library: reference or other public service departments; technical services; systems; major departmental or subject-specific libraries (medical, science, and so on); partial collections within the library such as government documents, periodicals, rare books, and audiovisual; and any other areas that may present unique perspectives on system use and interpretation. Each area representative will bring special information to the committee's work in terms of assessing user reaction to the system, explaining the technical reasons behind a system function, addressing the needs of unique user groups, or specifying the system restrictions for implementing changes in the help facility. The committee should also have links to any local library or institutional system oversight or policy committees that there might be (for example, a system implementation committee).

Evaluate the Existing Help Screens

Before any modifications are made, the existing help screen complex should be carefully reviewed and tested online. If there is any question about how a user might react to a particular searching function or corresponding help screen, student workers or other system users should be called on to test the screen(s). At any point of the screen revision process it is dangerous to assume how a patron might react to a screen. By testing out existing help screens at the beginning of the revision process, screen design committee members can assess the strengths and weaknesses of the screens as they are.

Make Printed Copies of All Help Screens

After help screens are initially tested, each screen should both be downloaded onto diskette to facilitate revision and printed off on paper for easier distribution and editing. Care should be taken to "catch" all help screens; some help screens will appear only at certain points in the search process or after certain error messages have appeared. Screens should also be kept in the order in which they appear in the system, grouped by function, and be labeled by type of screen and number (for example, "subj1" for the first help screen for subject searching). Screens should also be dated to avoid later confusion.

Consider Time Limitations

Before the screen design committee begins its work, it should consider how long the redesign will take, both in terms of revision and of the actual loading onto the system of the revised screens. Depending on how many help and information screens there are in the system, doing a close, careful, and substantial revision of the entire help screen system may take several months. Furthermore, and again depending on the system itself, programming and loading new screens into the system could take a considerable amount of time; in some systems, the help screens must be entered using the system's assembler language, thus requiring substantial programming time. If a system is to be available to users at a certain date, the redesign should be planned as early as possible.

Contact Other Libraries

Other libraries using the same system may have already revised their help screens. By contacting some of these institutions, the screen design committee can determine what help screens have worked best in other settings. Through user group newsletters, electronic mail systems such as BITNET and ALANET, and letters and telephone calls, librarians can get copies of help screens that are being used by other institutions. Effective structure and wording from these samples can be incorporated into local help screens as the redesign process progresses.

List Unique Library Characteristics and Customized System Features

One of the primary reasons for revising help and information screens is to reflect unique library information and to incorporate customized system features. References to particular department libraries and library services, for example, may need to be mentioned in the help screens. Patrons searching for items from particular library collections may need special help in searching and interpreting system commands and responses. Furthermore, most systems have been adapted for local library needs, such as setting unique default operators for multiterm searches and upper limits for record displays. Screen redesign should take into account all of these individualized features, making sure that each screen consistently and accurately reflects the current state of the library and the functionality of the system.

Consider All Users of the System

Before setting to the actual revision of the screens, the screen design committee must consider how system features affect the various user groups of the library. How in-house users and remote users will interpret commands and screens needs to be considered. In addition, the help requirements of inexperienced users as well as frequent system users should also be considered. Special user groups (medical library users, media collection users, and so on) may need different kinds of information from help screens than the general user population; for this reason, representation from these special departments on the screen design committee is important.

Consider Other In-house Automated Systems

If a library has end-user search systems in addition to the online catalog, such as CD-ROM databases or BRS/After Dark or Knowledge Index, these systems could be referenced in the online catalog help and information screens. Directing patrons, for example, to the ERIC computer to find journal articles and research reports in education that cannot be found via the online catalog can be an important unifying and clarifying function of the help screens. This kind of cross-referencing is particularly important to avoid confusion if the online catalog also provides access to abstracting and indexing databases.

Consider Other User Aids

Online catalog help screens can also refer to other user aids, in addition to help screens, available to patrons. Through the online catalog help and information screens, patrons can be directed to printed documentation such as booklets, searching aids such as separate computer-aided instruction and simulation for the catalog, catalog information desks, and reference desk assistance.

Consider All Search Modes; Understand the Search Software

When revising help screens, the designer needs a clear and thorough understanding of all search modes, commands, system responses, error messages, and search software intricacies. Special and less-frequently used capabilities of the search software, such as "tricks" for moving forward and backward in search ranges and creative ways of combining search statements, should be mentioned in the help screens.

Distribute the Revision Tasks

Finally, after considering all the above variables in system use and design, the screen design committee can begin the process of editing and revision. Because reviewing each help screen one-by-one by the whole committee is incredibly time-consuming, dividing up the help screens by function and delegating revision to teams of two committee members will help move the process along. Each team should consider both minor wording and editing changes, in addition to major revisions. Teams can look at what other libraries have done, consider local needs, and follow the text and page layout guidelines presented in this chapter.

Teams can make revisions on the paper copies of help screens (or create completely new help screens) and then transfer changes to diskette so that those changes can be easily edited and, ultimately, transferred to the system itself.

Review Changes and Additions Made by Teams

As a group, the committee should review individual changes made by teams, establishing early on that this review be fairly quick; it is easy to get bogged down in semantics and wording discussions and lose sight of the flow of the entire series of screens.

Pay Attention to Examples Used on Help Screens

In addition to checking for overall consistency in presentation, committee review of the screens should pay particular attention to the types of examples of searches and system responses used on the screens. Examples from a variety of subject disciplines and of a range of search modes should be included. The needs of special user groups can be addressed through corresponding examples of searches. Of course, it is important that examples follow the conventions of good taste as well; sexist, racist, and otherwise inappropriate or offensive examples should be avoided.

Circulate Paper Drafts of Screens

Before revised help screens are tested on the system "live," screens should be circulated to various departmental and area representatives to check for inaccuracies and inconsistencies.

Incorporate Changes into the System and Test

Once the paper copies of the changes have been checked and revised, the new help screen system can be loaded onto the online catalog. The help facility will need to be tested again, much like the original help screens were tested at the beginning of the revision process. A variety of librarians and users should look at the revised screens to make sure that they respond to the system smoothly and address any searching problems that a user may have.

Revise Screens Again

After "live" testing, the screens may need to be changed again, although the review of paper copies should have caught any major problems in the help screens.

Keep Track of Updates to the System

Even though the screen design committee has completed its mission once the final help screens are loaded into the system, the committee nonetheless needs to keep track of any updates or changes to the system software. A minor change in system software, such as changing a command M for "more" to N for "next," could affect an entire range of help screens. Not reflecting changes in the help screens could cause great confusion as searchers try to enter contradictory commands.

The ability to revise online catalog help and information screens locally contributes to an automated library system that is clearly adapted to the particular needs and searching idiosyncrasies of individual libraries and users. Close understanding of the system, its various users, and library collections will make locally designed help screens more effective. During the revision process, a wide range of library staff and system users should be consulted and called upon to test help and information screens. Finally, the guidelines for help screen functionality and screen layout and design as outlined earlier in this chapter will make the help facility easy to follow and most useful for patrons and librarians alike. At a 1985 Council on Library Resources (CLR) conference, "Online Catalog Screen Displays," Anne Lipow composed special lyrics to the tune of Dvorák's "Humoresque" reflecting screen design guidelines:

"Guidelines for Screens"

Say it short and say it clearly.

   Make the length of labels merely

12-20 characters, no more.

   Keep the users always knowing

Where they are and where they're going;

   Form a healthy system metaphor.

"Cluttered screens are such a mess

    and cause the users undo stress,"

Mental modeler Christine Borgman writes.

    So when thinking 'bout your path, use

Only screens endorsed by Matthews;

    Thus your OPACs will attain new heights.

CLR's refined our role, then.

    User Intimate's our goal, then.

Let's go home and use what we now know.

    After all is said and over

One small problem's left to cover –

    Where – oh where – to find sufficient dough?

(Lipow, 214)

CONCLUSIONS

Help screens are often taken for granted by librarians and system users alike: librarians may assume that the help facility provided with a system will not be used by many searchers and, therefore, shouldn't be considered as part of an overall system instruction program. System users, on the other hand, often assume that the help facility will, indeed, be helpful. In some situations, such as remote users and in libraries during low-staff periods, patrons may rely on help screens as their sole means of searching assistance. As systems increase in complexity by adding more dynamic and powerful searching capabilities, help screens may be relied upon even more as the quickest and most direct type of point-of-need help.

In a recent study, Lesley Trenner compared 16 search systems according to six criteria in order to evaluate the comparative quality and user-friendliness of each system. Types of systems covered included commercial online systems such as DIALOG and BRS, which provide online access to remote databases; public access automated catalogs; retrieval packages for mainframe computers; retrieval packages for microcomputers, such as dBASEII and Inmagic; and CD-ROM bibliographic retrieval systems. The criteria used to evaluate each system were the following:

1. Online "help" should be available at all times,

2. It should be easy both to enter and exit the help facility,

3. The help facility should be well constructed and reveal its structure to the user,

4. Help should be well presented,

5. Help information should be well written and the language used should be friendly,

6. Help should accommodate more than one user level.

Trenner assigned points to each category and each system he evaluated, with a maximum total score of 15 over all categories.

Trenner's conclusions and recommendations were clear. The CD-ROM product that he evaluated (SilverPlatter's LISA, which shares search software and help facilities with all SilverPlatter products) scored the highest in all categories. Microcomputer help facilities were second; online public access catalogs that Trenner evaluated fell third; mainframe-based search systems, other than OPACs, scored fourth; and, online retrieval systems were last. Trenner recommends that system developers involve users in the design of help screens and that nonprogrammers should be used to develop the content and the approach of help screens. Overall, Trenner concluded that help in automated retrieval systems is often inadequate, even though "useful, friendly help can both support and encourage users" (Trenner, 136).

For each automated information retrieval system that a patron encounters in the library (and, in some cases, beyond the library walls), the librarian must be familiar with the help facility that a system offers. By directing patrons to use a good help facility, the librarian is encouraging the patrons' independence in library use. By telling system designers that a weak help facility needs to be reworked, the librarian is also taking an assertive role in system design. Help facilities are an important and dynamic part of overall system functionality.

Works Cited

Bakowski, Vicki Bloom, and Lisa E. Moeckel. "The Impact of Local Tape Databases on the Library: The M(I)DAS Touch." *Online* 14, no. 4 (July 1990): 38-41.

Beech, David. *Concepts in User Interfaces: a Reference Model for Command and Response Languages*. Lecture Notes in Computer Science, no. 234. New York: Springer-Verlag, 1986.

Borgman, Christine. "Online Catalog Screen Displays: A Human Factors Critique." In *Online Catalog Screen Displays: A Series of Discussions* edited by Joan Frye Williams, 135-51. Washington, D.C.: Council on Library Resources, 1986.

Cribbs, Margaret A. "Monitoring Color in Libraries." *Online* 11, no. 6 (November 1987):113-19.

Durrett, John, and Judi Trezona. "How to Use Color Displays Effectively: A Look at the Elements of Color Vision and Their Implications for Programmers." *BYTE* 7 (April 1982): 53, as quoted by Nancy K. Herther in "Color Displays and Information Retrieval." *Online* 11, no. 6 (November 1987): 120-21.

Elsbernd, Mary Ellen Rutledge, Nancy F. Campbell, and Threasa L. Wesley. "The Best of OPAC Instruction: A Selected Guide for the Beginner." *Research Strategies* 8, no. 1 (Winter 1990): 28-36.

Evans, Nancy. "Development of the Carnegie Mellon Library Information System." *Information Technology and Libraries* 8, no. 2 (June 1989): 110-20.

Galitz, Wilbert O. *Handbook of Screen Design Format*. 3d ed. Wellesley, Mass.: QED Information Sciences, 1989.

Hildreth, Charles R. *Intelligent Interfaces and Retrieval Methods for Subject Searching in Bibliographic Retrieval Systems*. Washington, DC: Library of Congress, 1989.

-----. *Online Public Access Catalogs: The User Interface*. Dublin, Ohio: OCLC, 1982.

Lipow, Anne G. "Final Comments." In *Online Catalog Screen Displays: A Series of Discussions*, edited by Joan Frye Williams, 207-14. Washington, D.C.: Council on Library Resources, 1986.

Machovec, George S. "Locally Loaded Databases in Arizona State University's Online Catalog Using the CARL System." *Information Technology and Libraries* 8, no. 2 (June 1989): 161-71.

Matthews, Joseph R. "Suggested Guidelines for Screen Layouts and Design of Online Catalogs." *Library Trends* 35 (Spring 1987): 555-70.

Matthews, Joseph R., and Joan Frye Williams. "The User Friendly Index: A New Tool." *Online* 8, no. 3 (May 1984): 31-34.

Norman, Kent. "Critique of Online Display Screens." In *Online Catalog Screen Displays: A Series of Discussions* edited by Joan Frye Williams, 117-34. Washington, D.C.: Council on Library Resources, 1986.

Trenner, Lesley. "A Comparative Survey of the Friendliness of Online 'Help' in Interactive Information Retrieval Systems." *Information Processing and Management* 25, no. 2 (1989): 119-36.

Wilson, Flo. "Article-Level Access in the Online Catalog at Vanderbilt University." *Information Technology and Libraries* 8, no. 2 (June 1989): 121-31.

4

Instruction for and with CD-ROM

Linda Brew MacDonald

Optical disc technology is one of the newest information formats to reach libraries. Introduced in 1985, this medium uses a thin plastic disc with a reflective coating to store information in digital form. The disc is read by a laser beam in a player, which may be an external drive connected to a controller card in a microcomputer or an internal drive housed within the computer's case. With appropriate search software installed, the microcomputer can search, display, and download or print out information from the disc. *The New Papyrus: CD-ROM* by Steve Lambert and Suzanne Ropiequet, *CD-ROM and Other Optical Information Systems: Implementation Issues for Libraries* by Nancy Eaton, and *The Librarian's CD-ROM Handbook* by Norman Desmarais all provide excellent overviews of the mechanics of optical disc systems.

Despite its recent introduction, this technology has been quickly accepted by many libraries. The 1988 OCLC study of microcomputers and optical discs in libraries stated that 84 percent of the academic and research libraries polled owned at least one CD-ROM title (Herther 1989, 102). Kristine Salomon of Oakland University did an independent study of the installation and acceptance of CD-ROM products in 150 academic libraries across the United States; responses indicated that 68 percent subscribed to CD-ROM services, while only 34 percent of these libraries offered end-user online services like BRS/After Dark and WILSEARCH (Salomon, 206).

Many librarians are concerned about the library instruction requirements for these new materials. In this chapter we assume that you want to teach patrons or staff how to use some of the optical disc products currently available and intended for use in libraries, such as the Electronic Encyclopedia, WILSONDISC General Science Index, or Bibliofile. The discussion includes special characteristics of the optical medium that make it useful for library instruction, teaching content and methods appropriate to various users, and the issue of putting optical discs in context with other information sources such as online and print formats.

SPECIAL CHARACTERISTICS

Several aspects of optical disc technology make this medium especially useful for certain kinds of library instruction. First, we should clarify some terms: *optical disc technology* is the broad name for a family of different kinds of discs that can be read by lasers. There are discs with audio and graphics capabilities; Bibliofile's Intelligent Catalog for public access now includes talking help screens. The larger 12-inch optical discs are called *laser discs*; the first version of InfoTrac used laser discs and players, and could serve several workstations at the same time. Most of the products available for libraries today, however, are based on one particular type of optical disc, the *compact disc* or *CD-ROM,* for "compact disc-read only memory." Compact discs are only four and three-quarters inchex in diameter, but can store very large amounts of data; one disc can hold more than 150,000 pages of text, or six years of the ERIC database, for example. The "read only memory" phrase means that once the disc is produced, the information stored on it can only be read. New information cannot be added, nor can the data on the disc be altered or erased, although it can usually be copied to a floppy or hard disk. There are other kinds of optical discs, including some that are erasable or that the user can write to, but this chapter discusses CD-ROMs because most of the products now available for and installed in libraries use that form of the technology.

Wide Variety of Products

Although they are very new in comparison to print, CD-ROMs offer a wide variety of products for libraries. Publishers are adding titles in optical disc format so quickly that an exact count is not possible, but there are at least 350 products currently available. Publications that will help you investigate CD-ROM products, vendors, and disc drives include the most recent editions of *CD-ROMs in Print* by Meckler, *The CD-ROM Directory* by TFPL Publishing, and *Optical Publishing Directory* from Learned Information. The *CD-ROM Databases Product Directory*, a list of products and companies, has been published in several issues of *CD-ROM Librarian*; this directory includes citations to product reviews, a valuable feature when you are considering subscribing to a CD-ROM database. DDRI, publishers of the monthly *CD Data Report* and the annual *CD-ROM Sourcebook,* introduced the CD-ROM Sourcedisc in 1989. This innovative application of the technology includes a catalog of CD-ROM titles, simulations of selected products, and the full text of two books and 20 articles on optical discs.

There are compact disc versions of familiar reference tools like Art Index and ERIC and products, such as Bibliofile, designed for cataloging. The EBSCO Serials Directory could be used both in reference and acquisitions. Resources for the student at every level include the Electronic Encyclopedia for elementary grades, Readers' Guide Abstracts for high school students, and PsycLIT for undergraduates and graduates. Public library users might appreciate Magazine Index or National Newspaper Index; business professionals may use ABI-Inform or Datext; doctors, nurses, and medical students may depend on MEDLINE to cover recent journal articles. With such a range of products to choose from, librarians should be able to find one or more to interest the special group they want to instruct.

Varied Levels of Search Complexity

Just as compact discs cover many subject areas, they also offer various levels of search software complexity. Many products have separate search interfaces for novice and experienced users. WILSONDISC, for example, offers three distinct search options: BROWSE mode, for searching by subject heading; WILSEARCH, for completing an onscreen work form with implicit logic; and WILSONLINE, for using the full power of commands. DIALOG OnDisc has a menu-based search system for beginners and a command-driven mode for experts. How do these options affect library instruction? When CD-ROM products are placed in open-access, public areas, they draw many users. It is vital to have clear, entry-level search systems like WILSONDISC BROWSE or Information Access Company software so that users can proceed with limited assistance if staff are not constantly on hand to help. On the other hand, full-featured search programs can be used to teach and practice online searching, as discussed in chapter 5.

Storage Capability

Stephen Harter and Susan Jackson have stated that "the combination of small physical size, high storage capacity, and random access to data make optical discs potentially superb formats for publishing large databases such as MEDLINE, Dissertation Abstracts, and ERIC" (Harter and Jackson, 517). With CD-ROM technology, the limits of search simulations as practice tools for teaching online searching can be overcome. You can design an instruction program that includes practice sessions on optical disc databases, and students will have access to a large enough number of records to make search strategy development and modification meaningful. Although many of the larger databases are published on two or three discs covering different time spans, the current disc is usually most popular; an archival disc may be used at another workstation for practice or demonstrations.

Fixed Costs

Unlike online services, optical disc products are sold discretely or by subscription. Their fixed costs are probably the single most significant advantage to CD-ROMs as instruction tools. Many of the benefits of computer-assisted library resources are now available without the connect time, citation, and telecommunications charges that have made even the cheapest online services too expensive for many instruction programs. Users can be encouraged to practice, to explore the system's capabilities, to use ondisc tutorials. Students who are anxious about mastering the intricacies of search commands and computer keyboards need not worry about the "meter running" associated with online systems. CD-ROM products can be searched whenever the library decides to offer them, unlike the end-user online services, which are often available only during evening hours.

Attractive Technology

"Who could dislike a technology that dances to your door humming hits from MTV and agleam with all the colors of the rainbow?" asks Barbara Quint (Quint, 32). Although the earliest optical disc products were modelled to resemble online services, publishers have revised their first versions and designed the newest products to take advantage of computer graphics and color monitors. CD-ROM systems are attractive to users for reasons that go beyond devices like WILSONDISC's "light show" introductory screen. Users can conduct fast, efficient searches of several years of a database, can use keywords instead of subject headings (with most systems), and can take away a printed list of citations or other material, depending on the product. In a recent study at Cornell University, students were instructed on the use of both CD-ROM and print versions of ERIC; more than 90 percent preferred the optical disc version and felt it was relatively easy to use (Stewart and Olsen, 51). It is rewarding to design library instruction for a resource that many users find inherently appealing.

IS TRAINING NEEDED?

Let's assume that the purchase of a new CD-ROM system has been authorized for your library. Whether it is an encyclopedia or an index intended for installation next to the reference desk, or a technical services product that will be used only by library staff, one of your most important concerns will be training. There are arguments for and against training for optical disc products.

Why Train?

Vendors argue that training is not required for their products, citing the effort they have put into designing "user-friendly" software interfaces. Librarians at Texas A&M University, however, found it helpful to create a teaching presentation for InfoTrac, one of the simplest optical disc products. InfoTrac did not offer Boolean logic, field qualification, print options, or any of the sophisticated search capabilities that might be expected to cause problems for new users. The librarians felt instruction was needed to "reinforce tentative on-site searches by new users," increase searching efficiency, and illustrate common mistakes. Their computerized presentation emphasized "learning about subject headings and sub-headings, dealing with cross-references, analyzing and revising searches" (Charles, Waddle, and Hambric, 91-92).

Another argument against training is the users' own resistance to instruction demands. Unlike online search terminals, which have traditionally been placed in controlled areas like reference offices, CD-ROM workstations are often installed in open-access locations. Students at the University of Vermont expressed impatience and resentment at having to complete a short training program in order to use SilverPlatter ERIC, PsycLIT, and Agricola, which are available in an automated reference center near the reference desk. Some recent studies of the ways people learn to use microcomputers indicate that they prefer to solve problems on their own, turning to outside help as a last resort. Nancy Herther observes that "the help system must allow users to seek it out and not impose itself on the users" (Herther 1988, 121).

Costs are another factor in decisions about training. Since optical discs are purchased by subscription, there is no charge for time spent on the system. Why not let patrons learn to search by practicing and exploring on their own? This option is especially attractive when you calculate the expenses of having librarians design and produce teaching materials, conduct workshops and classes, or provide individual assistance with searching. Most library instruction programs are already burdened with teaching demands; how are staff members to find the time to create effective instruction for CD-ROM resources?

Reasons for providing training are more compelling than the arguments outlined above. CD-ROM products require the effective use of microcomputers, unfamiliar to many library users. Public, school, academic, and special libraries all have to recognize and cope with their users' computer ignorance or anxiety, the well-documented fear of computers that handicaps many people (Herther 1988, 120). Keyboards are complex; function keys may be poorly labeled or confusing; the screen contrast may need adjustment; the printer may suddenly make a funny beeping sound. Constance Mellon has recently done a study of college students' attitudes toward library research demonstrating that if their anxiety and confusion are not allayed, many will avoid using the library at all (Mellon, 138).

Optical disc search software is often both powerful and complex. A full-featured program may include Boolean logic, field qualification, truncation, word proximity operators, keyword searching, various display and print format options, and even online access. When these functions are presented on a screen full of cryptic notations and markings, with flashing windows opening and closing in response to commands, even the experienced online searcher may be confused. As trained searchers know, being able to remember and use commands and operators correctly is only part of the process. Composing the question, identifying its main concepts, and choosing search terms are key skills in searching that are best learned through an instruction program. Studies of end-user searching on BRS/After Dark have confirmed that "users have difficulty using Boolean logic, analyzing concepts and selecting appropriate terminology, evaluating results, and modifying search formulations appropriately" (Harter and Jackson, 519). Research done at Cornell University and Plymouth State College indicates that formal instruction does help new searchers to use CD-ROM databases more effectively (Stewart and Olsen, 52; Bostian and Robbins, 17).

If CD-ROM products are installed in library offices and used primarily by librarians or staff members, training and scheduling for their use will be part of their integration into library operations. If the optical discs are reference or public catalog resources and are placed near the reference or circulation desk, however, library staff may be overwhelmed with requests for assistance. At the University of Vermont, placement of three WILSONDISC workstations in the reference area has increased pressure on the librarians at the desk; although the Wilson software is very reliable, patrons need help frequently with database selection, search strategies, and jammed printers. Librarians at Cornell University have found that "CD-ROM use sometimes threatens to overwhelm our desk service. It is easy to spend time helping one or two users without noticing the line forming at the Reference Desk" (Coons and Stewart, 35). Good library instruction materials can answer some of the basic questions and give the beginners a chance to get started on their own.

Library instruction is also your best defense against "answer machine syndrome." Many people have inordinate faith in computers as reliable sources of complete information. Coupled with ignorance about library materials like indexes and catalogs, this attitude leads naive users to confuse and misuse CD-ROM products, searching for literary criticism in the WILSONDISC Readers' Guide and for musical scores on PsycLIT. Recent studies of InfoTrac and librarians' experiences at the University of Vermont confirm that many users will choose the speed and convenience of an optical disc product over print resources, even when the database is not appropriate for the topic. "A related concern is that users are likely to have false confidence in the results of their searches because they think they have employed the full capability of an electronic retrieval system when they have only used it at the most superficial level" (Harter and Jackson, 525).

Because instruction teaches users to search more efficiently and quickly, it may help solve the problems of scheduling and waiting for busy workstations. Unless you connect workstations with a local area network (LAN) or install a multiplayer system, each product can be used only by one searcher at a time, and open access workstations will quickly become very busy. We schedule the use of ERIC, PsycLIT, Agricola, and ABI-Inform at the University of Vermont, although walk-in use is permitted if no one has reserved the terminal. When large classes are assigned to use ERIC, PsycLIT, or one of the WILSONDISC databases, lines of waiting students are common. Our workbooks, computer-assisted instruction (CAI) program, flip charts, and handouts contribute to keeping the demand for personal assistance manageable. Most students who have been trained can complete their searches within the half-hour appointment limits (15 minutes for WILSONDISC).

Should Training Be Required?

Once you have decided that training will be needed to help your staff, students, or patrons learn to use optical disc products, you must address another concern: should the training be required or merely offered? As mentioned above, when the product is destined for use by staff only, proficiency in its use will be essential and instruction will be a normal part of its introduction into library operations. But when you are installing a CD-ROM resource for end users, the issue is different. Libraries frequently require that end users who want to search online services complete a training program, even when the user pays for part of the search costs. Although we began our end-user search service at the University of Vermont with the same training requirement for both optical and online systems, after three years of experience we have dropped the requirement for the CD-ROM products.

Required training assumes that the student will complete a course of instruction, gain understanding and beginning level skills, and then polish those skills through practice and use of the system. That is the process followed by information professionals; we learned to search not in classes or vendors' workshops but by searching. We have observed, however, that our end users don't search frequently or repeatedly. They search to find information for a speech or paper, or to fulfill a class assignment, and then may not search again for several months. When they do return, they remember very little of the instruction from the workshop, CAI, or workbook completed so long ago. We decided that it was not fair to demand that our users invest one and a half hours in training when they were not searching enough to maintain their skills. We have concentrated on point-of-use materials at the terminals and personal assistance instead, since these approaches are equally suited to the first-time user or the infrequent searcher who just needs to be reminded which function key runs the printer.

There is one exception to this rule: when a professor assigns a search to every member of a large class, we require that each student complete a short workbook and CAI program before searching. We have had hundreds of beginning education and psychology students search on ERIC and PsycLIT to complete an assignment in one or two weeks. The instruction program and sign-up schedule for half-hour appointments make this situation manageable for both students and staff.

Research done by Julia Rholes and Naomi Caldwell-Wood compared the search performance and satisfaction of students trained to use SilverPlatter ERIC by a one-hour workshop or a four-page handout. They concluded that "the large percentage of successful searches and high satisfaction scores reported would seem to indicate that the classes are not essential for the successful implementation of the ERIC SP [SilverPlatter] service" (Rholes and Caldwell-Wood, 7).

WHAT TO TEACH

Your first step in deciding the content of your instruction materials is to become thoroughly familiar with the optical disc product. Analyze the user interface, the software that communicates with the CD-ROM system. Is it designed for a particular audience? To some extent, this is governed by the nature of the product. For example, the EBSCO Serials Directory is designed primarily for staff use in reference and acquisitions; EBSCO's software writers can assume that the system's primary users will have some knowledge of library terminology and functions. Information Access Company, on the other hand, intends its National Newspaper Index for users with no search experience at all. IAC software developers provide very limited search, display, and print options.

Does the system have several modes, designed for various levels of experience? DIALOG, WILSONDISC, and other vendors offer both menu-driven and command-driven interfaces. Is there effective ondisc help? Is there an ondisc tutorial program to which you can refer new searchers? Finally, what is your subjective impression of the product? Is it easy or difficult to learn and to use?

Stephen Harter and Susan Jackson observe that "a trade-off normally exists between the complexity and power of a retrieval system and its ease of use; the more capabilities a system offers the more difficult it is to master. Not only are there more commands and capabilities in terms of sheer numbers, but the decisions regarding which capability to employ when and precisely how are also much more difficult." (Harter and Jackson, 518) Your instruction program must be designed to help users make these difficult decisions.

Hardware and Software

Since optical discs are computer-assisted reference tools, your training has to cover certain basic information users must know to operate the systems. Users have to understand the keyboard and peripherals, such as the printer. In some libraries, users are allowed to change the discs in the CD-ROM player, and must be taught how to do this correctly. New searchers have been known to put the optical discs into the floppy disk drive on the microcomputer! You will have to orient people who are not familiar with microcomputers to finding information and directions on the monitor screen. Why should an inexperienced user know what the cursor is and why it is significant? Function keys are another mystery. Your training materials must decode their cryptic messages; handouts, posters, and keyboard templates are good ways to convey this information. In addition, you need to explain the search protocols of the system and the display or print options for reviewing the results of the search.

Concept Jungle

When you start to list the skills new searchers have to learn, you may feel you are entering a "concept jungle." Your teaching topics may include some or all of the following broad areas, depending on the number of optical disc products you offer and how complex their search systems are:

1. Recognize subject area of topic

2. Select appropriate database

3. Understand database structure

4.   Formulate topic

5.   Isolate main concepts

6.   Use Boolean and positional operators

7.   Use truncation, field limits, set numbers

8.   Review search results

9.   Modify search strategy as required

10. Understand and use output

Even if you decided to require that your users complete a formal training program, it would take hours to cover all of these subjects in detail, even though one study has shown that end users believe they can learn to use CD-ROM systems in 5 to 15 minutes (Lynn and Bacsanyi, 20-21). If you agree that training should be optional for most users, your task is even more difficult, since your handouts, CAI, workshops, or other teaching formats have to be attractive, succinct, and designed for all levels of interest and experience. How can you cope?

Easy Searching

One method that librarians can use to select the essential elements from large amounts of teaching material is to focus on the concepts that users must understand in order to begin searching. Robert Wagers has proposed a model for "Easy Searching" that covers all of these basic concepts (Wagers, 79). His short list of teaching objectives corresponds closely to those developed informally at the University of Vermont for new users of optical disc and online services:

1.   Select a database.

2.   Write a search statement and divide it into concepts.

3.   Compose a "quick and dirty" search with a few terms, the logical operators *and* and *or*, and one adjacency operator.

4.   Display results in a trial format for evaluation.

5.   Print the final results in a format with all required fields.

When compared with the wide range of capabilities offered by many CD-ROM products' search interfaces, this list may seem very limited. Where is truncation? What about searching in special fields? Wouldn't positional operators be more useful than *and*? Remember that these are the basic competencies for end users; you can also design more advanced training materials for searchers who want to learn more. In our experience at the University of Vermont, few users search frequently enough to progress beyond these basic operations. End users who do want to go beyond the entry level commands learn by practice, use the vendors' manuals, or ask for personal assistance. We plan to produce advanced instructional workbooks and CAI for the CD-ROM products.

One advantage of the "Easy Searching" model is that many of the skills it teaches are transferable from one system to another. You must select a database, compose a search statement, and identify its main concepts whether you are searching the Electronic Encyclopedia, Bibliofile, or MEDLINE. Most systems use the connectors *and* and *or*, either by command or by implicit logic; understanding how they work to narrow or broaden a search is fundamental knowledge. Another advantage is that library staff can be expected to reach this basic level of competence with as many systems as the library offers, in order to assist users as necessary; learning the full complexities of several optical disc and online systems will tax even an experienced searcher's "random access memory."

Whether you use an approach similar to "Easy Searching" or find some other way to adjust the content of your instruction to the limitations of time and attention users are willing to invest, you will need to differentiate between using the system and effective searching. Patrons may be able to start the system, enter terms, and print off citations, but their searches may be incomplete or unsuccessful. Stephen Harter and Susan Jackson note: "Librarians should be alert to the likelihood that although little initial guidance may be needed for users to begin using a system, this does not mean that they will be able to conduct skilled or even minimally effective searches. To what degree this is possible depends on the nature of typical information needs, the power and complexity of the system considered, and the design of the user/system interface. It is essential to determine the minimum level of knowledge and skill–with implications for education and training–that users in a given library environment must achieve to satisfy adequately their information needs using a given system" (Harter and Jackson, 520).

HOW TO TEACH

The key to designing successful, appropriate instruction for optical disc products is to take a user-centered approach. CD-ROM technology is a new and important development of microcomputer applications in libraries, but the characteristics of the medium should serve the training program, not control it. Harter and Jackson emphasize the importance of determining teaching objectives according to the needs of users in a specific library. Nancy

Herther agrees with this view: "Users want support that is centered on them and their needs, and not, as so often happens, to have programs designed around some particular function of the system. User-centered support programs allow users to create their own networks of support because they are task or user-centered, not technology-oriented" (Herther 1988, 122). She also observes that few training programs are well planned or based on research. Handouts, posters, and other materials are often produced to "put out fires" as problems arise when users work with the systems.

The Bailey/Howe Library at the University of Vermont is an academic library that also serves many members of the surrounding community. We have identified three distinct types of users with different backgrounds and information needs: individuals, individuals from classes, and classes or groups. We have planned a training program that offers various media to meet the needs of each type of user, although all teaching materials are available to all learners. We will discuss the three types and the media best suited to their needs in detail in the following sections. It should become clear that user-centered instruction is a model that can be applied to optical disc products in all major types of libraries. Public and special libraries are likely to have primarily individual users; school libraries may have more classes or groups, depending on how the CD-ROM resources are provided. Staff members also constitute a special user group with distinct demands for education and training.

Individuals

The individual user is probably the biggest challenge to your ingenuity in creating instruction materials and programs. In libraries where optical disc resources are offered on an uncontrolled or public access basis, you may have very little knowledge of the user's background and interests. Public libraries serve the widest possible variety of users; in special, school, and some academic libraries, you may be able to assume some consistencies of subject specialization, age, or grade level. You will not have complete information, however, in the following important areas:

1. Purpose. Is the user just browsing or doing detailed research?

2. Library skills level. Can you assume any knowledge of indexes, abstracts, catalogs, bibliographic elements?

3. Library affiliation. Some libraries differentiate levels of service; can you spend half an hour helping this person while others wait?

4. Preferred learning style. Some users like print, some want computer-based instruction, some prefer personal assistance. How many bases can you cover?

5. Attitude toward automated resources. Is the user eager to explore another computer application or must you cope with apprehension and anxiety?

Instruction for the individual should focus on point-of-use materials, vendor-supplied documentation, CAI, and personal assistance.

Point-of-Use Materials

Point-of-use aids include handouts, posters, charts, and similar materials that you keep or display at the workstation. They are vital to teaching individuals because they often provide the new user's first information about the optical disc product. Point-of-use materials meet Nancy Herther's criteria for good user support: they are nonintrusive until the users themselves seek guidance, and are also "local, easy to use, and clearly accessible" (Herther 1988, 121). Handouts, posters and similar aids are available when library staff may be busy or not assigned to the workstation area. They are also easy to alter, to reflect software and other product changes.

Point-of-use aids should be colorful and attractive, to draw attention naturally, but also extremely clear and concise. State the name and character of the CD-ROM product boldly: "Here is WILSONDISC General Science Index, for periodical articles about the sciences." All posters, charts, and handouts should be done in the largest type size possible and illustrated with examples. People do not want to read lengthy instructions, and tiny print is deadly. Examples are a much better means of showing what happens when certain commands are used, especially if they are drawn from actual searches.

Whenever you are unsure of the individual user's background, you must assume total ignorance of microcomputers, library resources, and CD-ROM products. Don't use any jargon unless you explain its meaning, and check every detail. Test your materials on end users; their comments, reactions, and problems will be your best guides to revising point-of-use aids.

At the University of Vermont we have created a laminated flip chart to introduce users to searching WILSONDISC. Choosing a database, selecting terms, and entering them through BROWSE, WILSEARCH, and WILSONLINE modes are covered in 20 pages, which feature large print and many examples. Figure 4-1 shows a single page, to demonstrate how a handout can combine product-specific information and general research guidance.

Figure 4-1. WILSONDISC Guide Page

■ Always check the top of the WILSONDISC screen to see what database is being searched, what search mode is being used, and how the search is progressing.
   To change the database or search mode, press the F2 key until the WILSONDISC Main Menu appears.

■ Read the instructions at the bottom of each screen; these will help you search, display results, and print references.

■ Don't give up if you don't find what you need on WILSONDISC. There are many other sources that you can use for information on your topic.

■ Ask for help at the Reference Desk.

Copyright Bailey/Howe Library, University of Vermont.

Vendor-Supplied Aids

Optical disc vendors frequently supply a wide variety of teaching materials with their products, including keyboard templates, posters, and manuals. The keyboard templates, which label function keys and other important key locations, are often very useful. You will have to judge the posters for clarity, conciseness, and application within your own library and workstation area. Some are colorful and well designed, but others are too cluttered and confusing to help new users.

Vendor manuals are often produced in an appealing format, as small loose-leaf binders to make updating easier as software upgrades are issued. Too many manuals, however, are written in much too detailed and complex a style to be appropriate for beginning searchers. The writers seem to be determined to teach every intricacy of the complex software; even when a special tutorial section is included to explain the basics, it is often buried among chapters of installation and configuration instructions. A recent survey at Texas A&M University confirmed that only one-third of the end-user respondents used the vendor manual for assistance with SilverPlatter ERIC. Of this group, fewer than 4 percent gave the manual a high grade for clarity; on a scale of 1 to 5, 75 percent rated it "3" or less. "Since it is not easy to look things up in this manual, staff prepared a four-page handout that described basic search commands, Boolean logic, and special features with examples. From staff observations, these HELP sheets seemed to be used more frequently than the longer manual" (Rholes and Caldwell-Wood, 6). Manuals may be most useful for staff reference; experienced searchers trying to remember the capabilities of six or more systems may need to check how nested logic is entered or whether the default print format can be altered. You can translate the detailed information from the manual into brief handouts more suited to the needs of new searchers.

Several new products indicate that vendors have noted these criticisms and are responding to them. Pemberton Press, publishers of *Laserdisk Professional*, has marketed Quick Reference CommandCards for four of the most popular CD-ROM systems: DIALOG OnDisc, WILSONDISC, SilverPlatter, and OCLC CD450. These 8½-by-11-inch laminated cards cover only the basic search steps for each vendor's software; for example, the Easy Menu mode is explained for DIALOG OnDisc, but command language mode is omitted. The type is too small and they do not show sample searches, but the graphics are attractive and the format very durable. The American Psychological Association (APA) has produced a set of three small booklets to help end users search PsycLIT on CD-ROM, or PsycINFO on BRS/After Dark or Knowledge Index. *Searching PsycLIT on CD-ROM* is excellent: the clear, concise text includes a sample record from the database and good search examples. For beginning end users, the authors could have omitted the Venn diagrams of Boolean logic and the list of Content Classification Codes printed in tiny type. APA offers the booklets at cost (75 cents each) and encourages photocopying of the text, which is not copyrighted.

CAI

Computer-assisted instruction programs for optical discs may be offered in several formats: on diskette; on mainframe, if your institution offers instruction through that medium; or as part of the information stored on the disc itself. Several vendors have written innovative CAI tutorial programs; SilverPlatter's instruction covers basic commands and takes about 20 minutes to review. At the University of Vermont we refer beginning searchers to the SilverPlatter tutorial; combined with the handout specific to each database, the program gives the individual user a good basic introduction to searching. CAI programs have several advantages and disadvantages for teaching the use of optical discs. The program may be interactive, with questions that must be answered correctly before moving to the next section, in order to check student comprehension and progress. Computer graphics can be added to highlight commands and results, which will appear exactly as they do in real searching. "Canned" search topics, however, often lack interest; it is very difficult to choose subjects for demonstration searches that will intrigue a wide variety of learners. If you write your own CAI, the project will be time consuming and expensive, as discussed in chapter 7. Once written, a CAI program may be very difficult to revise when software or product lines change.

Since optical discs already offer powerful search software for large databases at no connect cost, there is no reason to develop a search simulation program like those discussed in chapter 5. You are more likely to want a simple overview of the basic commands, function keys, display and print options, and search examples–a handout with the added benefits of automation! Like handouts and other point-of-use aids, CAI programs are helpful for individuals because they are nonintrusive but available when needed.

Personal Assistance

Personal assistance, provided by librarians, assistants, staff, or student monitors, is the best form of optical disc instruction for individual users. It is interactive, "context sensitive," and flexible. Only another person can recognize the user's comprehension, puzzlement, or anxiety and adjust his or her responses accordingly. Good teachers can also be tactfully intrusive if necessary. At the University of Vermont, librarians at the reference desk can oversee the three WILSONDISC workstations and offer help if the user presses the wrong keys several times, causing a distinctive beeping sound, sits staring at the same help screen for more than a few minutes, or shows other signs of confusion. Furthermore, many learners prefer personal help. Nancy Herther states: "Users in most studies prefer fellow humans as trainers to printed or online sources of information. Users want to seek clarification, interact to dispel computer anxiety, and talk through a procedure with another person" (Herther 1988, 122). Librarians at Wayne State University, summarizing results of a survey of user preferences in instruction methods for CD-ROM products, report that "individualized instruction on demand was highly rated as a desired instructional method" and "remains the ideal teaching method" (Lynn and Bacsanyi, 19).

Unfortunately, providing personal assistance is expensive, as every administrator who has tried to staff the reference desk and run a library instruction program knows. How many assigned shifts can be handled by a department? If CD-ROM products are placed near the reference desk, should the staff on duty be increased or reassigned? Is there enough funding for student monitors' wages or for nonprofessional help? Extended shifts are no answer; the quality of help, like that of reference service, declines over time. The most patient tutor can only explain the basics of searching logic and system protocols only so many times before developing a strong desire to "boot" something other than the software.

You will need to design adequate training for all staff members responsible for helping end users. Although most staff members will not have to develop a high level of expertise with every system, each person must be able to:

1. Operate, demonstrate, and troubleshoot the hardware

2. Explain the system software

3. Teach basic search strategy development

4. Recognize when the optical disc resource is not appropriate and refer the user to other materials or to the reference desk for help

Communication skills and a user-oriented approach are two frequently overlooked facets of staff training. Role playing, discussions, and peer tutoring are good methods to use to help staff learn how to convey their knowledge to end users (Hendley, 102). At the University of Vermont, reference librarians and assistants provide personal help with CD-ROM products in the reference area and in the Automated Reference Center (ARC). We also employ five or six student monitors in the ARC each semester. The monitors are trained individually, using a procedures manual, workbook, CAI, vendors' manuals, and lots of discussion and practice.

Summary

The individual user is best served by a mixture of instructional media and materials: some designed for learners who like automation, others for those who prefer print. Some form of assistance must be available when personal help is not provided, if the optical disc products are open to public access.

Individuals from Classes

Librarians at school and academic libraries are most likely to encounter individuals from classes. This group of users presents special challenges to your instruction program. The situation may have some characteristics, however, that will help you design teaching materials:

1. There are often large numbers to teach. In an academic library, a faculty member may assign all students in one of the introductory level courses to do a search on an optical disc system. At the University of Vermont we have had to schedule as many as 200 students for ERIC or PsycLIT within one week.

2. Assigned tasks are common. All of the individuals from the class may have to find and read five articles on a topic, for example.

3. The group has a similar focus. Education students will often be assigned to use ERIC, and psychology students to use PsycLIT.

4. Individuals from a class may have some background to understand the product. The faculty member may give a presentation on the resource and its importance in the students' field of study.

5. Time constraints are also common. The faculty member may not be able to fit a library instruction session into the class schedule, even though the assignment may be due within one or two weeks.

How do you design teaching materials for large numbers of students who need to learn to search quickly? A program based on workbooks, CAI, and practice sessions is one method of meeting the special needs of this user group.

Workbooks

Workbooks are short manuals that include exercises to explain the text material and provide practice. The advantages and disadvantages of workbooks for teaching database searching are discussed in detail in chapter 5. Workbooks require active learning involvement; the user supplies the topic and proceeds through the steps of developing it into a search strategy by completing the exercises. Answers should be checked to uncover areas of misunderstanding and sections that may not have been completed.

Workbooks can be given to a faculty member to be handed out and discussed in class or picked up by students at the library or search center. They can be completed by students at their convenience and need not be done in the library, which is a great benefit when serving hundreds of users in a brief time frame. They are, however, difficult to revise if ordered in bulk and time consuming to design and produce well.

CAI

Both diskette and ondisc tutorials can be used to reinforce the concepts and skills introduced in the workbook. Since CAI requires the use of microcomputers and provides the opportunity to add graphics and other screen effects to highlight lessons, it makes an excellent bridge between the written workbook and actual use of the optical disc product.

CAI programs require workstations, however, which can be a limiting factor in their use to teach large numbers of students. If the CAI is an ondisc tutorial, using the CD-ROM for viewing it precludes any other searcher from gaining access to the system unless there is a network available. Diskette-based CAI can be run on less powerful personal computers without compact disc players; many academic and school libraries have microcomputer labs that provide adequate workstations for many students. You will need multiple copies of diskette CAI to serve large numbers of students. A flexible approach, allowing users to sign out CAI diskettes to use at home or to copy the program onto their own floppy disks, will help compensate for a shortage of library computers.

SilverPlatter has responded to subscriber complaints about inability to use their ondisc tutorials at heavily scheduled CD-ROM workstations. Since the fall of 1989 programmers have been developing tutorials to distribute on floppy diskettes; the instruction program for MEDLINE has been completed and released. Optional ondisc tutorials will be phased out as diskette versions become available. The new CAI will "simulate interaction with the compact disc and show software screen displays, prompts, and messages." They will also allow the company to enhance the graphics and effects within the teaching programs (see figure 4-2; SilverPlatter release, June 1989).

Figure 4-2. SilverPlatter MEDLINE Tutorial on Diskette

```
SilverPlatter            MEDLINE (R) 1/88 - 6/89        Esc=Commands F1=Help

                                                                    1 of 2
  AB: In Germany pleural mesothelioma occurs annually in 100-200 patients who
     had usually been working in the asbestos industry. In 100 mesotheliomas,
     evaluated radiologically, 6 | presented pleural effusions and 82 ↑ pleural
     tumour. This may result in  | etracting the hemithorax. Radiothera|y has a
     palliative goal. Applying 4 | Gy may reduce pain and may inhibit  |luid
     production. The irradiated  |ol┌──────────────────────────────┐un|  tissue,
     which necessitates careful  |re│ We'll use a Lateral Search     │  H│man-;
  MESH: Asbestosis-epidemiolog └──│ to select mesothelioma and     │
     Mesothelioma-epidemiology; Mes│ the plural mesotheliomas        │
     Mesothelioma-radiotherapy; Pal│ directly from the record.       │
     Pleural-Neoplasms-epidemiology│                                 │
     Pleural-Neoplasms-radiotherapy│ Press spacebar to continue.     │
  MESH: *Mesothelioma-; *Pleural-└──────────────────────────────┘

                                                                    2 of 2
  MESH: Bronchi-drug-effects; Bronchitis-etiology; Bronchitis-pathology;
     Chronic-Disease; Female-; Human-; Male-; Middle-Age;
     Pulmonary-Emphysema-etiology; Pulmonary-Emphysema-pathology; Siberia-

Menu:  OPTIONS     MARK RECORD     SELECT TERM     FIND     PRINT     DOWNLOAD
Press CTRL F2 to select terms fENTER to select; TAB for another menu option
PgDn for more; CTRL F10 for next; CTRL F9 for previous
```

Copyright SilverPlatter Information, Inc.; reprinted with permission.

Practice Sessions

Practice sessions employ the best features of optical disc products for library instruction. Since CD-ROMs are purchased by subscription, practice time is not costly and need not be carefully assigned and controlled, as with the online services. If there is no other person using or waiting to use the terminal, new searchers can practice as long as they wish. Most of the current literature, however, reports that CD-ROM workstations are very busy; you should assess the level of activity your facility can handle before requiring practice sessions for large numbers of students (Anders and Jackson, 31; Coons and Stewart, 40). Some librarians feel that "if the intended audience for an optical disc system is *all* interested end users, the likelihood is that more than one system (and copy of databases) will be needed, especially if users are encouraged to take their time and explore their information problems fully" (Harter and Jackson, 522).

Although workbooks and CAI are essential preparation materials, users learn CD-ROM searching "by doing." You can guide their explorations and begin to cope with time limits by designing brief exercises to be completed during practice sessions. Your exercise questions should be planned to demonstrate basic features of the system, such as using *and* and *or*, and displaying and printing citations. You can use these structured searches to build confidence and to lead to the user's own topics. The APA's *Search PsycINFO: Student Workbook*, a fine example of this approach, contains numerous exercises and activities.

Current Example

At the University of Vermont, we use a combination of workbooks and CAI to teach individuals from classes. The 12-page workbook covers only the basic elements of defining and expressing a search topic, combining concepts with *and*, *or*, and *not*, and displaying and printing citations. Our workbook does include command charts for several compact disc products and checklists for searching. We tell students that we hope they will keep the workbooks for reference while they are learning to search. Brief exercises for practice sessions are to be added in a new edition of the workbooks and are intended to form the first part of the student's first search. Our CAI was written to demonstrate the functions discussed in the workbook. Students complete the CAI on dual floppy drive personal computers in the ARC to avoid pressure on the busy optical disc workstations.

Classes or Groups

School, academic, public, and special librarians may choose to instruct classes or groups in using optical disc resources. Teaching groups or classes has some benefits and drawbacks that should be analyzed in choosing methods of instruction:

1. Class or group members have some interest in common. Members of the class are self-selected by their desire to know more about searching optical discs or, in academic and school settings, by interest in a subject like English or engineering.

2. The class environment is preferred by many learners.

3. The class period limits time available for teaching. Many class times are set at 55 minutes or less; voluntary workshops should not take more than two hours.

4. Large groups make it difficult to involve students. Small classes facilitate discussion and demonstration of student search topics.

5. Class attendance may be voluntary or required, which has an important effect on the level of interest and commitment participants have.

Classes and groups present special problems and opportunities in teaching the use of optical disc products. How can you show 30 restless people how to use ABI-Inform in less than 50 minutes and have them want to go out and start searching after the class? Effective methods for this situation include lectures, demonstrations, and practice sessions.

Lecture

The lecture is an essential component of teaching classes or groups to use optical disc resources. You can use this method to present lots of information, if it is well organized. You can explain how to analyze a topic to determine whether the CD-ROM resource is the best place to research it. Put the optical discs in context for your users by reviewing print, online, and other materials suited to their subject area; literature students, for example, need to know the differences in years covered by the print, online, and CD-ROM versions of the *MLA International Bibliography*. Here is your opportunity to review and explain the protocols and rules for your search service. Users will be more likely to respect restrictions on the amount of time they can spend on the system or the number of citations they can print off if they understand the reasons behind your limits.

Lectures are also a good medium for conveying and generating enthusiasm for optical disc technology and products. Users who are anxious about microcomputers and automated workstations may be reassured by your explanation of the mechanics of the system and willingness to answer questions. Lectures are not without disadvantages, however. They are not the best ways to teach the specifics of commands, logical operators, and function keys. Most people have a fairly short attention span for listening to straight discussion of this detailed information, especially if they have no experience with the system. Your lecture should be brief, and illustrated with examples. Simple handouts showing a sample record from the database, basic commands, and samples of search strategies including operators (as in figure 4-3) will help keep classes oriented and provide a convenient place to take notes.

Figure 4-3. ABI/INFORM Class Handout

```
UMI/DATA COURIER          ABI/INFORM          MAY 1985 -- APR 1990
```

Previous Activities	Item Count
[1] TE(labor costs) or TE(payroll costs)	408
[2] clothing industry	593
[3] [1] and [2]	7

Search term(s):

To Search: Enter key word or phrases, press ↵ .   F1=Help   F2=Commands

```
88-43103
Title:     Why Made-in-America Is Back in Style
Authors:   Weiner, Elizabeth; Foust, Dean
Journal:   Business Week (Industrial/Technology Edition)  Iss: 3078
           Date: Nov 7, 1988  pp: 116-120  Jrnl Code: BWE  ISSN: 0007-7135
Terms:     Clothing industry; Production costs; US imports; Labor costs;
           Productivity; Profit margins; Manycountries; Quotas
Codes:     8620 (Textile & apparel industries); 9180 (International)
Abstract: Employment in apparel and textiles has begun to increase, and imports
   of both are down 8% through August 1988 compared to the same period in 1987.
   The shift has been caused principally by competitive pressures that are
   making fast delivery the key factor in the garment industry.  Breakthroughs
   in automated sewing machines are reducing turnaround time and labor costs,
   and data processing links instantaneously report purchases from stores to
   designers and fabric suppliers.  In addition, leveraged retailers and
   manufacturers do not want to tie up cash with long lead times, big
   inventories, and large markdowns that come with overseas manufacturing.
   These realities are causing Asian and European manufacturers to set up shop
   in the US.  However, substantial business also is headed for the Caribbean
   and Mexico, and Canada is gearing up for clothing production as well.
   Charts.
```

Copyright UMI/Data Courier; reprinted with permission.

Demonstration

A demonstration of the optical disc system is the ideal partner or follow-up to the class lecture. You have talked about how fast and efficient the CD-ROM product is and how it can handle topics with several main concepts; now you can let the system sell itself.

The equipment required to demonstrate CD-ROM products is similar to that for showing online searching, which is discussed in detail in chapter 5. To do interactive, live demonstrations you will need a microcomputer with a graphics adapter and port, an internal or external CD-ROM drive, and a liquid crystal display (LCD) unit or video projector. A portable microcomputer with an internal CD-ROM drive and a modem would be very useful in an active online and optical disc instruction program taught in several classroom locations or where classes are held outside the library.

Demonstrations are an excellent way to involve learners in classes or groups. You can proceed directly from the lecture, in which you may have created several sample search strategies based on topics supplied by the students, to demonstrating how the searches work on the system. Naturally, students have much greater interest in their own subjects than in any prepared search you can devise. Even if the search is unsuccessful, you can use the results to comment on modifying the strategy or exploring a range of other library resources.

At the University of Vermont demonstrations are used to teach classes of up to 30 undergraduate or graduate students how to use compact disc products like WILSONDISC Art Index, SilverPlatter ERIC, and UMI ABI-Inform. We have a Compaq II Plus portable microcomputer, a Philips 110 external CD-ROM drive, a Kodak Datashow LCD projection unit, and an overhead projector, all of which are stored on a small rolling cart that can be moved from one classroom to another. This setup includes a modem that makes it possible to show online tutorial services and our public access catalog to classes and groups. We have found demonstrations to be an effective, popular component of library instruction sessions, both subject-specific class presentations and workshops on CD-ROM and online searching.

Librarians at Plymouth State College compared the search results of new end users trained by four methods: no instruction, handouts, lecture, and lecture with live demonstration. Their study concluded that "the only level of instruction that resulted in a significant difference was live demonstration of a few searches" (Bostian and Robbins, 17).

Some technical hints may help you streamline your demonstrations:

1. Use an out-of-date or archival copy of the optical disc product for classes. Some vendors let you keep superceded discs as updates

arrive; using older discs avoids taking current discs out of users' hands.

2. If there is a hard disk on the microcomputer used for classes, set up subdirectories for each CD-ROM product you plan to demonstrate, then write simple batch files that will start and run the system. Simplify the process as much as you can, especially if several librarians need to use the same setup for teaching.

3. Always try to allow time to test the demonstration before your class begins. If possible, have the microcomputer, projection unit, and CD-ROM product running while you lecture. Then all you need to do is turn on the overhead projector or video projector to start the show.

You can also plan your demonstration, download searches from the compact disc, edit the results, add text and graphics, and create an automated program complete with narrated script. This approach is suited for situations where you need to convey the same information to many classes or groups and want to standardize your instruction. Downloaded demonstrations using presentation software do not require a CD-ROM drive to show the program. Librarians at Texas A&M University have used Show Partner software, an IBM PC microcomputer, and a Kodak Datashow LCD projection system to create a 20-minute program to teach the use of InfoTrac. They emphasized subject headings and subheadings, cross-references, and analyzing and revising searches; their demonstration included two complete sample searches designed to show the system's features and common search mistakes. They concluded that "the application of high-quality user instruction to large groups can provide students with the knowledge they need to make InfoTrac and other laserdisk databases effective research tools. Demonstrations produced with software such as Show Partner and shown in classrooms by using large-screen projection systems such as Datashow can provide creative, flexible tools for educating end-users" (Charles, Waddle, and Hambric, 95)

Practice Sessions

Lectures and demonstrations lead naturally into practice sessions, since optical disc products demand that students learn various skills best mastered through experience. The advantages and disadvantages of this method have been discussed above, but large classes present some special problems. Students will not be able to practice immediately, when their interest is likely to be highest, so you should have some means of scheduling their searches. It is best to have the schedule available at the end of class, to capitalize on that interest. Practice should be required if possible and appropriate to the specific class; your ability to require it as part of an instruction program will depend on your search facility.

Exercises can be used to lead into assigned or free searches. Many students appreciate the guidance of a structured approach to their first efforts. Once they have completed your exercise questions and seen the system perform successfully, they should have confidence to begin their own research. This type of support is particularly helpful for products that do not offer software interfaces designed to accommodate novice searchers.

At the University of Vermont a program including lectures, demonstrations, and practice sessions was developed to teach a class of 15 school librarians how to search WILSONDISC and SilverPlatter CD-ROM products. The exercises (see figure 4-4) were an important link in transferring the students' understanding of the theories and concepts of automated information retrieval to experience with the individual systems.

Staff

Whether the CD-ROM product you are introducing is designed for reference consultation by end users or acquisitions processing by technical services personnel, staff training is an important aspect of your education program. As Stephen Harter and Susan Jackson point out, "an extensive staff orientation and education program may be required, and many costly hours must be allotted for staff participation. Training sessions and ample practice time will be required for every reference system the library acquires. This staff training will be a significant issue in terms of time and money involved, and librarians will need to consider how this training will be provided" (Harter and Jackson, 520).

Background

You have one significant advantage in creating training for staff compared to designing instruction for end users: you know their background. When staff members have used microcomputers for word processing, spreadsheets, statistics, or any other applications, you can build on that foundation of knowledge to teach optical disc skills. If your students are reference librarians already familiar with online searching of several systems, you can draw their attention to similarities between the known and new software. Recent research has shown that training for automation is more successful when the instruction programs are differentiated based on the amount of experience learners have had with computers in general (Herther 1988, 121).

Figure 4-4. WILSONDISC Class Exercise

1. Choose a topic in which you are interested. Use BROWSE search mode to find at least five citations on your topic or related to it.

2. Use the Print Screen key to print the screen that shows your search request before you enter it.

3. Remember to use F8 if the display has an asterisk next to your subject heading.

4. Print at least five of the citations from your search. Comment on whether you found a useful subject heading for your topic.

5. You can use other subject headings listed below the citation(s) to get related articles.

6. Now use WILSEARCH mode to search for your topic. Use the connector ANY at least once to search for synonyms or related terms.

7. Use the Print Screen function to print the screen that shows your search terms before you enter them.

8. Print at least five citations from your WILSEARCH exercise; try to include some that differ from the group you printed after your BROWSE search. Comment on the two modes: ease of use, flexibility, speed. Explain why the two modes give different search results.

Copyright Bailey/Howe Library, University of Vermont.

You should also be aware of staff members' attitudes toward the CD-ROM product. Were they involved in the decision to select and purchase it? How do they feel about its effect on their work? End users are primarily voluntary searchers whose participation in training is based on their own interest; when they are students assigned to complete a search, it is usually only a small part of their work for the course. But library staff will *have* to work with the product, and in some cases its implementation may completely alter the way they accomplish their tasks. You can promote a positive atmosphere and dissipate negative feelings by explaining the reasons for the product's selection, its strengths and weaknesses compared with other resources, and potential effect on the department and library (MacDonald, 7).

Levels of Expertise

You may be able to set reasonable teaching goals by analyzing the degree of expertise each staff member needs to have and instructing them accordingly. Public services staff, as mentioned above, need to have a fairly high level of competence with all of the products offered to end users, since they may be required to help searchers with a wide variety of problems. They need to know not only the commands, function keys, formats, and other specifics of each system, but also the skills of defining topics, identifying main concepts, and designing search strategies. When the CD-ROM product is intended for use only by the staff, you may be able to train most users to a basic level and identify one or two interested people for more advanced instruction. Then the "experts" can serve as problem solvers for their colleagues.

Many optical disc products have software interfaces designed to accommodate novice, intermediate, or experienced searchers. You will need to choose the one most appropriate for the staff to learn. If a novice or menu mode is available, be sure that it offers all functions staff members need to use before you teach it. If they will have to use the expert or command interface, you may prefer to teach it from the start, even though more instruction effort may be required.

Teaching Methods

You may combine several of the teaching methods discussed above for staff training. How many staff members need to learn to use the CD-ROM? If you are introducing a product to eight or more people, you may want to use a lecture and demonstration to begin. Workbooks or manuals with exercises will be essential in many programs; every staff member will need a copy of the essential information from the vendor's manual, such as function key and command charts. CAI programs can be very useful where you are training several staff members but do not have a CD-ROM workstation for each one or a local area network. If you are teaching one person, perhaps a newly hired reference librarian, personal assistance and practice may be the best approach.

Whatever methods you choose, a well-developed staff training program should be one of your first concerns. Librarians report that, based on their experiences implementing optical disc services, it is a mistake to concentrate teaching efforts on end users exclusively. At Cornell University, instructors have realized that "everyone on the staff needs to learn more about CD-ROM than we previously thought. Formalized in-depth training for our Reference Desk information assistants, and refreshers for librarians, are now being planned." (Coons and Stewart, 40) At the University of Vermont, we have developed an organized instruction program for the student monitors who assist end users with both online and optical disc resources. In addition, the library administration has become so concerned about staff training for automated systems that a training coordinator has been designated to organize instruction throughout all departments.

GOING BEYOND TRAINING

Your new CD-ROM system has arrived and has been installed. You have made clear, colorful signs and composed concise point-of-use aids. Workbooks will be delivered from the print shop tomorrow. Your CAI will be ready in just a few days; the instruction librarian says there are just one or two rough spots she wants to smooth over. Lecture notes and overheads are ready and everyone knows how to connect the projection unit to the microcomputer for demonstrations. Staff have had their instruction and have been given adequate time to practice with the new system. What could be missing?

Now is the time to review all of your instruction materials with one objective in mind: how well have you put the optical disc resource in context with other materials and services in your library? Throughout this chapter, we have used the terms *training, instruction,* and *teaching* synonymously, but you must not overlook the need to go beyond the specifics of the system. When you are absorbed in the intricate complexities of function keys, special punctuation, and quirky logical operators, you are likely to design instruction that is entirely self-contained. You may describe the operation, software, protocols for use, and every other aspect of the CD-ROM version of *Sociological Abstracts,* for example, and never refer to the print or online forms or to other library resources in the social sciences.

Importance of Context

How important is this aspect of user instruction? Just visualize the number of microcomputer terminals available to end users in your library. There may be terminals for an online catalog, for end-user online searching, for educational software, or for word processing and other applications, depending on the type of library and stage of automation. Faced with increasing numbers of computer screens, users are more and more likely to become confused and anxious.

A recent survey of academic libraries indicated that 58 percent of the respondents had part or all of their catalog online. Of the librarians polled, 35 percent felt that users would be confused by multiple computers. Many of those who felt users would not be confused worked in libraries without online catalogs or CD-ROM products (Salomon, 211). Experienced librarians report errors that demonstrate users' misunderstandings very clearly. From questions asked and searches left on computer screens, we find students searching "Compact DISCLOSURE for a journal title in the library, searching in AGRICOLA for articles on killer whales or looking in ERIC for books about Roberto Clemente" (Coons and Stewart, 37). These users may be able to choose terms, operators, and function keys without hesitation, but their knowledge is useless when applied to an inappropriate optical disc resource.

Getting the Message Across

Nancy Herther expresses the importance of going beyond training: "Support should be evolutionary as well as compensatory. It is important to help users understand some technical issue or answer specific questions, but users also want and need background information to help them develop a frame of reference for understanding and better using computer systems" (Herther 1988, 122). In our experience at the University of Vermont, many users do *not* want background information or a discussion of library services when they first confront optical disc products. Their initial interests and approaches are very specific: "Which button do I push to make it print?" "Do you have a computer just like that one, but for history?"

How can you get beyond specifics? First be sure that your own view of the CD-ROM is a contextual one. Think of its relationships to other versions of the resource and its place among the services your library offers. Write down its advantages and disadvantages; pretend you are a naive searcher and do some research on inappropriate topics to see what kinds of results appear. Remember, some of your users may place great faith in whatever the computer prints out, and some optical disc products like Magazine Index, Readers' Guide, or Newsbank may have a few citations on almost any topic you can imagine.

Now insert messages about context everywhere they apply in your instructional materials. Most of these notes and reminders will be brief, although a longer explanation would be possible in a lecture or presentation comparing various technologies or services offered by the library. You can use all of the methods outlined in this chapter to teach CD-ROM technology in context. Your point-of-use materials may need just a line or two reminding users to ask at the reference desk for assistance if their needs are not met by the optical disc product. Workbooks and CAI should be concise, but still provide ample opportunities to note that various formats of information are available. You can design exercises that compare and contrast optical disc and print or online versions of the same resource. And, of course, personal assistance or class lectures give you a good chance to discuss the limitations of each product and suggest alternatives (Mensching 1989, 90-91).

Librarians have developed innovative ways to include context information in teaching materials. For example, at the University of Vermont we place brief reminders to ask for help at the Reference Desk in flip-charts for WILSONDISC, handouts for SilverPlatter and ABI-Inform, workbooks, and CAI. Class lectures always contain a discussion of optical disc technology in comparison with other information formats, in general terms and with reference to specific products. We also train our student monitors to refer users to reference librarians for help with problem searches. The automated presentation produced at Texas A&M University "reminds students that InfoTrac is not always the most appropriate tool available and that supplemental resources can be used" (Charles, Waddle, and Hambric, 92). Vicki Anders and Kathy Jackson, also at the Evans Library at Texas A&M, discuss the care with which staff explain the relationship of ERIC online and ERIC on CD-ROM to students who are convinced they are two different databases. They conclude that "various kinds of services can co-exist and, in many ways, they enhance each other. Users who are first attracted to a laserdisk database only to discover that it does not cover their topics then ask questions and learn about the BRS and Knowledge Index programs" (Anders and Jackson, 31).

"A Wonderful Opportunity"

Bill Coons and Linda Stewart, at Cornell University's Mann Library, provide an excellent overview of a teaching program designed to go beyond training. Their instruction "occurs within the framework of our information literacy program. Information literacy may be defined as the bundle of information concepts, knowledge and skills required to function in society. Teaching it involves communicating the power and scope of information to students and instructing them in how it is organized, retrieved, and managed. . . . Our goals for the students are that they: understand the role, power and uses of information in a democratic society; understand the variety of contents and format of information; develop the capability to retrieve information from a variety of systems and in various formats; and develop the ability to evaluate, organize and manage information for various purposes. CD-ROM is a tool which has provided Mann with a wonderful opportunity to expand the resources used in our information literacy program" (Coons and Stewart, 36-37). Optical disc technology offers the same opportunity to every librarian interested in teaching the full range of information resources.

Works Cited

Anders, Vicki, and Kathy Jackson. "Online vs. CD-ROM–The Impact of CD-ROM Databases upon a Large Online Searching Program." *Online* 12 (September 1988): 24-32.

Bonta, Bruce, and Sally Kalin. "CD-ROM Implementation: A Reference Staff Takes Charge." *Reference Services Review* 17 (Summer 1989): 7-11, 93.

Bostian, Rebecca, and Anne Robbins. "Effective Instruction for Searching CD-ROM Indexes." *Laserdisk Professional* 3 (January 1990): 14-17.

Charles, Susan, Keith Waddle, and Jacqueline Hambric. "Using Presentation Software to Train Laserdisk Database Users." *Laserdisk Professional* 1 (November 1988): 91-95.

Coons, Bill, and Linda Stewart. "Mainstreaming CD-ROM into Library Operations." *Laserdisk Professional* 1 (September 1988): 29-40.

Harter, Stephen, and Susan Jackson. "Optical Disc Systems in Libraries: Problems and Issues." *RQ* 27 (Summer 1988): 516-25.

Hendley, Margaret. "Staff Training in an Automated Environment: Keeping the Patron in Mind." *Canadian Library Journal* 46 (April 1989): 101-3.

Herther, Nancy. "Microcomputer Technology: Helping Users Cope." *Online* 12 (September 1988): 120-22.

-----. "Those Lingering Doubts About CD-ROM." *Database* 12 (February 1989): 102-4.

Lynn, Patricia, and Karen Bacsanyi. "CD-ROMs: Instructional Methods and User Reactions." *Reference Services Review* 17 (Summer 1989): 17-25.

MacDonald, Linda Brew. "Training Staff to Use Optical Disc Products." *Access Faxon* 1 (Spring 1988): 6-8.

Mellon, Constance. "Attitudes: The Forgotten Dimension in Library Instruction." *Library Journal* (September 1, 1988): 137-39.

Mensching, Teresa. "CD-ROM: The Aladdin's Lamp of Library Technology?" *Research Strategies* 7 (Spring 1989): 90-92.

Quint, Barbara. "How Is CD-ROM Disappointing? Let Me Count the Ways." *Wilson Library Bulletin* (December 1987): 32-34, 102.

Rholes, Julia, and Naomi Caldwell-Wood. "ERIC SilverPlatter: Is It User-Friendly?" Paper presented at the Annual Meeting of the American Library Association, San Francisco, June 27-July 2, 1987. ED 286522.

Salomon, Kristine. "The Impact of CD-ROM on Reference Departments." *RQ* 28 (Winter 1988): 203-15.

Stewart, Linda, and Jan Olsen. "Compact Disk Databases: Are They Good for Users?" *Online* 12 (May 1988): 48-52.

Wagers, Robert. "Can Easy Searching Be Good Searching? A Model for Easy Searching." *Online* 13 (May 1989): 78-85.

Watson, Paula. "Cost to Libraries of the Optical Information Revolution." *Online* 12 (January 1988): 45-50.

5

Online Tutorial Services:
Connecting Searchers and Information

Linda Brew MacDonald

Several vendors of online databases currently offer instructional or tutorial services to teach end users how to conduct their own searches. These services, which include DIALOG's Classroom Instruction Programs, BRS's Instructor, and WILSONLINE's Educational Rate, have certain features in common. All are offered at reduced rates, currently in the range of $15 per hour. Multiple passwords (usually 10-12) are offered at no extra charge, allowing a reasonable number of students to practice at one time. The tutorial services, unlike the end-user services, are available during the daytime. One important restriction applies: the tutorial services must be used for bona fide teaching, and in some cases the librarian must sign an agreement guaranteeing that this rule will be observed. It is not appropriate to use these services to avoid the higher costs and limited hours of some of the end-user services like BRS/After Dark and Knowledge Index.

The tutorial services are special purchase packages intended to make online time available and affordable for search practice and instruction. They provide access to the regular search interface and to a selection of databases; the service software has not been enhanced with such features of computer-assisted instruction (CAI) as additional help screens, question-and-answer exercises, or step-by-step demonstrations. This chapter considers how these tutorial services can be used in instruction, how to design materials to complement them, and some factors, such as costs and security, that influence their implementation.

BACKGROUND OF TUTORIAL SERVICES

Major vendors like DIALOG and BRS developed online tutorial services before there was an active, sizeable end-user market. The original systems were designed for professional searchers, and learning them required highly specialized training provided by the vendors themselves through the familiar one-day workshops. The workshops were conducted with materials designed especially for teaching: overheads, handouts, sample exercises, and short manuals for attendees to take home with them.

The first tutorial services were developed for use in library schools, as online searching became a more essential component of library education. BRS's Library School Program and DIALOG's Classroom Instruction Program, both introduced in the 1970s, are examples of this type of service. By convincing the database producers to forgo royalties in exchange for building a group of knowledgeable new users, the vendors were able to offer access to a variety of databases for extremely low prices. Since the services were intended to be used in formal teaching programs at the graduate level, support materials like workbooks, exercises, and student manuals could be devised by the instructor. Mead Data Central's Library School Program is the newest entry in this area.

In 1982 the introduction of the first true end-user services, BRS/After Dark and DIALOG Knowledge Index, changed the situation completely. The library school programs were offered to teach users who were familiar with citations, indexes, and the organization of knowledge in libraries. The end-user services were intended for home computer searchers, who did not necessarily have any library skills. To reach these users, vendors had to develop more elaborate training packages, including manuals, workbooks with exercises, videotapes, and demonstration diskettes, in addition to offering the traditional one-day seminar or workshop.

Available Tutorial Services

A variety of tutorial services is available to libraries that want to use this method to teach searching. Here are brief descriptions, costs, and contact addresses for some of the better-known programs. All of the programs are intended for teaching end users, from elementary school students to business and medical professionals. Some can also be used to develop or refine skills for library staff as well.

BRS Instructor
BRS Information Technologies
8000 Westpark Drive
McLean, VA 22102
(800)955-0906

The Instructor Program, which replaced the Library School Program in 1985, is a well-developed teaching service that connects to more than 50 current databases on BRS. It is available for use in "any supervised classroom program" from elementary school through graduate level. Up to 12 passwords may be requested; the cost is $15 per hour including telecommunications if Telenet or Tymnet is used. Both command and menu search modes are available, making it possible to instruct new librarians on command-level BRS and end users on the same system that is used for BRS/After Dark. The *BRS Search Service User's Manual* can be purchased at a discount, and subscribers can also attend an introductory BRS training session at no charge. Training videos have been produced and are currently available.

DIALOG Classroom Instruction Programs (CIP)
DIALOG Information Services
3460 Hillview Avenue
Palo Alto, California 94304
(800)334-2564

The widest range of tutorial services is offered by DIALOG. Certain features of the Classroom Instruction Programs are common to all of the services: cost of $15 per hour including telecommunications, up to ten passwords available at no extra charge, and the restriction that programs be used in educational institutions "in conjunction with formal programs of classroom instruction about online information retrieval." DIALOG CIP, formerly a library school instruction service, now provides access to more than 280 current databases. Targeting undergraduate and graduate school users, this program uses the command-driven interface. Complimentary training sessions for two instructors at a DIALOG System Seminar are provided with each subscription. Support materials, in addition to the regular user's guide, include the *DIALOG Lab Workbook* and the *Introduction to DIALOG* videotape. A self-paced CAI program on diskette has recently been introduced. DIALOG maintains the ONTAP (ONline Training And Practice) databases for practice use.

DIALOG CLASSMATE CIP is intended for students in elementary and secondary schools, but is equally useful for training end users to search Knowledge Index, DIALOG's simplified search interface. Connecting to about 60 databases, CLASSMATE CIP has information in a variety of subject areas and contains both full-text and index files. DIALOG offers special "Teach the Teacher" seminars for instructors who want to use CLASSMATE CIP. There is a full range of documentation, including the *CLASSMATE Teaching Guide*, *Student Workbook*, and the *Knowledge Index User's Workbook*. An inexpensive IBM PC-compatible demonstration diskette is also available.

DIALOG BUSINESS CIP complements the DIALOG Business Connection, a menu-driven service designed for end-users seeking corporate and financial information in five "applications": corporate intelligence, financial screening, sales prospecting, products and markets, and travel planning. Business CIP instructional materials are: the self-instructional *User's Guide*, case studies, student practice exercises, and lesson plans. DIALOG MEDICAL CIP supports a similar service, DIALOG Medical Connection, which offers access to bioscience, medical, and science and technology databases.

Dow Jones News/Retrieval Service Academic Rate
Dow Jones & Company
P.O. Box 300
Princeton, NJ 08543-0300
(609)452-1511

One of the best bargains in tutorial services is the Dow Jones News/Retrieval Academic Rate. Qualifying schools include "all public, private, and parochial primary and secondary institutions, and all accredited, degree-granting, non-proprietary public, private and parochial institutions of higher education." In addition to the business news and stock market information for which the service is famous, Dow Jones provides access to the Academic American Encyclopedia, Peterson's College Selection Service, Magill Book Reviews, Cineman Movie Reviews, and Sports and Weather Reports. Most of the databases contain condensed text, excerpts, or statistics, making this service an excellent complement to those that give access primarily to bibliographic citations. With its broad subject coverage and menu mode search software, Dow Jones is ideal for elementary and secondary schools; they can purchase one password for $150 per month. Colleges and universities must buy at least three passwords. For these flat rates, academic subscribers have unlimited access to all of the Dow Jones files except five financial and investment databases, 24 hours a day and seven days a week. Text-Search Services cost an additional $15 per hour. A minimum commitment of three months is required, so schools can discontinue the service during summer. Teaching materials include the *Dow Jones News/Retrieval User Guide*, printed quick reference cards, and posters.

Einstein
LEARNING LINK National Consortium
Central Educational Network
1400 East Touhy Avenue, Suite 260
Des Plaines, Illinois 60018-3305
(708)390-8700

Einstein, developed by Addison-Wesley, is a user-friendly, "plain English" interface connecting to BRS, Data-Star, DataTimes, DIALOG, VU/TEXT, and WILSONLINE. Currently used for teaching online searching from the elementary to the undergraduate level, this service offers a wide range of databases of interest to students, faculty, and librarians. First-time subscribers must order a Starter Kit, which includes the *User's Manual*, *Database Directory*, *Teacher's Guide*, and 50 single-search passwords. Unlike most of the other tutorial services listed here, Einstein does not offer an hourly connect rate; additional sets of single-search passwords are available at $5 apiece. There is a discount on publications and passwords for users who also subscribe to the LEARNING LINK service.

VU/TEXT in Education
VU/TEXT Information Services, Inc.
325 Chestnut Street, Suite 1300
Philadelphia, Pennsylvania 19106
(800)323-2940

VU/TEXT is the largest vendor of full-text databases of newspapers, newswires, selected journals and articles, and international information from QL Search (Canada) and PROFILE (Europe and Asia). The VU/TEXT IN EDUCATION service offers access to the full range of databases except QL Search, PROFILE, and a few financial resources. Subscribers can search more than 40 newspapers; selected articles from regional business journals; full text of *Time*, *Fortune*, and other periodicals; and newswires, including the Associated Press. The VIE program costs $16 per hour, including telecommunications. VU/TEXT will supply a single password that will allow a "limitless number of students to access the system simultaneously" or multiple passwords to track individual searches. The service has a full range of support materials, including a free *VU/TEXT User Guide*, two *Mini*

Guides, a teaching guide, and free training for one instructor at a regularly scheduled workshop session. *Ready Reference Guides* and database lists for each student will also be provided. VU/TEXT IN EDUCATION is designed to be used "in a class providing formal instruction in online information retrieval" and is aimed at the undergraduate and graduate level student. A brief questionnaire indicating the number of students participating, dates for online use, and a course brochure or syllabus must be submitted with the subscription agreement.

WILSONLINE: Educational Rate
H. W. Wilson Company
950 University Avenue
Bronx, NY 10452
(800)367-6770

The Educational Rate provides access to all WILSONLINE databases except Library Literature for $15 per hour, which includes telecommunications. This service is only available to high schools, and a proposal letter outlining the instruction program must be sent with the subscription request. There is no limit to the number of passwords that will be issued. Wilson provides access to more than 20 databases, including the MLA Bibliography. Readers' Guide Abstracts, General Science Index, Education Index, and Book Review Digest are examples of files that would be appropriate and popular in many secondary school libraries. The WILSONLINE software is powerful but straightforward; some useful features are online help, online thesaurus, and multifile searching. Wilson does not provide special training materials for the Educational Rate service. Their user aids for WILSONLINE are the *WILSONLINE Tutorial manual* (free), *Quick Reference Guide* (free), *WILSONLINE Guide & Documentation*, and a video, *Online Searching*.

APPLICATIONS IN INSTRUCTION

Access to end-user online services is not the commonest form of electronic technology offered by libraries. Although college and university libraries are the most likely providers of this type of service, a recent survey of 150 college and university libraries showed that only 34 percent made end-user services like BRS/After Dark or WILSEARCH available. By comparison, 68 percent of these libraries subscribed to CD-ROM services, and 100 percent had access to full-service DIALOG or BRS for mediated searching (Salomon, 206).

In libraries that currently offer or plan to provide end-user online search services, however, the question of how to provide training in their use is vital.

There are many approaches to teaching people how to search, and several bibliographies have been compiled that list research concerning the best programs and methods of end-user online instruction (Batt; Huston, 14-33; Lyon; Walker).

Content: Skills versus Concepts?

Before examining the technological issues involved in using the tutorial services, you should determine the content of your end-user training program. Although your own instruction will be tailored to a specific situation, depending on what services your library offers and who your students are, examining some of the general guidelines available will help you organize your ideas. Dennis Hamilton's "Library Users and Online Systems: Suggested Objectives for Library Instruction" lists 30 instructional objectives under four main headings: understanding the system, planning the search strategy, operating the system, and interpreting the search results. The objectives are detailed but not related to any particular service: "The user will be able to identify the elements of a search display and will be able to determine which elements are relevant in retrieving the needed information" (Hamilton, 196). These excellent guidelines were designed to provide an outline for both individual and classroom instruction, and to help teachers prepare instructional aids in all media.

Some researchers differentiate between two types of learning end users must master in order to become competent searchers. Mary Huston identifies "procedural search instruction" or "search training," which concentrates on system mechanics and how-to operations, and "conceptual search instruction" or "search education," which involves the search strategy or plan for the whole search (Huston, 16). Ralph Alberico makes a similar distinction between "tactical knowledge" of technical procedures and "strategic knowledge" of the analytical and intuitive bases for search decisions (Alberico, 8). Both instructors believe that system-specific training has been emphasized at the expense of conceptual education in many end-user instruction programs.

Librarians at Cornell University's Mann Library have developed an end-user instruction program that combines these two elements, the "educational or concepts curriculum" and the "training or skills curriculum," into an effective synthesis. Their approach stresses concepts that help students understand the nature of automated information retrieval systems, so that they can apply the skills learned on one system to others. Since users of many libraries have to cope with different search systems for an automated catalog, end-user online services, and CD-ROM products, the issue of learning transfer is a vital one.

The guidelines for the Mann Library end-user education program are clear and concise (Lippincott, 185, 189):

The Concepts

For a sophisticated understanding of any electronic bibliographic system, users need to develop understandings in the following conceptual areas:

- What a database is

- What a bibliographic record, its fields, and access points are

- How to divide a topic into component parts (sets) for development of a search strategy

- How to use controlled vocabulary and free text terms effectively

- How Boolean operators or connectors are used to link terms or sets

The Skills

An end-user instruction program that totally ignores skills would certainly be detrimental to novice users. According to Lippincott, skills that can be taught include:

- Logging on and off the system

- Keyboard mechanics

- Input and output procedures

- Locating materials identified through the search

Your instruction program should not emphasize skills at the expense of concepts. It is easy to become absorbed in teaching the intricacies of a single system, even at the beginner level. Detailed studies of end-user behavior indicate, however, that a clear understanding of the content and organization of a database, including a mental image of how the information is arranged, makes it easier to learn system mechanics and search skills (Linde and Bergstrom, 98-99).

The time you spend determining content and teaching objectives will be well invested, since you must recognize several constraining factors in end-user training. First, end users, unlike library professionals, do not value search proficiency highly in itself. They are not willing to spend much time learning to search and, once trained, seldom practice searching frequently enough to maintain their skills. Both you and your students will be more satisfied with your instruction if you define realistic goals that combine concepts and skills appropriate to their needs (Balius, 76).

Methods: Hands-on Practice

The consensus of opinion is that the most effective element of the education program is practice time on an online system. In spite of the development of several computer-based alternatives, including search simulation programs, there is no substitute for online access. "This 'hands-on' online searching is important for both intermediaries and end-users. Students who have prepared and carried out a search have a better understanding of the process involved than those who have observed a demonstration" (Fjallbrant, 235).

There are three main methods of using the tutorial services to teach online searching: demonstration, practice in class, and individual practice. Demonstrations are appropriate when the purpose of instruction is to introduce searching, to show the online resources available, or to review the capabilities of a system. Classroom and individual practice is the task the tutorial services were designed for, and they are ideal for this purpose.

Tutorial Services in Demonstrations

One way to share the interactive dialogue and excitement of finding pertinent references with a group of learners is an online demonstration. This method requires a microcomputer, access to a telephone line, telecommunications software, a password for one or more tutorial services, and a mechanism to display the images on a screen or wall.

Microcomputer

A wide range of microcomputers are suitable for use in demonstrating online searching. A portable computer is especially valuable when sessions need to be given in several different classrooms, or to take the demonstration to locations outside the library. A hard disk or hard card eliminates the need for keeping track of numerous floppy disks, since the required software programs can be stored in memory. If an internal modem is used, instead of an external one, there will be one less piece of equipment to carry and connect. The microcomputer must have the proper graphics capabilities and connections available for the projection unit you plan to use. In the case of the Kodak Datashow, which is a liquid crystal display (LCD) unit, an IBM color graphics adapter (CGA), IBM enhanced graphics adapter (in CGA mode), or other 100 percent compatible graphics adapter is required; the Datashow connects to a 9-pin RGB display port on the computer. If you are purchasing new equipment, be sure to check with the vendor of the projection unit for these requirements; you want the whole system's setup and operation to be as simple and reliable as possible.

Telecommunications Software and Passwords

Communications software must be available, on diskette or hard disk, to connect your demonstration microcomputer with the online tutorial services. CROSSTALK, ProComm, SMARTCOM, and Bitcom are only a few of the many programs that handle telecommunications. You will want to select a communications program that provides all of the standard features for online searching, such as logging on, downloading, and printing captured files. The best program for demonstrations is one that can be customized, so that complex operations like changing the communications parameters or logging on can be done with function keys or short batch files. One interested staff member can learn the program in detail and then set it up so that other instructors need only type KI to start a demonstration of Knowledge Index, or enter a few key strokes to change from pulse to touch dialing. Good software will allow users without sophisticated programming skills to make these modifications (Bell 1989, 64). Communications software programs are reviewed frequently in both library and personal computing literature.

Your passwords for the tutorial services may be stored in the telecommunications software for ease of use, and should be masked (automatically or by customization) during your demonstrations. If the microcomputer is used for other purposes in addition to demonstrations, safeguard the security of the passwords by erasing them from the memory or by using diskettes for the communications software.

Display Mechanism

Currently, there are three alternatives for projecting real-time computer output: large-screen monitors, video projectors, and LCD projection pads. Large-screen monitors replace the small monitor on the microcomputer so that groups of up to ten people can watch a display comfortably; however, they cost between $7,500 and $10,000. Video projectors are available in monochrome or color output, can display 4- to 12-foot diagonal images on a screen, and cost between $3,000 and $10,000. They require a darkened room and are too heavy to be considered portable. LCD projection pads are lightweight units designed to sit on top of a standard overhead projector. They display the computer monitor's text or graphics output clearly up to about a 12-foot diagonal image, and their contrast is sharp enough that dim room lights can usually be left on. Most LCDs project in monochrome only, although color units are available. Weighing about five pounds and costing between $750 and $1500, LCDs offer an affordable and portable means of using the tutorial services to demonstrate online searching (Phillips, 73; Davis and Miller, 5).

Downloaded, Scripted, or Spontaneous Demonstration?

You can create a completely planned demonstration that runs like a slide show, organize a live demonstration that follows an outline, or sign on to the online service and improvise. Each approach has advantages and disadvantages, and all have been tried by instruction librarians with varied results.

Librarians at Northwestern University have used both dial-in live and downloaded, text enhanced demonstrations to teach Knowledge Index and the NOTIS online catalog. They prefer the prepared package, citing its transportability to classrooms without telephone lines, and the ability to put copies of the disk on reserve for students to review. The sequenced instruction program also ensures better control and consistency, and "eliminates the hazards of telephone line problems or other unexpected problems that interfere with the flow of the lecture" (Baker and Steffen, 227).

Instructors at the University of Pennsylvania's Lippincott Library have used an IBM PC and a Sony universal video projector to enhance end-user training sessions. First, they used the video projector with the PC STORYBOARD software package to create a series of text and graphic screen images, including a down-loaded sample search on BRS, to accompany lecture sessions on online searching. Trainers found that students were more attentive to video displays than they had been to overhead transparencies, and survey results showed that students' ratings of the training session as "excellent" or "very good" rose from 61 percent for the transparency presentation to 76 percent for the video version (Batista and Einhorn, 22). Class sessions now include live demonstrations on BRS Instructor, CLASSMATE, and the Dow Jones News Retrieval Service; the librarians ask for topics from the class, which generates "much more interest than a downloaded search" (J. Newland, telephone communication, 1989).

Stephen Bell, also at the Lippincott Library, prefers live online demonstrations and lists benefits of the scripted and spontaneous versions or a combination of both. In contrast to downloaded search presentations, live sessions provide a realistic image of online searching, are more stimulating, require flexibility, and may save time since no advance creation of materials is needed (Bell 1990, 42).

At the University of Vermont's Bailey/Howe Library, demonstration equipment includes a Compaq II Plus portable microcomputer, an overhead projector, and a Kodak Datashow LCD projection pad. Stored on a small rolling cart, this setup can be moved to any one of several classrooms within the library. Telecommunications software on the Compaq's hard disk contains automatic log-on information for BRS Instructor, DIALOG CLASSMATE, WILSONLINE, and the Dow Jones News Retrieval Service. We demonstrate live searching on the tutorial services for classes in many subjects, and for up to 30 students. In many cases, the online demonstration is part of a subject-specific library orientation class. For example, an Art History professor may ask to have a session taught on library resources for research in American architecture. In addition to reviewing a list of selected reference materials, the instructor demonstrates searching on Art Index and Artbibliographies Modern, taking topics from the class and using the success or failure of the example to discuss aspects of searching and library research. At least 15 to 20 minutes of the standard 50-minute class period should be reserved for this type of demonstration, since it produces many questions and comments.

Summary

The combination of tutorial services with some form of projection system is ideally suited for teaching classes in online searching. Since the teaching services correspond very closely to the end-user systems, most of the commands and protocols can be demonstrated exactly as they will be used in searching. If the demonstration is live, students get a better idea of the speed, power, and complexity of the systems. Having a student enter commands at the terminal while you lecture is a popular way to show that beginners can handle the equipment. Disconnection, line noise, and other common online service problems may be encountered, which you can use to give a realistic view of online disadvantages.

This approach has been used successfully at the Bailey/Howe Library in training a class of 15 school librarians to search BRS/After Dark and DIALOG Knowledge Index. First, the instructor lectured with overhead transparencies showing the commands for each service. Then the students formulated and reviewed search strategies on topics of their own choice. The class chose three searches for the instructor to demonstrate online, explaining the results and modifying the strategies as required. The students felt that the class demonstration gave them experience and confidence with the online services, and helped them to prepare for their unsupervised practice searches.

Tutorial Services for Practice in Classes

Since direct experience with online systems is the best way to learn searching, some training programs provide practice time on the tutorial services as a portion of classes or workshops. This approach can be modeled on the traditional full- or half-day seminar given by the major vendors and database producers. At these seminars, the training begins with a lecture overview of the material, then online practice time is provided, supervised by the instructor. At a full-day workshop, the group meets again to review their experiences or to study the service or database in greater detail, and the seminar ends with more free practice time.

In designing classes and workshops for end users, you must work within a limited time frame. One recent survey indicated that the longest single instruction session end users would attend was two hours, and that they preferred the total course of training to take not more than three to six hours (Sewell and Teitelbaum, 243). At Chalmers University of Technology in Sweden, a required undergraduate course on both manual and computerized information retrieval takes only 14 hours, divided into a two-hour lecture, two four-hour laboratory exercises, and four hours for preparation of a bibliography (Hasslow, Hermansson, and Kihlen, 88).

Content

To stay within reasonable time limits, you will have to decide on a clear set of teaching objectives and eliminate all but the most essential information. You will have to make difficult decisions about the best way to give library users a realistic view of searching and its place in the wide range of information sources available to them. In our experience, there are two major problems to consider. First, there is not enough time in a one- or two-hour class to cover anything but the basic concepts and skills of searching, especially if practice time is offered. Second, people attending our workshops want to learn the mechanics of searching, including the function keys, commands, and operation of the printer. Graduate students, faculty, and professionals often know the primary literature of their fields in detail, and will find other ways to locate information if the process of learning to search online is too frustrating.

When you have determined the content of your workshop, be sure to include learner participation by requesting topics from the class and working them into search strategies as a group. Overhead projectors with transparencies you can write on, marker boards, and blackboards are useful for sharing this kind of search preparation in class. Online time should follow the lecture or group work immediately if possible, so that students can see how the strategies they have created in class perform on the service (Witiak, 51).

Microcomputers

The availability of microcomputers may be another constraint on providing practice time as part of classes or workshops. While the simplest of dual floppy-drive computers will be adequate, each workstation must have a modem, be attached to a telephone line, and should also have a printer available. Depending on classroom space, two or three people can share each workstation, although one for each student is best. In school and academic libraries, microlabs may be used for practice sessions if telephone lines are accessible.

Telecommunications Software and Passwords

The basic guidelines listed earlier apply to classes as well. Any full-featured communications software program can be used, provided it is not copy-protected. You will want one copy for each workstation, and the software can be kept on diskettes, which the instructor hands out at the appropriate time in the class session. Adding a start-up menu screen and simple batch files that log on to the tutorial services automatically will make it easier for new searchers to begin and will protect the security of your passwords. For most of the services, you will need a separate password for each workstation; eight to ten can usually be assigned to instructional accounts without an extra charge.

Current Examples

At the Bailey/Howe Library, we require training for use of the end-user services BRS/After Dark and Knowledge Index. We offer a one-and-one-half-hour workshop every week during the semester. Sessions are held in a classroom in the Automated Reference Center (ARC), where five microcomputers with dual floppy drives are available for practice. Attendance is limited to ten students to make class participation and group work possible. The content of our sessions is very elementary, since we emphasize that the workshops are basic classes to prepare searchers with no experience. We use overhead transparencies, marker boards, and the Kodak Datashow to illustrate search strategy development on topics provided by the students.

We use Bitcom software on diskettes for the practice searches, and have created a short introductory menu that tells the students what services are available and what to type to search them. When they type KI or BRS, simple batch files start the Bitcom program and select the correct telephone numbers and automatic log-on sequences. This experience is good preparation for using our end-user services, which are set up with very similar menus and batch files on a workstation in the ARC.

A supervised individual practice search is also a required part of our training program. When there are only two or three participants in the workshop, the instructor may offer the option of extending it for another half hour and doing the practice searches as part of the class. In a larger class, two or three members may choose to stay and practice if the instructor can extend the session. We find that it is difficult to cover even the basic commands for two services in a short workshop, and that one teacher cannot provide enough attentive supervision to more than a few students doing their searches at the same time.

The computerized information laboratory sessions at Chalmers University of Technology Library follow a similar pattern. After a short lecture covering the advantages and disadvantages of online searching, students review commonly used commands on the ESA-IRS system and develop search strategies. Instructors demonstrate selected databases online. Workshop attendance is limited to 12 students, with two instructors, so that they can work alone or in groups on their strategies. At the end of the class, students do 15-minute practice searches. The librarians at Chalmers feel that direct online experience enables the students to "obtain up-to-date material on a topic of high interest and that the references found can be used in their research projects" (Hasslow, Hermansson, and Kihlen, 92).

Tutorial Services for Supervised Searches

Many authorities agree that one-to-one personal assistance is the ideal method for training beginning searchers. Dena Gordon, of Data Courier, states that "the best way to teach online searching is to take people by the hand and in an intimate and relaxed setting show them how to search" (Gordon, 10). One method of combining individual teaching with hands-on practice is to offer or require at least one supervised search as part of your training program. The supervised search can follow a lecture, demonstration, written exercises or some other form of instruction, or may be the only teaching method used.

Advantages and Disadvantages

Instructors counseling individual searchers are able to tailor their comments to the student's level of knowledge and special interests, avoiding the problems of frustration and boredom that more formalized methods may produce. One-to-one training seems labor intensive, but almost no preparation time is required if the teacher is very familiar with the system. Individual training may not take much more time per person than small group workshops that include practice time, and it is the method preferred by many new searchers (Sewell and Teitelbaum, 242). Since the tutorial services provide access to current files, the supervised search can be both a learning experience and a way to get valuable references for the student.

Content

The topics covered during a supervised search will vary, depending on whether the search is the last component in a structured training program or the only teaching method. The actual online time should be used to demonstrate and practice the capabilities of the service. Students should not sign on without adequate preparation, including some discussion of the advantages and disadvantages of online searching, database content and selection, basic commands, and search strategy development. Some librarians provide extensive presearch counseling sessions to cover this information and include discussion of the library's end-user protocols, such as time limits, appointments, and costs (Janke, 16). At the least, each student should come to the supervised search with a completed strategy on paper. Reviewing this strategy before going online gives you an opportunity to correct basic mistakes and misconceptions.

Once online, you should let the student execute the search as planned, commenting on and explaining the results as appropriate. Here the student may discover the limits of careful preparation; learning to modify an unsuccessful search online will illustrate the power of interactive searching better than any lecture or explanation can do. The service's basic functions should be tried: selecting terms, displaying and printing citations, changing databases, getting help. The essential operations of the communications software should also be practiced. Many end users have lost their results because they could not turn on the printer or open a file for downloading to diskette.

Microcomputers and Software

One of the virtues of supervised searches is that any available computer with a modem and access to a telephone line can be used, provided it is in a quiet enough location to allow the instructor and student to talk and concentrate. The software should be the same program that is used for the end-user services, and search manuals, database guides, and other aids should be readily available near the terminal.

Scheduling

Scheduling the search appointments is one of the most troublesome aspects of offering or requiring supervised practice sessions. Student, instructor, and microcomputer must all be available for the half hour, hour, or more that is needed. Fortunately, most of the tutorial services are accessible during both day and evening hours. While it is ideal for the practice session to be done immediately after the class, workbook, CAI, or other training has been completed, this is often impossible. Busy librarians cannot do practice searches on a walk-in basis, but equally busy students often have trouble fitting search appointments into their class or work schedules. One solution is to make a calendar of times when librarians are available for searches. Depending on the size of the library and the number of librarians, this may involve a commitment for each instructor of one or two hours per week, which may or may not be used for search training. The calendar should be posted near a sign-up sheet, which students can use for appointments as soon as they finish their other training. Where the number of end users requesting practice searches is very small, you may be able to make individual arrangements with them.

Training the Instructor

The value of supervised practice sessions depends on the knowledge and attitudes of the instructors who provide them. Only those librarians who are interested enough to learn the services thoroughly, patient enough to cope with new searchers, and able to convey confidence and enthusiasm for the process should be teaching. Kenneth Murr, of the Clemson University Library, observes that "as with most other bibliographic instruction programs, lack of interest or knowledge in the subject is easily detected by the attendees who then lose interest. A reluctant teacher is worse than no teacher at all" (Murr, 363).

You will have to explain not only the search commands but also the telecommunications software, terminal operation, and sometimes even the keyboard to beginners. While all staff members must have basic familiarity with the services offered in a library that provides end-user searching so that they can approve strategies, suggest appropriate databases, and correct simple mistakes, the instructors must be fluent with the system. This expertise can be gained by attending training sessions given by vendors or by other instructors, reading the service manual, and practicing. You should make a special effort to keep current with the features and databases on the end-user services, since they sometimes differ slightly from the ones on the tutorial services. Vendor newsletters are a good way to keep up with the changes.

Current Examples

Teachers in the Department of Instructional Resources of the Montgomery County Public School System in Maryland have used supervised searches effectively in an in-service training course on online searching for library media specialists. With enrollment limited to 15 participants and seven microcomputers available, every student was assured of individual practice time. The course was divided into five three-hour sessions, every one including a lecture-demonstration, hands-on practice, and a follow-up discussion. Students signed on to local bulletin boards, CompuServe, and DIALOG, using both bibliographic and full-text databases. Evaluation forms indicated that "since they learned best by doing, the combination of individualized hands-on practice and group discussion had been a particularly valuable learning experience" (Dowling and Pruitt, 33).

Beginning searchers at the University of Vermont must complete either a workbook and CAI or attend a workshop before scheduling their required half-hour supervised practice searches. Students must bring a completed search planner form to their appointments. After reviewing search strategies, students log on to DIALOG CLASSMATE or BRS Instructor using Bitcom software on diskette. The diskettes for the tutorial services are kept at the secretary's desk in the reference office, adjacent to the classroom, for security. We have eight passwords for each service, and we change them at least twice each year. Students practice all of the basic commands, including selecting, displaying, and printing documents, changing databases, and getting online help. We also use this opportunity to explain the reasons for some service limits; for example, because BRS charges for the citations displayed or printed, the greatest number of citations an end user can print is 40. Students comply with the rules much more readily when they understand the reasons behind them.

After weeks of wrestling with problems scheduling practice searches, we have developed a system that works in our medium-sized department. We circulated a calendar to the eight librarians who would be doing practice searches and had each one sign up for at least two hours of time during the week to be in the reference office and available for an appointment. Students who complete their workshop or workbook/CAI training are told to sign up immediately in the ARC for a practice search. Although sometimes their searches must be delayed for several days, making the appointment minimizes the number who only partially finish the program. We have found supervised practice searches to be the most valuable part of our search instruction program, and have seen great improvement in the quality of search planners and search results produced by our end users since this requirement was made.

DESIGNING MATERIALS TO COMPLEMENT SERVICES

Since even the specially priced online tutorial services are very expensive, you will need to design and produce a variety of materials to prepare users so that their connect time will be used as efficiently as possible. Librarians have been teaching and learning database searching for more than ten years, and end users have been learning for at least five; many approaches have been tried, tested, and evaluated. Materials commonly used with the tutorial services to teach online searching include search planner forms, workbooks, manuals, exercises, and CAI packages. CD-ROM products and videotapes are the newest online teaching devices.

Search Planner Forms

A well-designed search planner form is more than complementary; it is essential to your instruction effort. In our experience at the University of Vermont, no single aspect of teaching online or optical disc searching is more useful to the beginning searcher than this form. We use it as the backbone of our teaching program. The workbooks and workshops are planned around the steps required to complete the search planner properly. Each online end user is required to fill out one of these forms completely and have it approved by a reference librarian before signing up for a search appointment. Richard Janke, writing about end-user instruction at the University of Ottawa Libraries, comments: "it is sound procedure to devise a blank search form tailored to your user-friendly system's interface. In the presearch counseling session, the librarian then uses this form to show the client how to devise a workable search strategy, by filling it in with appropriate terms and Boolean operators. Even the online print commands can be illustrated in this fashion" (Janke, 16).

Design

You will first need to examine as many search planner forms as you can, analyzing their strengths and weaknesses. Many of the vendors' teaching materials contain sample forms, which you can adapt to your own purposes. Other librarians will also share examples of forms they have designed for end-user instruction. When creating your search planner:

1. Cover each step in the search preparation process. For example, our planner is divided into the following sections: writing a topic statement, selecting the main concepts, listing alternate terms for the main concepts, choosing a database and service, formulating the search statements with Boolean operators and system commands for search and display/print, and logging off the service.

2. Don't include any extra material. The search planner is not the place to elaborate, explain, or theorize. Find other ways to remind

searchers of system commands, function keys, and similar information.

3. Think like a complete beginner. We have recently changed the method of listing alternate concept terms from vertically to horizontally to make it simpler to translate them into search statements. This change was based on the comments of our students.

4. Keep the form on the front of one page if possible. This restriction will help you simplify the planner. The reverse side can be used for a sample of the properly completed form, which new searchers find very helpful.

5. Include necessary rules or restrictions on the form if appropriate. Our search planner form contains spaces for the reference librarian's signature after approving the strategy, a notation that downloading to diskette is acceptable, and a waiver of the limit of 40 citations per session. Student monitors can check at a glance that these steps in the preparation process have been completed.

6. Include as much white space and writing space as possible.

7. Construct the form to support exactly the services you offer, at the level of complexity best suited to your searchers. You need only examine the examples included in this chapter (figures 5-1 and 5-2) to see how widely forms may vary, yet still be suited to the specific services they support.

8. Tailor your workbooks, workshops, CAI programs and other materials so that they reflect and explain the search planner form. These materials need not follow the form exactly, but the presentation of information, vocabulary, sequencing, emphasis, and other elements of teaching should support the importance of carefully planning an online search. The form is the outline of the process.

A good search planner form will make it easier for your beginning students to work online, will help experienced end users remember essential steps and commands, and will help organize your instruction program.

Figure 5-1. Bailey/Howe Library Search Planner Form

BRS/AFTER DARK OR KNOWLEDGE INDEX SEARCH PLANNER

YOU __MUST__ HAVE THIS FORM REVIEWED BY A REFERENCE LIBRARIAN BEFORE YOU SEARCH.

1. State your search topic briefly: _____

_____

2. Think about your topic and circle the two or three most important parts, or concepts, above.

3. Write each concept you circled in a space, then list synonymous or related terms next to it, if applicable. If a thesaurus is available for your database, use appropriate terms from it also.

First Concept   _____ OR _____ OR _____

Connector   _____

Second Concept   _____ OR _____ OR _____

Connector   _____

Third Concept   _____ OR _____ OR _____

4. Insert connectors **OR, AND, NOT** between the concepts above.

5. Select the best database(s) for your topic. The ARC monitor can provide a list of databases. Select a service (**BRS/After Dark or Knowledge Index**); fill in the database label(s).

Database:_____Service:_____Label:_____

6. Write the search statements you will enter to find, display, and print your first sets:

1. _____

2. _____

3. _____

4. _____

5. _____

What command will you use to logoff the system? _____

PLEASE ASK THE ARC MONITOR FOR ASSISTANCE WITH THIS FORM AND WITH SEARCHING!!

_____ Librarian Reviewed   ( ) Diskette Download OK   ( ) 40 Citation Limit

Copyright 1990, University of Vermont, Bailey/Howe Library, Reference Department.

Figure 5-2. DIALOG CLASSMATE Worksheet

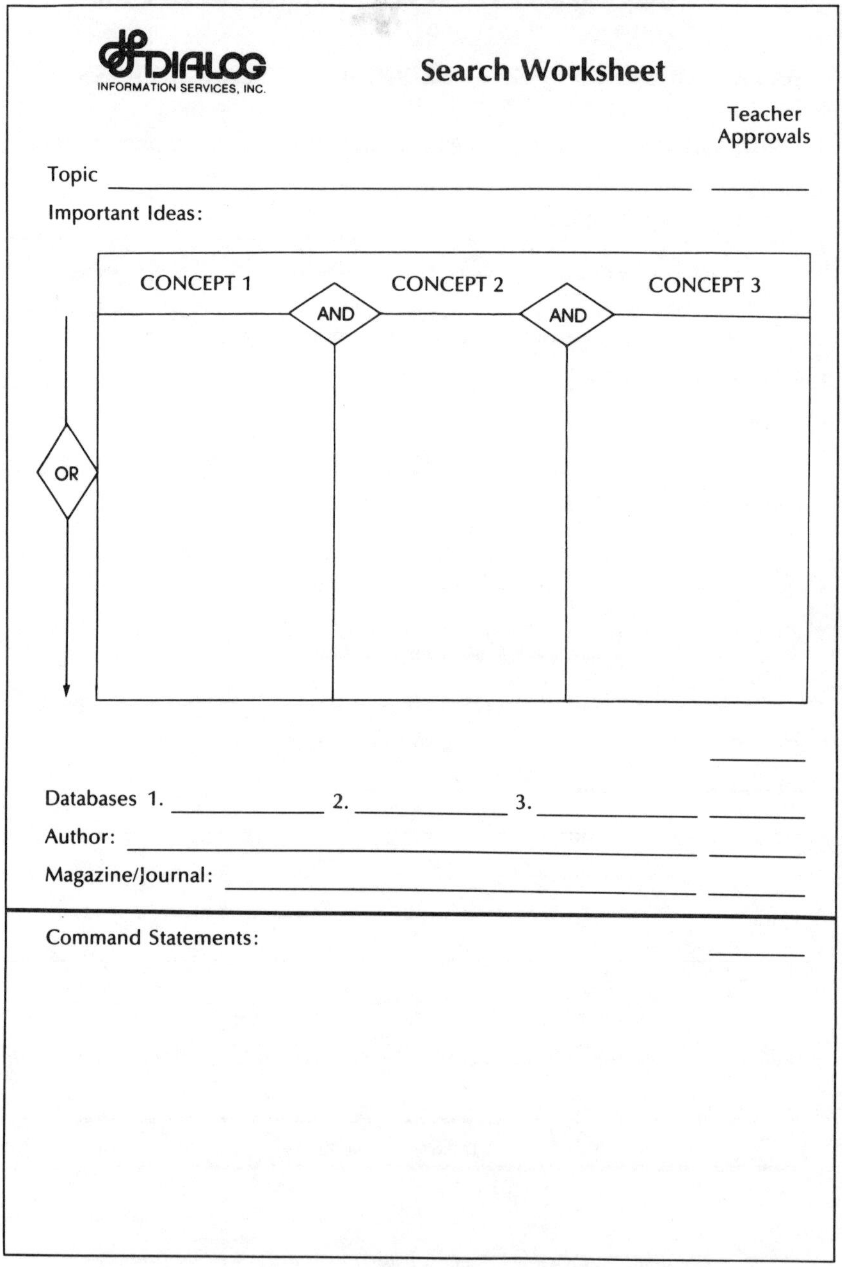

DIALOG
INFORMATION SERVICES, INC.

Search Worksheet

Teacher
Approvals

Topic _____ _____

Important Ideas:

CONCEPT 1	AND	CONCEPT 2	AND	CONCEPT 3

OR

_____

Databases 1. _____ 2. _____ 3. _____ _____

Author: _____ _____

Magazine/Journal: _____ _____

Command Statements: _____

Copyright DIALOG Information Services; reprinted with permission.

140

Workbooks

By *workbooks*, we mean written guides that explain or describe the system, search strategy development, or software, illustrated with examples and including exercises. Workbooks do not need to be glossy or expensive publications, and it is better if they are not too long. The workbook used for end-user online service training at the Bailey/Howe Library is only 12 pages long, photocopied on both sides, with a colored paper cover, and stapled in one corner.

Advantages

Workbooks, from the polished ones like DIALOG's *CLASSMATE Student Workbook* with multicolored type, cartoon illustrations, and three-ring binder to our own simple version, have many advantages. They are relatively inexpensive to produce, even in large numbers. You can be general or specific in the text, writing about the universe of electronic knowledge or how to use the semicolon in command stacking on BRS/After Dark. You can and should use lots of examples, even downloading and printing real searches to show how commands operate. Exercises are very important. One of the benefits of workbooks is active user involvement. The user supplies the topic and develops it, step by step, into a search strategy. Instruction can be broken down into manageable segments. Workbooks are also free of time constraints; users can complete them at their own pace. Answers to exercise questions can be checked and evaluated, and mistakes discussed to clarify misunderstanding.

Disadvantages

Workbooks also have disadvantages. They do not use microcomputer technology, may be boring, and can seem unrelated to searching. They must not be too long; students won't read through detailed explanations of things they don't know how to do. Imagine reading two pages on using a manual transmission and then going out to drive a car! Workbooks are difficult to revise if a large run has been ordered from the printer. This happened at UVM when we dropped the requirement that students take formal training in order to use CD-ROM products. If you add a service or change policies, or if a vendor changes software – as when DIALOG introduced "Menu Mode" on Knowledge Index – you may be left with hundreds of out-of-date workbooks. You may be able to add new information by inserting one or more pages, or use up old workbooks, as we do, with selected classes that are told about their inaccuracies.

Design

Designing your own workbook is a challenge, but the process is worth the effort. It is important to set aside plenty of time, since you will want to test and revise your text and exercises. At the Bailey/Howe Library, writing the first online searching workbook took most of one librarian's time during a one month winter intersession. Revising and rewriting the second version took about one month during summer session. Some guidelines for designing workbooks are:

1. Work from a model like DIALOG's *CLASSMATE Student Workbook* or the American Psychological Association's *Search PsycINFO Student Workbook*. Analyze how the vendors present lessons, when the more advanced commands are introduced, and what examples are used. Notice that instruction is broken up into units, followed by examples and exercises that reinforce the learning.

2. Set reasonable goals. Think about the minimum number of commands and steps you need for basic-level searching. Learners become confused if you try to teach them too much too soon. This is a mistake most vendor's manuals make; they can't bear to leave out any of the exciting features of their system. But *you can*.

3. Design several levels of expertise: perhaps a basic workbook, to be required, and one or more advanced levels that would be optional. Most students who become frequent searchers will want to learn more.

4. Use lots of white space, illustrations, and examples.

5. Be specific; teach only the services you offer. People don't want much general information about online retrieval, they want to get started searching.

6. Be flexible and analyze your own work. Use the workbook to train new staff members. Revise frequently. Look for other libraries' approaches; they may suggest improvements for your own.

A workbook is a manual with exercises added. Learners in a recent study that compared three methods of teaching online searching liked using manuals and learned as well from them as they did from CAI and slide/tape presentations (Hutchins, Anders and Jaros, 190). Workbooks can also provide "comfort value" to novice searchers, if they include charts of commands, function keys, and other information that people want to have readily available when they are searching. The low-technology workbook is still an excellent tool to introduce users to high technology. (See figure 5-3 for a sample workbook page.)

Figure 5-3. Bailey/Howe Search Workbook Page

SECTION FIVE: COMMAND SUMMARY CHART

Function	Knowledge Index	After Dark
Select database	BEGIN label	Type label after prompt
Search for terms	FIND terms	Type terms after prompt
Show citations	DISPLAY s1/m/1 (set #/format/range)	D;1;s;1
Print citations	TYPE s3/m/1-20 (set#/format/range)	PC;3;m;1-30
Disconnect	LOGOFF	O

SECTION SIX: WRITE SEARCH STATEMENTS

The last step in planning your search is to write out the search statements you will type into the computer when you are online. Search statements include commands, search terms, and connectors.

Example using Knowledge Index commands:

find artificial sweeteners or sugar substitutes or aspartame

find safe or safety or dangerous or healthy

find s1 and s2

display s3/m/1

logoff

Copyright 1988, University of Vermont, Bailey/Howe Library, Reference Dept.

CAI

Since the general question of computer-assisted instruction in library education is treated in detail in chapter 7, this discussion will concentrate on those programs and studies directly related to teaching online searching. CAI programs of various types and levels of complexity have been used for at least ten years to train new searchers. A distinction is commonly made between programs that allow actual searching on a small database of records and those that do not. There is some confusion in the library literature because the terms *computer-assisted-learning module*, *simulation*, and *emulation* are used by different authors to describe the development and use of programs with the same functions. In this chapter, *simulation* will be used in the broadest sense to describe both programs that teach and demonstrate the process using downloaded or sample searches, and those that provide search software and a database.

CAI search simulation programs have been developed and used successfully in public, academic, and special libraries to teach online searching (Foster, 167; Large and Armstrong, 95; Perkins, Spann, and Buchan, 202). There is a wide range of styles and levels of complexity, from very simple, step-by-step text lessons that fit on one floppy diskette to mainframe-based simulations that provide large, searchable databases and access for many users. You will have to decide, based on the level of resources available and the number of users that need training, what kind of CAI fits within your training program.

Current Examples

In view of the cost and effort required to design your own CAI, you should investigate both in-house and commercial products to see whether an existing program will meet your needs. Even if you decide to produce your own, reviewing the style and content of the range of programs available will give you good ideas about what is effective in CAI training. Many libraries will share their in-house CAI; we have developed a program at the Bailey/Howe LIbrary for teaching end users to search BRS/After Dark and Knowledge Index which we copy for other libraries on request. This single diskette simulation does not include search functions; it is a "run-time" version of Dan Bricklin's Demo program, which was used to write the CAI. The run-time version will play our program but will not allow the user to write a program of their own, which would violate copyright restrictions.

In-House CAI

Jocelyn Foster has described the development of a simple CAI program for use in teaching public library patrons in selected libraries in Ontario how to use Info Globe. This program was written with OAK courseware, which runs on IBM PC-compatible microcomputers and allows for both multiple-choice and typed-response questions. The CAI program had to be designed for people with no computer experience who would be willing only to give a short amount of time to the training session. The final version had six sections and took 35 minutes to one hour for novices to complete. "As well as explaining the basics of command language, the instruction covered the strategic necessities of a search: judging if Info Globe was appropriate for the topic, choosing vocabulary, restricting the search, and checking results and revising if necessary. Each section of the instruction ended with a few review questions, and the final section reviewed the whole search by asking participants questions" (Foster, 163). Foster's report, which includes the results of a detailed survey of end users' satisfaction with this training method, gives an excellent analysis of the effectiveness of this type of entry-level CAI.

A more complex program, based on the European ESA-IRS system, has been developed at the College of Librarianship Wales. The microcomputer-based Online Search Trainer has three modules: an eight-lesson instruction program, a search function, and a section on strategy techniques. The eight lessons cover the online environment, database structure, and commands; the command lessons include tests that display explanations in response to wrong answers. The search function uses the basic commands, as well as truncation, field searching, and limits, on a database of 600 records from INSPEC. The strategy section poses exercises to be carried out in the second module; the program can track the user's search and comment at the end, suggesting improvements. This is a good example of a more ambitious CAI that includes search capabilities but does not require large computer storage for the program, which runs on an IBM PC-XT with 256K RAM and a ten-megabyte hard disk (Large and Armstrong, 95).

Commercial CAI

DIALOG offers a demonstration diskette for Knowledge Index that contains three learning modules (see figure 5-4). The introduction describes the online environment and explains a sample citation; "Learning Key Commands" reviews the basic commands in an interactive program that poses questions and suggests review in response to wrong answers; and a "Practice Session" allows searching on a very small database of about 50 records from ABI-Inform. Though limited by its single diskette format, this is a clearly outlined, attractive program that could be used as CAI in training for CLASSMATE as well as Knowledge Index, and the cost is less than ten dollars (see figure 5-4).

Figure 5-4. Knowledge Index Demonstration Diskette

```
You have entered an incorrect response. Remember, you want to
search for documents that include BOTH INSURANCE AND HEALTH.
Therefore you should use the logical operator AND with the two
terms. The right response would be one of the following:

    FIND INSURANCE AND HEALTH

    FIND HEALTH AND INSURANCE

The order of the terms has no effect on the results of the
search.
```

(C)ontinue (M)ain Menu

Copyright DIALOG Information Services; reprinted with permission.

In July 1989 DIALOG introduced *The Microcomputer Tutorial*, a three-to four-hour program on four diskettes, designed to teach the basics of searching the regular interface. This interactive CAI includes testing, feedback, simulated searches, and online exercises in the ONTAP practice databases. With an instruction book, search worksheets, and quick reference cards, it is an excellent example of vendor-produced CAI.

The Information Focus, from McGraw-Hill Educational Resources, takes a very different approach to teaching online searching. Designed for use in elementary and secondary schools, this is a stand-alone program for Apple microcomputers. The 15 lessons progress from general information about telecommunications, through simulated sign-ons to bulletin boards and electronic mail systems, to database searching. Support materials include student workbooks and practice disks that contain six small, searchable databases. The simulations are all generic examples, and the package is not intended to imitate any major vendor. This CAI would be useful in a program intended to teach the basic principles of telecommunications and online searching, but special assistance might be required to help students make the transition from such general background information to a specific online service.

CAI programs can be very powerful teaching tools, but even the most complex simulations do not replace hands-on practice with the online systems (Wood, 33). Students that have had the chance to practice with CAI programs, however, may be more relaxed and better prepared to use their time on the online tutorial services efficiently.

Optical Disc Exercises

With a little imagination, optical disc products can be used to teach online searching, and there are significant advantages to this approach. Many CD-ROM products have full-featured search software, some of which closely resembles online search services. Most CD-ROM search programs, for example, include Boolean operators, truncation, field limitation, and ondisc indexes. CD-ROM users must also learn to display and print off citations, although many products handle these operations through function keys rather than by commands. Since the storage capacity of optical discs is so high, these products offer very large, searchable databases; since they are sold by subscription, there is no connect-time charge for using them.

"Direct" versus "Indirect" Learning

Unfortunately, very few CD-ROM products' search interfaces correspond exactly to online services. In fact, newer optical disc software tends to diverge farther and farther from online models as designers experiment with windowing, split screens, and other graphic innovations. New searchers will find it much simpler to transfer learning from practice sessions on CD-ROM discs to online searching if the systems are the same, or nearly identical, as on the hybrid CD-ROM products. Hybrid CD-ROMs include automatic access to their vendor's online service in their software; DIALOG OnDisc and WILSONDISC are leading examples of this type of CD-ROM product. WILSONDISC offers three search modes: BROWSE, WILSEARCH, and WILSONLINE. The user can move from disc to online searching in any search mode by pressing the F7 key, if the library decides to allow direct access at the workstation. Since the search interfaces are exactly the same, you must be careful to teach the differences between ondisc and online database coverage and currentness, so that the online service is not used inappropriately.

When you use optical disc products to teach the concepts basic to online searching, "indirect" learning is required unless the systems are identical. The CD-ROM product may offer all of the functions you want to teach, such as Boolean operators and field qualification, but the commands for using them will be different from those of the online service. New searchers may become so confused that the benefits of practicing on the CD-ROM product are outweighed by the strain of remembering not only the theory, but the specific commands for each interface. On the positive side, library science postgraduate students who had searched Library and Information Science Abstracts on CD-ROM "showed noticeably better skills and attitudes [in an online search class] than previous cohorts of students," an improvement attributed to "confidence gained in having already transferred and developed basic search skills from one interactive system to another" (Day, 406).

You will have to decide on the value of optical disc exercises in your online search training program. If you are teaching only one dial-out service, like Knowledge Index, it may be more effective to have students practice on a CAI or tutorial service that replicates the system, to minimize confusion. If you are covering a range of search services and products, requiring students to master a variety of specific commands plus the underlying concepts of searching, CD-ROM exercises may be more useful.

Current Examples

DIALOG has recognized the potential of optical disc technology as a training medium for online searching. The DIALOG OnDisc Discovery Training Toolkit, introduced in 1989, is a package containing DIALOGLINK Communications and Account Manager software, OnDisc Manager search software, documentation, and a CD-ROM disc with selected records from eight OnDisc databases, including ERIC and Medline. Students can practice on the CD-ROM using command language searching that is identical to the online version; the OnDisc Easy Menu mode approximates, but is not the same as, the online Menu mode. This product could be cost effective in teaching large numbers of end users to search online.

During fall semester 1988, 15 school librarians took a continuing education course, "Optical Disc and Online Resources for School Libraries," at the University of Vermont. The course was planned so that the Electronic Encyclopedia, WILSONDISC databases, and SilverPlatter ERIC were introduced before the online services. Students were required to complete practice exercises and searches on the optical disc systems as part of their course work, and were encouraged to practice on the CD-ROM. Parallels were drawn between the searching, displaying, indexing, and output functions of the optical disc and online resources, with special attention paid to subtle differences among system commands. In their course evaluations, many students remarked that the practice sessions on the optical disc products had increased their confidence and helped them to do the required searches on BRS Instructor and CLASSMATE. They also commented that they felt "tense and anxious" when searching the online services, due to the time limit of one-half hour allowed for completing their assignments. They stated clear preferences for having at least one optical disc product in their own school libraries, since they felt it would be easier for their students to learn searching through practice.

Videotapes

BRS, DIALOG, and Wilson have produced videotape training programs for their search services. The "BRS Video Training Course" and the "Introduction to Searching Dialog" demonstrate and discuss only the basic search services, not Knowledge Index or BRS/After Dark, and therefore would be of little use in a program designed to teach these interfaces. Where end users are preparing to use regular BRS or DIALOG, the videos may make effective complements to other training methods. "Online Searching: An Introduction to WILSONLINE" covers both the menu-driven WILSEARCH interface and WILSONLINE, and has been recommended to introduce end users to searching and assist in their instruction (Karetzky, 364; Quint, 19).

DECIDING HOW TO OFFER TUTORIAL SERVICES

You will need to analyze several factors before deciding the most appropriate ways to use the online tutorial services in your search instruction program. Although the ideal method may be to offer hands-on practice to every new searcher via a supervised practice session, in reality time and money constraints may make other applications more feasible. You will want to consider the number of users you need to teach, how much you can budget for the services, and how to maintain password control and security.

Number of Users

The answer to "How many users are too many users for hands-on access?" will be different for every library, depending on the number of instructors, workstations, and passwords available. Most of the tutorial services will provide eight or ten passwords at no extra charge, so adequate password access is usually not a problem. One or two librarians working in a special library that serves a limited number of users interested in learning to search may be able to use one-to-one practice sessions as the main component of their teaching program. In school, public, and academic libraries where the number of students is larger, time will become a major obstacle to offering or requiring supervised practice sessions. If a group of librarians share the responsibilities for teaching, more hands-on time can be provided. But at the Bailey/Howe Library, just one faculty member suggesting that a specific database would be of value to an introductory-level class of 80 students results in a demand for 40 hours of search instruction through half-hour sessions. Even with six reference librarians available for scheduling practice searches, finding six and a half hours of "free" time within a few weeks to train each member of the class is extremely difficult. When the number of students is too high to be handled individually, the tutorial services may be best used for demonstrations. Small groups or classes are another possibility, but it is difficult for one librarian to provide assistance to more than a few students searching at the same time.

Costs of Training

Although the tutorial services are inexpensive compared to the end-user and full-power search services, the cost of using them in a teaching program will be significant. Carol Tobin points out that "bibliographic instruction programs are usually poorly funded with no separate line item in the budget. The costs usually come out of the general reference budget and the time and dedication of the librarians. Computer searching requires equipment and the searches themselves can run into some money, even on an instructional use contract" (Tobin, 72). She suggests several methods for meeting the problem, including charging student lab fees and asking academic departments to subsidize the charges. There is justification for such charges, especially when the library would not be able to offer search instruction at all without them. Most of the tutorial services provide access to a wide range of up-to-date databases, so that practice searches will get valuable citations or other materials for the students. The library budget must cover the costs of demonstration searches, however, and should support the costs of required hands-on training as far as possible.

How much does an active instruction program cost? Using the Bailey/Howe Library as an example, let's look at the costs for BRS Instructor and DIALOG CLASSMATE for October 1988. We employ these two services for demonstrations, classes, and supervised practice searches. October is a moderately busy month in the academic calendar for bibliographic instruction; in 1988 a total of 25 separate classes were scheduled, including course-specific sessions and workshops on online searching, most of which featured online and optical disc demonstrations. Fifteen school librarians also did half-hour searches on CLASSMATE for their continuing education course; the number of individual practice sessions is unknown. Cost of the BRS Instructor service was approximately $100, while the CLASSMATE charges were $270. Costs for January, a much slower month for instruction demands, were $10 for CLASSMATE and $40 for BRS Instructor.

A recent survey of user preferences for search instruction methods indicates the importance of providing access to tutorial systems. Researchers polled faculty, graduate students, and staff who had learned to use National Library of Medicine databases by a variety of training methods. Asked to list their first three choices, 53 percent selected one-to-one instruction first, followed by hands-on experience (45 percent), and self-paced instruction on the computer (38 percent). When asked how they had *actually* learned to search, however, 73 percent of the respondents answered "trial and error" (Sewell and Teitelbaum, 242). Since all of these methods demand use of the online services, money spent by the library in providing access to them is a popular and essential investment.

Password Control and Security

The steps you need to take to ensure password security will be determined by your decisions concerning telecommunications software, workstations, and protocols for your instruction program. Unauthorized password use must be controlled to avoid the possibility of one or more searchers running up enormous bills before your invoices reveal the problem. You should also guard against computer "viruses," destructive programs designed to erase files or do other damage to your microcomputer once they are installed from a floppy disk or through online access to a bulletin board or other shared utility. You can plan to protect the passwords and equipment whether you use a hard disk, floppy disk, or release the passwords to students.

Hard Disk Protection

Hard disk security is an issue when a microcomputer is used for several applications, including online searching. For example, you may use a portable microcomputer for demonstrations and classes, with the tutorial passwords installed in appropriate telecommunications software; the same portable may also be used for word processing, spreadsheet statistics, and other purposes within the library and at home by colleagues and others. At another library, a workstation in the reference area may be set up for public access to several software packages, including the instructional services, which are used for practice searches. In these instances, both the passwords and the hard disk itself need to be secured. Here are some common precautions:

1. Write a simple menu program that calls the telecommunications software and starts an automatic log-on procedure. Don't teach software functions that are not essential to searching; there is usually no need to point out how the log-on is carried out or where the passwords are stored.

2. For better protection, use a brand-name menu program that controls access to the disk operating system (DOS) and offers various degrees of protection to programs on your hard disk. Some examples are AutoMenu, Hard Disk Menu III, and EZ Menu (King, 44).

3. Use the features of the telecommunications program to mask the passwords so they don't appear in demonstrations.

4. Supervise end-user access so that new searchers don't have the opportunity to "rummage" through your software. If all of your practice searches are carried out with a librarian present, this will not be an issue. If the workstation is used for CAI or other do-it-yourself purposes, it will be.

5. Keep viruses out of your computer and keep users from copying your software by supervising whenever they download to a diskette. Insist that all diskettes placed in your microcomputer be formatted, empty ones.

6. Be wary of downloading software programs or other information from public-access bulletin boards, which are common sources of computer viruses. This aspect of security has become such a concern that VIRSCAN, VSTOP, and many other software programs are now available to check for hidden viruses. Personal computing literature discusses the problem and current solutions in detail.

Floppy Disk Protection

If you have several microcomputers available for use with the tutorial services, or in a microlab situation, you may prefer to keep telecommunications software and passwords on floppy disks. Guidelines for their security include these measures:

1. Choose a safe, central storage place for the diskettes and keep them there. Be sure each instructor collects the diskettes handed out in class and returns them to the storage area, and informs you immediately if one is missing.

2. Select a telecommunications program that is simple and straightforward, and use it only as a tool for searching. There will be a few special situations where your teaching program may cover a detailed analysis of telecommunications functions. But for most librarians working with end users, James Koga's observations are pertinent: "My belief is that the best software for this purpose is the one that limits the user's options the most and keeps their minds on the searching, not the software" (Koga, 66).

3. Create a simple menu program with batch files to call the communications program and start the automatic log-on process.

4. Once you are familiar with the software, you may be able to remove files needed to configure the system but not required to run the program, thus blocking access to passwords. You may also be able to use DOS or other utilities to make files "read only" or even to hide them.

5. Reformat the diskettes regularly and reinstall the program files from a master copy. This practice will help guard against viruses and clean up unwanted reference files left on the disks.

Signing Out Passwords

In some cases, such as special libraries, continuing education classes, and school libraries, you may decide the most efficient way to provide the opportunity for search practice is to sign out passwords to students.

1. Be sure to keep exact records of your password assignments.

2. Make certain that everyone understands the restrictions you place on practice time, citations, and related issues. You may want to write up a brief form listing the rules, with a statement to the effect that the searcher agrees to pay costs for usage above the limits. Having the student sign this form and take a copy gives you a method for negotiating if the password is abused.

3. Place a time limit on the life span of the passwords. Decide on a suitable period within which they must be used, then change them.

Summary

One simple habit will help to protect your passwords' security on hard disk, floppy disk, or paper: change them frequently! Most of the online tutorial services make it easy to alter your passwords as frequently as you wish. Taking advantage of this function is good insurance against receiving surprising invoices. You will also want to examine your bills in detail, paying special attention to the activity log for each password. At the Bailey/Howe Library, we discovered that a password for Dow Jones News Retrieval Service had been stolen when the search log showed that the service had been used at three o'clock in the morning.

FUTURE OF END-USER ONLINE SEARCHING

With the advent of CD-ROM products, "local online," sophisticated networks, and other means of database access, will the end-user online systems continue to be important library services? The answer depends, of course, on the individual library and its users. Where budgets are limited, as in many public and school libraries, a "pay-as-you-go" service may be the best option. Online services also provide the widest possible range of databases to meet the needs of a variety of users. Imagine trying to imitate the breadth of subject areas covered through Knowledge Index or the Dow Jones News/Retrieval Service by purchasing CD-ROMs!

The tutorial services make it possible to introduce elementary and secondary students to online searching. Where end-user online access is offered in academic, public, or special libraries, the tutorial services can be the cornerstones of a well-designed instruction program that recognizes the importance of practice. They are one of the most valuable of the teaching technologies for libraries.

Works Cited

Alberico, Ralph. "Media for Online Instruction." *Small Computers in Libraries* 7 (July/August 1987): 8-11.

Baker, Betsy, and Susan Swords Steffen. "Microcomputers and Bibliographic Instruction." *Reference Librarian* 7 (1989): 223-32.

Balius, Sharon. "Changing Perspectives Evolving from Diverse End-User Applications." In *Bibliographic Instruction and Computer Database Searching*, edited by Teresa Mensching and Keith Stanger, 75-78. Ann Arbor: Pierian Press, 1988.

Batista, Emily, and Deborah Einhorn. "Training the End-User: Enhance Your Presentation Using Microcomputer Graphics." *Proceedings of the 8th National Online Meeting*, New York, 5-7 May, 1987, compiled by Martha E. Williams and Thomas H. Hogan, 21-27. Medford, N.J.: Learned Information, 1987.

Batt, Fred. *Online Searching for End-Users: An Information Sourcebook.* Phoenix: Oryx Press, 1988.

Bell, Steven. "Using the 'Live Demo' in Online Instruction." *ONLINE* 14 (May 1990): 38-42.

-----. "Customizing Communications Software for End-Users." *ONLINE* 13 (March 1989): 62-66.

Davis, Scott, and Marsha Miller. "New Projection Technology for Online Instruction." *Technicalities* 8 (February 1988): 3-6.

Day, Joan. "CD-ROM – An Online Training Tool?" *Education for Information* 6 (1988): 403-10.

Dowling, Karen, and Ellen Pruitt. "From Bulletin Boards to Boolean: Using Online to Teach Online." *ONLINE* 11 (May 1987): 31-33.

Fjallbrant, Nancy. "Recent Trends in Online User Education." *Iatul Quarterly* 2, no. 4 (1988): 228-36.

Foster, Jocelyn. "Computer-Assisted Instruction: Putting It to the Test." *Canadian Library Journal* (June 1987): 161-68.

Gordon, Dena. "Online Training for the End User or Information Consumer." Paper presented at the Midyear Meeting of the American Society for Information Science, Lexington, Ky., May 22- 25, 1983. ED 245697.

Hamilton, Dennis. "Library Users and Online Systems: Suggested Objectives for Library Instruction." *RQ* 25 (Winter 1985): 195-97.

Hasslow, Rolf, Eva Maria Hermansson, and Elisabeth Kihlen. "Online Education of Engineering Undergraduates." *Iatul Quarterly* 1 no. 2 (1987): 86-94.

Huston, Mary. "Search Theory and Instruction for End Users of Online Bibliographic Information Retrieval Systems: A Literature Review." *Research Strategies* 7 (Winter 1989): 14-32.

Hutchins, Geraldine, Vicki Anders, and Joe Jaros. "End User Perceptions of Teaching Methods." *Proceedings of the 8th National Online Meeting*, New York, 5-7 May, 1987, compiled by Martha E. Williams and Thomas H. Hogan, 183-90. Medford, N.J.: Learned Information, 1987.

Janke, Richard. "Presearch Counseling for Client Searchers (End-Users)." *ONLINE* 9 (September 1985): 13-21.

Karetzky, Stephen. "Videocassette Kits for Instruction in Online Searching." *College & Research Libraries News* 49 (June 1988): 360-64.

King, Alan. "The Seven Deadly Sins of Microcomputing." *ONLINE* 13 (July 1989): 40-44.

Koga, James. "DIALOGLINK: More Shortcuts and Quick Tips." *ONLINE* 13 (July 1989): 64-69.

Large, J. A., and C. J. Armstrong. "A Self-Contained Training Package for End-Users of Bibliographic Databases." *Iatul Quarterly* 1, no. 2 (1987): 95-101.

Linde, Lena, and Monica Bergstrom. "Impact of Prior Knowledge of Informational Content and Organization on Learning Search Principles in a Database." *Contemporary Educational Psychology* 13, no. 2 (1988): 90-101.

Lippincott, Joan. "End-User Instruction: Emphasis on Concepts." In *Conceptual Frameworks for Bibliographic Education: Theory into Practice*, edited by Mary Reichel and Mary Ann Ramey, 183-91. Littleton, Colo.: Libraries Unlimited, 1987.

Lyon, Sally. "End-User Searching of Online Databases: A Selective Annotated Bibliography." *Library Hi Tech* 2, no. 2 (1984): 47-50.

Murr, Kenneth. "Training the End User's Helper." *Proceedings of the 8th National Online Meeting*, New York, 5-7 May, 1987, compiled by Martha E. Williams and Thomas H. Hogan, 361-65. Medford, N.J.: Learned Information, 1987.

Perkins, Miriam, Melvin Spann, and Patricia Buchan. "MEDTUTOR: A Microcomputer-based Training Program for MEDLINE." *Bulletin of the Medical Library Association* 77 (April 1989): 201-4.

Phillips, Brian. "Projecting Real-Time Video Output." *DATABASE* 11 (August 1988): 71-73.

Quint, Barbara. "New Technologies for Training Online Searchers: A Review of New Industry Products." *Database Searcher* 4 (January 1988): 15-24.

Salomon, Kristine. "The Impact of CD-ROM on Reference Departments." *RQ* (Winter 1988): 203-15.

Sewell, Winifred, and Sandra Teitelbaum. "Observations of End-User Online Searching Behavior over Eleven Years." *Journal of the American Society for Information Science* 37 (July 1986): 234-45.

Tobin, Carol. "Online Computer Bibliographic Searching as an Instructional Tool." *Reference Services Review* (Winter 1984): 71-73.

Walker, Geraldene. *End-User Searching: A Selection of the Literature for 1983-1988.* An ERIC Synthesis Paper. ED308877.

Witiak, Joanne. "What Is the Role of the Intermediary in End-User Training?" *ONLINE* 12 (September 1988): 50-52.

Wood, Frances. "Microcomputer-based Training Aids for Online Searching." In *Information Technology in the Library/Information School Curriculum*, edited by Chris Armstrong and Stella Keenan, 32-36. Aldershot, England: Gower, 1983.

6

The Audiovisual Renaissance

Margaret W. Gordon

Audiovisual technologies instruct the viewer by using image projection accompanied by narration; the standard formats are slides, film, videotape, and videodisc. The approach is personal, may be adapted to any subject material, and has a respected history in the educational community. A review of the literature from the early 1980s to the present reveals a wealth of information on the technological and educational fine points of audiovisuals in the classroom. Libraries have successfully incorporated slide and tape formats in their bibliographic instruction programs.

The advent of the computer in the library has brought with it not only new things to teach but new ways of teaching them. In the audiovisual field this has led to a blurring of distinction between many of the formats. The standard uses, of course, still pertain: photographic images produce well on both slides and video. Innovations, however, have increased the options for the older technologies.

New software makes it possible to capture images from a computer screen or to download them directly to another program. These images can then be programmed to play back like a slide show, with or without accompanying narration. Computer projection units, such as Kodak's Datashow, project images from a computer by using an overhead projector; thus, any computer-generated program can be shown to a larger audience (Phillips). A videotape can be made from any slideshow, and can even receive images directly from the computer. Hypercard programs now make it possible to translate photographs or slides into computer images and thus incorporate them directly into a computer program.

The array of possibilities for using these technologies is almost without limit. At times, their capabilities infringe upon the realm of computer-assisted instruction (CAI). Despite the confusion, the standard formats of slide shows and videotapes prove themselves to be reliable, effective, and henceforth exciting and innovative methods for instruction. This chapter discusses the different options for using audiovisual methods as teaching tools for computer users and makes suggestions for getting started.

The simplest form of audiovisual training is a slide show conducted and narrated by a librarian. Slides of computer screens and other resources can be combined with slides of text and graphics, and the slide show can then be automated and coordinated with a taped narration. This type of slide-tape presentation is relatively inexpensive to produce and exceedingly versatile.

Another type of slide show involves the downloading of computer screens to create a simulation of a computer search. The slides can be programmed to advance at set intervals, or may be controlled by a librarian who provides narration. The demonstration may be shown on one or more video monitors, or a video projector may be used for larger audiences. One software program that will do this is Dan Bricklin's Demo Program (Sage Software, 3200 Tower Oaks Blvd., Rockville, MD 20853). Images from computer screens can be captured directly from other programs, or may be created using Demo software (see chapter 7). The Reference Department at the UCLA Biomedical Library has developed its own software program, called Show, to produce slide show demonstrations from downloaded searches (Deeney). Neither of these programs includes images other than from computer screens.

Many graphics packages include the screen capture capability mentioned above, so that downloaded searches can be incorporated into the program. In addition, they offer the full range of graphics options, from boxes and fonts to pictures and animation. The Van Pelt Library of the University of Pennsylvania uses a graphics package called PC Storyboard to create a video training session for end users that combines the realism of an online search with instruction from librarians using clever graphics (Batista).

The luxury of film and all of its attendant paraphernalia is, for all practical purposes, reserved for the Hollywood moguls. On the other hand, the advent of video as an affordable alternative has placed cameras in the hands of thousands. Videotape is an extremely versatile medium that can capture almost any message and project it to a wide audience. If the equipment and expertise necessary to produce a video are not available in-house, they can be hired.

While a video camera has no difficulty in filming a close-up of a computer screen, it is also possible to produce a videotape directly from your computer's output. If your video recording unit has dubbing capabilities, you can also add narration to the program (Planton). This option offers the same possibilities as a slide show simulation.

Videodisc offers the same image storage option as videotape, but with greater capacity, longer durability, faster accessibility, and at a greater cost. A series of images stored on either videotape or videodisc can be made interactive. This requires the image storage medium, a TV monitor or computer screen, a controller (so that the software has access to the images), appropriate software, and a means of receiving input. Input can be received from a keyboard, mouse, touch screen, or light pen. The program responds to these commands by branching to, or calling, other stored images. Many programs used for authoring CAI packages can also be used to create interactive video programs.

Although it is less expensive in terms of equipment to store images on videotape rather than videodisc, there are disadvantages. Videotape will produce an unstable still frame, and the need to rewind or fast forward in order to call the appropriate image is awkward. There is also a marked lack of tape durability for programs that receive heavy use.

Interactive videodisc is the Rolls Royce among audiovisual training options. It is durable, and interactive to a degree that makes even a live demonstration seem passive. By combining preprogrammed instruction with the versatile possibilities of video, it is certainly the most promising, and consequently the most expensive, option available in computer-assisted learning. Used primarily in the corporate world and by government agencies, production costs remain prohibitive for the educational sector. If you are interested in interactive videodisc, you should investigate the options by contacting software producers and courseware publishers. The journal *Instruction Delivery Systems* publishes a yearly buyer's guide to interactive products and services (Communicative Technology Corporation, 50 Culpeper Street, Warrenton, VA 22186, ISSN 0892-4872). In his book *Authoring Systems*, Peter Crowell also lists information on over 60 authoring systems.

ADVANTAGES

What are the advantages of the audiovisual medium over other methods? The obvious advantage of any program over a live presentation is that staff is freed from such repetitive tasks as teaching routine instruction sessions. A video or slide presentation not only fills that role but ensures that the training is consistent from one session to the next. Few methods will prove as economical as that in which staff time is saved in the long run.

A presentation can be custom designed to demonstrate the strengths and the vagaries of the local online public access catalog. It can guide users through the collection of in-house databases or provide instruction in other collections or services unique to an individual library. It can be designed to reflect the strengths or weaknesses of a particular group, such as business students who already have considerable experience in one database, or continuing education students who may have had no previous experience with computers. A presentation may also be designed to strengthen areas of instruction that are weak or nonexistent, such as programs to off-campus users of the online public access catalog (OPAC).

Video provides a sense of immediacy and realism that is second only to a live presentation. In its simplest form it can be just that: a taped recording of a live demonstration that fulfills its function over and over again to a large audience. Sound, image, and movement combine to provide a direct link to the audience that is more personal and vivid than written materials or computer screens.

Information is presented in several ways: motion video, freeze frame, graphics, text, and narration. It is this combination of media that enhances the message. For teaching a computer program to a user, the instruction moves beyond the computer screen to include other levels of perception. A patron watching a computer demonstration on video also hears the commentary and advice of the narrator. A freeze frame adds explanatory text. Subtitles, highlights, and arrows reinforce the narration. The visual image of a diagram provides a detailed explanation of a difficult concept. Special effects such as color distinguish the input from the output so that the patron is not confused during the demonstration. Highlighting search words helps the patron understand how the records were retrieved.

An audiovisual medium makes visual connections that reach beyond the scope of other methods. It shows end results: for example, a shot of a successful OPAC search is followed by a map of the library so the patron can locate the material. Audiovisual takes the audience to the print index, to the mainframe computer with database tapes, to the microcomputer where the database is searched by the patron. It offers the audience a visual portrayal of material that is difficult to describe verbally: database, record, citation, search.

Watching an instructional video on using an end-user search service, a patron first sees shelves of printed indexes. Next she sees the computer tapes from which the indexes are printed, along with a diagram that explains the role of the database provider, such as BRS, and the networks involved in accessing those databases. The image of a printed index citation is followed by the image of a database record on a computer screen. Words are highlighted in order to demonstrate logical operators in particular and search strategy in general. During an explanation of field limiters, the fields in a sample record are highlighted, followed by a shot of the BRS AidPage where field tag descriptions are found. A visual connection is made between the journal citation, the actual journal article, and its location in the library.

The patron sees a close-up view of a particular object or event, then steps back to put that object or event in context. These visual connections, accompanied by narration, provide the patron with a behind-the-scenes understanding of how the system works. Showing a computer search in the context of the materials being searched gives the viewer a wide perspective on the entire process. This inclusion of the process, as well as the end result, is a very personal, direct approach for the viewer who is learning new skills.

The most attractive asset of audiovisual presentations is flexibility; almost any subject is appropriate for a production, and it can be shown when convenient to both librarians and patrons. The production can be shown in a variety of settings: a library classroom, a regular classroom, on a continuous loop near the OPAC, or even in a patron's home. The proliferation of VCR machines makes it easier than ever to serve off-campus users of an OPAC by bringing the training to them.

When being viewed by individuals, videotape offers the added benefit of being self-paced. An individual, and even an entire class, can stop, rewind, and review the material as needed. Add to this the "motivation" factor: people *like* to watch television. It is an attractive medium that appeals to patrons as a source of information.

DISADVANTAGES

Video's popularity as a medium is also one of the disadvantages in using it as a training tool. Today's viewing audience is accustomed to sophisticated, professionally produced programs. A shoddy, amateurish work will stand out and lose the respect of the audience. An audience with high expectations is intolerant of low-budget work, no matter how important the message. When it is time to estimate the cost of an audiovisual production, the most important factor to remember is that a work that can only be poorly done is not worth doing. If the financial support is not available for a high-quality production it is best to look at other, less expensive methods of instruction.

With the exception of interactive video, audiovisual is a passive medium that does not directly involve the audience in practicing the new skills that are learned. This disadvantage can be overcome by supplementing the production with additional training or testing methods; however, this may defeat the goal of eliminating repetitive training tasks. A visual presentation cannot be studied the way that written materials can be. The subject material, therefore, should not be too complex for a person to understand in one viewing.

Once completed, a video production is difficult to update. Although a new sound track can be recorded to include new subject material, updating the visual sequence is time consuming and expensive. A slide presentation is much easier to adapt, and is a better option when the subject material is unstable and likely to change in the near future.

PRACTICAL APPLICATIONS

There are a variety of formats available for using audiovisual as a teaching tool. Factors to be considered when choosing between them include audience, costs, production time, and compatibility of the medium to the subject material. A slide-tape presentation is an excellent medium for an instruction session that traditionally requires the use of visual aids. These can be brought together in a linear format, just as they would be presented by a librarian, and linked together by a taped narration. Imagine a presentation that introduces the basics of searching the online catalog: shots of the keyboard with important keys highlighted, sample searches, sample pages from *Library of Congress Subject Headings (LCSH)*, a shot of the reference desk so the viewer knows where to ask questions, and even a diagram to show the location of books and other materials.

Complex topics are equally suitable for a slide-tape format. Anything that is best explained using charts, diagrams, or other stylistic representations will reproduce well on slides. Make a list of all of the concepts you have ever instructed using paper or blackboard. Most aspects of online searching, from logical operators to truncation, can be competently taught using this format. Additional visuals of thesauri or paper indexes combine to produce a well-rounded instructional session.

One possibility using video is to tape the standard lecture that is routinely given to users of the OPAC or other search services. While it does not take full advantage of the capabilities of the medium, such a presentation requires minimal editing and rehearsing. It is also useful in terms of feedback for the person who is making the presentation. A videotaped class introduces the option of interplay in the form of questions and answers between the "audience" and the instructor, but it is unlikely that such a session could be realistically improvised. Any production that moves beyond taping live action must be scripted and rehearsed. Taped discussion or interview formats can be lively and informative, but require complex editing in order to succeed.

A more personal approach is to tape an individual instruction session. The librarian guides the patron through the steps necessary to find information using the library's computerized sources. The presentation may focus on a specific research question, but should be general enough so that the viewers can apply the material to their own needs. For example, the

"Everyman" patron in the video approaches the reference desk with a question that requires the use of the online catalog, an index to periodicals on CD-ROM, and the automated circulation system. As the librarian instructs the patron, his explanations are general enough to be relevant to each viewer in the audience.

An even more immediate approach is straightforward instruction directed to the viewer. This format can include demonstration, graphic illustration of complex material, and narration addressed to the viewer without the fictitious patron to act as intermediary. At its best, this format gives the impression of a personal instruction session to each viewer in the audience. The tone is informative, authentic, and businesslike. Patrons feel that they are on an equal footing with the narrator, rather than merely an audience being entertained, and indirectly instructed, by a video.

One of the most attractive formats for appealing to a varied audience is a fixed display, such as is seen at trade shows. In a library scenario, a video monitor cleverly placed near the online public access catalog runs a continuous looping instructional video on the use of the catalog. The looping feature of the videotape naturally involves heavy use, and the tape will require frequent replacement. The only special equipment required is a playback tape deck that will run the tape on a continuous loop. A slideshow demonstration could be designed on the same principle, with the patron initiating the show by a keystroke.

COSTS

A low-budget production, unless it is done by experienced professionals, will invariably look like a low-budget production. On the other hand, it's unnecessary to invest in the trappings of a full-blown production by hiring professional actors or building a custom-designed set. Corners can be cut in many areas while maintaining overall quality.

Nevertheless, producing a video or slide production will not be inexpensive. The range of costs for video depends primarily on the amount of time and work that goes into it, especially during the filming and editing stages. There can be several thousand dollars' worth of difference between a 10-minute video and a 20-minute one. Extra frills, such as professional actors and color graphics, obviously run up the bill. These costs can be significantly reduced when many of the required tasks are taken on in-house rather than hired out. For example, a library could appoint one of its own to write the script, instead of commissioning a free-lance scriptwriter.

The reference department at Lee Library, Brigham Young University, chose to work with a private company and to use 16-mm film, which would then be transferred to videotape, "rather than compromise on quality. The only drawback was cost, which was estimated at $1,000 per minute. After some negotiation we agreed to pay $7,000 for a ten-minute video" (French). The Undergraduate Library at the University of California, San Diego turned to the campus media center and, using student actors, were able to keep their costs down to $350 per minute (Smith). The latter project was also partially funded by a local grant.

Costs for a slide-tape program might include the services of a photographer, slide production, and equipment. Equipment might consist of a slide projector(s), a dissolver, and a cassette or tape deck. Additional expenses include any professional assistance hired to process and coordinate the sound and slides. The Northwestern University Library produced a slide-tape orientation program for $3,000, using an in-house photographer and having the slides and sound produced commercially (Cubbage).

If there is no one in-house with the expertise and equipment required to take still photographs, a professional photographer should be hired for any or all of the shots needed. She can also follow through on the production of slides. Commercially produced graphics and text are an added expense, but will give the finished product a polished and positive look. A media center can prove helpful at every stage, from taking the photographs to coordinating the tape.

It is neither necessary nor desirable that special equipment be purchased. It is only necessary that the library own the equipment necessary to show the production once it is ready. The entire production can be commissioned, or certain steps of it may be while the library undertakes other steps in order to save money. One producer may be hired to oversee the entire production, from planning and design through editing and distribution, much as an architect or contractor is hired to oversee the construction of a home. Or you can do the contracting yourself by completing the design process and then looking for bids on the remainder of the project. Each step of the project may be commissioned separately: script writing, shooting, sound, editing.

The final cost of audiovisual productions depends on such a variety of factors that it is impossible, without a well-formulated and specific plan, to round it out even to the thousands. A general sequence of steps that will enable you to draft a rough plan for your production includes analyzing the library's needs and defining the objectives for the training, choosing the format most suitable to the audience and to the subject material, writing the script and the storyboard, and determining the upper limit of your budget. Once this is done you can take the entire package to a professional who can help you to work out the technical details. You'll then have a chance to estimate more accurately the cost of the entire production.

WHERE TO GO FOR HELP

Where do you locate the equipment and expertise necessary to undertake your project? Most colleges and universities have in-house audiovisual media departments. This is an excellent facility to contact, whether or not your library is affiliated with the university. If you are affiliated, of course, there is the satisfaction of knowing that the media department has the best interests of you and the institution in mind; they are not working with a for-profit business motive.

Although they view themselves primarily as a university resource, some media centers may take on educational, nonprofit projects as time allows. At the very least they are an excellent source of contacts for other professionals in the area. A glance in the yellow pages under "video production services" (refer to the nearest large city if your town has little to offer) will give you an idea of how much there is to work with. In addition to production companies, there are many free-lance professionals who can be hired to assist at any stage, from camera work to sound dubbing to the creation of titles and graphics.

A less expensive option, but one that comes with no guarantees, is the gratis work of students in various fields. A student in the theater department of the local university, for example, may welcome the opportunity to practice her lighting techniques. Students in a video class at the same college might jump at the chance to take on a "real" project. Contacts can be made through the media department or by contacting the instructors themselves. The quality of the final product may be an outstanding gem from brilliant young minds, or it may be an unmitigated disaster. If yours is necessarily a low-budget project, it may be a risk that you find worth taking.

Equipment

Rapid change in the audiovisual technical fields, which makes much of the equipment obsolete within a few years, argues against buying, as opposed to renting, the technology. Only a well-established production company or free-lancer could hope to make this type of equipment pay for itself. The only equipment that a library should purchase is that which is necessary to show the final presentation.

To run a slide-tape presentation you will need a dependable video projector, a special cassette or tape deck that will produce audible beeps on the tape that can be picked up by the projector, and a dissolve unit if more than one projector will be used. If images will be downloaded from a computer, then appropriate hardware and software are necessary. The taped narration should also be commercially produced. Depending on where the presentation will be shown, you may need to buy a screen if there is no clean, blank wall to use instead.

Much of the equipment necessary for producing a videotape is determined by the level of quality desired. One of the first decisions that must be made is tape format. There is film, the most expensive choice available, which can later be transferred to tape for distribution. There are also a variety of tape formats, which range in price and quality from two-inch to VHS. Of these, VHS is lowest in quality, lowest in price, and most readily available. The flexibility of the format is perhaps its greatest strength; once duplicated, it can be shown in almost anyone's home, or in any setting with a monitor and a receiver. Other formats hold up better in terms of quality and duplication, but the ability to distribute them widely is limited.

For equipment such as cameras, lighting, and sound, the expertise with which they are used is as important as the quality (or quantity) of the equipment. For example, using more than one camera offers greater flexibility while shooting, but demands greater time and skill at the editing stage.

The production of sound and music presents its own problems. Sound may be recorded directly onto the tape during the shooting, which requires planning and care to ensure that it be done well, or may be recorded, mixed, and added to the tape later. In this case you will need microphones, a sound booth for recording the voice-over, a mixer, and the expertise necessary to make it all come together.

There are several possible options if you want to add background music. The copyright law restricts you from selling copies of the video if you have used copyrighted material. It is possible, of course, to get permission to use the material from the composer. This can be time consuming, but many educational media centers have been successful, especially when it is made clear to the composer that the project is educational and nonprofit. You may also find local artists who are willing to compose and produce a piece for a reasonable fee.

Editing time is one of the most expensive items on the video production budget. Nevertheless, the temptation to rent a video camera and to shoot and edit a program "in camera" should be strenuously avoided. No amount of planning and foresight can hope to achieve the results of professional postproduction editing, although they can make the job somewhat easier and less time consuming.

The choice of cameras, lighting, and lenses is important and decidedly affects the quality of the video. But instead of choosing the equipment, you should find someone with the experience who can do it for you. You should make decisions about what frills you want in the planning stage, but in the end the "contractor," and your budget, will make the final decisions about what to use and how to use it. The expertise to use the equipment is where your money should go. Whether you decide to hire one person or several, you are looking for someone who can take your concept and turn it into an effective, interesting, and instructional product.

Design

During the preproduction design process you will determine the overall objectives, the projected audience, the content, and the best format to represent them. The planning is the bare-bones framework of the production on which the completed project will be built. It is also necessary to complete the planning in order to seek out funding or to accept bids. Six areas need to be considered in the design process:

1. What are the needs of the library that the presentation is expected to fulfill?

2. Who is the projected audience?

3. What subject material will be included?

4. Which format is best?

5. How will the production be viewed and distributed?

6. What are the limitations of the chosen training option?

An analysis of needs has probably already been done if a library is considering ways to improve its instructional training. The following questions need to be asked: What problem is the production expected to solve? For example, is it expected to make it easier for freshmen to use the online catalog or to free staff from the repetitive, hour-long workshops given every semester? Is it expected to take the burden of basic how-do-I-get-started-on-this-machine questions off the shoulders of overworked reference librarians? In what way will it be more effective than the training system (if any) currently in place?

An excellent way to focus on what you wish to accomplish is to view the best and worst of what has already been done. Not only will you get ideas for scope, techniques, and subject material, but you will see the glaring evidence of how *not* to do an audiovisual production. The advice that you get from the success or failure of similar productions is more valuable than anything that can be read in an article or book. And, if your funds remain low, the viewing of several low-budget productions may convince you to abandon the project altogether in favor of a method more within your means.

Instructional videos produced by companies such as BRS and Wilson may provide you with some ideas, although the length, scope, and budget of those productions may leave you with some unrealistic expectations. An excellent resource is the wide range of audiovisual productions available for loan from the LOEX Library Instruction Clearinghouse (Eastern Michigan University Library, Ypsilanti, MI 48197).

Next comes a detailed description of the content necessary in order to fill the objectives of the training. You want to be specific, because the scriptwriter will rely on these points for guidance. List the skills that the audience will need to learn. If the objective of the program is to acquaint the viewers with the various CD-ROM products in the library, then they'll need a working knowledge of each product as well as a general introduction to search techniques. Specific skills include choosing the appropriate database, subject or keyword searching, displaying and printing records, and asking for help. A program with clearly defined objectives and specific goals will have a good chance of fulfilling the immediate needs of a training situation.

Although the content may determine the length of your presentation, it is far more likely that the length of the presentation has already been limited by your budget. Instead of trying to cram all the details of a half-hour video into a ten-minute one, think instead about paring the information down to the basics. It's unlikely that a viewer could absorb, much less maintain interest in, a 20-minute information-filled video. This may be a limitation, especially if the video is designed to replace a lengthier live instructional session; however, you may also find that the audience retains much more of the material.

AUDIENCE

Defining your audience is an important first step in determining the most appropriate format for your production. Who is the audience? Where are they? What do they already know? Video is a personal medium in which it's possible to communicate comfortably with the viewer. Is this appropriate for your audience, or would a more formal approach be better?

You must be thoroughly familiar with the knowledge level of your audience. You can't hope to reach them with your message unless you know how far to reach. A program discussing complex online search strategies will be lost on a group of college freshman with no database search experience, whereas a rudimentary "how to use a computer" show will waste the time of experienced faculty members.

It should be possible to design a program that appeals to a fairly wide audience and that will also be challenging to most. You will *not*, however, be able to train everyone with one program. A program that is too broad will probably offer little of value to many, while a presentation that is very specific in its focus will leave most people in the dark, and untrained.

Be aware of superfluous information that you think the audience ought to know. There is often a discrepancy between what the expert knows and wants to teach and what the audience feels it needs to know. Be objective. Unless they're librarians, your audience probably doesn't care how many journals are indexed in ABI/Inform, or whether dissertations are covered in PsycLit. Think of what the patron wants to learn when he views your presentation. His objectives are to retrieve appropriate information, display or print it, and find it in the library as quickly as possible and with a minimum of fuss.

The size and physical arrangement of your projected audience is important for several reasons. The advantage of a large audience is, of course, the financially sound notion of training as many people as possible at one seating. Showing a videotape in a large room requires several television monitors placed strategically around the room. It is tempting to use a large screen, but the distortion of the image may increase to the point that the message may be lost.

Slides are well suited to being shown on a large screen or wall without a significant loss of visual quality, accomodating a large number of patrons in one session. Smaller groups (five or fewer) can comfortably view a video image on a television screen. A group of this size, and especially a single viewer, also has the option of conveniently reviewing segments as often as necessary. It is awkward to schedule large groups for longer productions, especially if the video is in several segments.

WHICH FORMAT?

Choosing the format for your presentation and the style with which it will be written are inherent steps in the design process. The format you choose will determine the equipment necessary, and vice versa; you may find that your budget dictates the format you can realistically use. Whichever is the case, a list of equipment needs should be made as you decide. This should include the equipment needed not only during the production process but also at the viewing and distribution end. The best way to decide on format and style is to consider all of the options available through a few brainstorming sessions with other librarians involved in the project. You can then determine the best presentation format in terms of content, cost, and audience.

A slide show has definite advantages for a straightforward instructional demonstration. Elliot writes, "In instances where the programme involves predominantly static sequences . . . then a slide/tape . . . production may be more effective and considerably less expensive. Production costs are lower, and it may also prove a manageable first step into the use of audiovisual media" (Elliot, 2).

If an existing workshop or presentation has proven effective, then a slide program could be created to model it. The format and content of the presentation have already been designed, and existing materials could be used to produce the slides.

In addition to their suitability for viewing by large audiences, slides are also durable, and will put up with heavy use. In addition, should your subject material change in any way, the presentation can be updated with a minimum amount of fuss and bother by simply substituting new slides where necessary. Audiences are generally receptive to slide shows, especially if they reflect a professional quality of workmanship.

Clearly, a presentation consisting primarily of still shots, text, and graphics doesn't take advantage of video's full potential. On the other hand, an instructional emphasis on an action, rather than simply its consequences, demands a format that can communicate both sound and motion. Whereas a static medium such as a slide show presents images focused on tools and their results, video conveys the movement, development, and vitality of the process. The immediacy of the event is communicated to the viewer seemingly instantaneously.

The bottom line in choosing any of these methods is time, money, and content. Will the presentation save staff time, and therefore prove itself to be economically efficient? Will the cost of the production pay for itself in terms of the number of patrons trained balanced against the cost of staff time involved? Most importantly, can the presentation successfully instruct a chosen audience in the subject material, thereby fulfilling the objective of the training?

LIMITATIONS

It is wise to take a realistic look at the limitations of your program before you even begin its design. Since it is unlikely that all of your training problems will be solved with one production, supplementary material should be planned to fill in the gaps. Slides and video are essentially a passive medium, and there is no way to ensure that the material has been learned without some sort of follow-up. After screening a video training program, participants could be asked to complete a workbook in order to verify and reinforce their knowledge. Students who view a slide-tape presentation might walk away with a help sheet as a reminder of search basics and commands to help them get started. A demonstration program near the OPAC should have a pile of user's guides nearby for those who are still unsure of themselves. A video or slide-tape presentation could be followed by a wrap-up session with a librarian, who can clarify certain points and answer questions. This is also an excellent way to discover the limitations of the presentation in terms of what each viewer actually learns from the material.

You should be aware of common pitfalls during the design process. One of these is the temptation to pack too much information into an instructional session. The standard instructional rules of thumb indicate that if fewer facts are thrown at them, patrons will have a better chance of understanding them. As a corollary, don't get too involved in your story or plot; this only distracts the audience from the information. Avoid forced conversation, and rely instead on factually presented material.

Humor is a delicate tool that has been used in many videos in the hope that it will dispel the common notion that the library is a solemn, unfriendly place. While in some cases it has been used successfully, in others the entire show comes off as being cute, condescending, and gimmicky. Such shows also tend to show their age earlier than others, especially when they're based on some aspect of popular culture. A good way to test the appropriateness of an idea with a particular group is to ask some of its members. It's easier to accept criticism early in the design stage than it is with a final product in your hands.

Another danger to avoid is concentrating solely on the narration, to the exclusion of other techniques. Remember to *use* the medium you have chosen. This means don't just tell about a search, but show it to the viewer. Pan in on the printed sources and computer screens. Use the ability to go from the general to the specific and back again.

SCRIPT AND STORYBOARD

The production process involves writing the script and storyboard, producing the video or slides, and editing the final product. Both audio and visual, text and image, combine in order to present information in the most effective way. Bear in mind the classic advice of instructors: tell them what you're going to say, say it, then tell them what they just heard. Repeat the steps using the different formats available.

In the script you want to form the content into a logical sequence of instruction for the viewer. Current training methods may suggest the best way to proceed. Brainstorm with colleagues who teach the material daily. What methods work best for them? What phrases or explanations do they use when they instruct? How do they illustrate concepts such as database, descriptors, and logical operators? Remember to avoid library jargon; try to think like a patron and remember the user's immediate goals.

An effective means of conveying information is to move from the general to the specific. Explain the why, then demonstrate the how with a specific example. Showing the correlation with a print product is often appropriate.

Plan to show a visual of a paper source, such as a thesaurus, manual, or index when necessary. For people learning to use the online catalog, for example, it may be useful to show the card catalog, with a close-up of a single card, followed by a shot of the OPAC terminal with a close-up of the same book's record on the screen. Remember to show actions in context whenever possible. A spot to demonstrate using *LCSH*, for example, would first show a person using the books, pinpointing their location, then focus in on the source.

As the narration takes shape, think of logical places where such concepts can be illustrated. This is the beginning of the storyboard, the representation on paper of images that will accompany the script. What visual images can best be used to illustrate each concept? Will the viewer see only the computer screen, or should you cut away to a diagram? A relevant illustration can sometimes produce a more vivid understanding for a patron. Using a Venn diagram to illustrate logical operators is a typical example. Too many cutaways, however, can be distracting and may remove the viewer from the material at hand. With the script and storyboard completed, you can begin to make a detailed plan for the accompanying visual images. For a slide show, this is a reworked storyboard with a full description of each shot for the photographer to work with. A videotape will require a camera script, with a description of each shot's location and subject. The production coordinator you hire will help you with this, but it's useful to have a rough script to work from. Finally, have as many people as possible review the final draft of the narration to check for accuracy and to make suggestions. You don't want to find an error once the information is down on tape.

PRODUCTION

If your video is to be taped on location, which is certainly the cheapest and most realistic option, you'll need to block the actors for each shot and see that the area is cleared and that extraneous noise is kept to a minimum. It is best to schedule shooting for a day when the library is closed, if possible. Have a foresight session with colleagues to think of everything that could possibly, and that most probably will, go wrong. Are all necessary props at hand, and will the computer systems be in working order? Are there any background sounds, such as air conditioners or fighter jets overhead that could be picked up on tape? Has an additional day for shooting been scheduled in case everything does go wrong at once? Will the actors remember their lines? The remedy for this possibility is to rehearse, rehearse, and rehearse again. For a production to be credible, it must be well practiced. And it's never too late to smooth out dialog or movements once production is under way. Indeed, it is often the best time to notice problems or irregularities once everything has been brought together.

While it's unrealistic to shoot a videotape in its entirety "in camera," that is, to do without the final post production editing, a well-planned and scripted program requires a minimum of editing. Indeed, a certain amount of in-camera editing as a result of planning can significantly cut down on the post production editing process. It is possible to achieve a low-budget, high-quality program with thorough planning and realistic goals.

DISTRIBUTION

How will the final product be viewed? Is there an appropriate place in the library to schedule and accommodate the audience? Is equipment available for a permanent display, or will it have to be set up each time it is to be viewed? Is equipment available in classrooms if the program is to be mobile? If copies are to be lent to individuals, how many should be made? Will copies be distributed, or even sold, to interested parties outside the library?

Identify one person to schedule and distribute the final product. This will make it easier to keep track of equipment, as well as to avoid conflicts in scheduling. Decide how many copies will be made of a videotape or if additional copies of a slide presentation are necessary.

Is there adequate equipment on which to show the presentation once it is finished? Equipment necessary for a portable demonstration may differ from that required to outfit a stationary setup in a library classroom. A demonstration designed to run in a public area needs to be considered in terms of security and durability. All equipment on which the presentation is to be shown should be evaluated for quality. It would be a waste to spend thousands on a good quality production only to have it shown on below-par equipment.

EVALUATION

The surest way to evaluate a training program is to do a follow-up interview with recent viewers. Part of this interview should include a technical evaluation of the content in order to see whether viewers have learned the skills put forth in the training program. Personal interviews are obviously staff intensive, but there is no better way to evaluate a passive training program that has no built-in testing module. A brief test should ascertain how much of the material the viewer has absorbed.

The interview should also give some insight into the viewers' overall impressions. These impressions are more difficult to quantify. Did the program meet their expectations? Was the content presented in a logical manner that made sense to the viewer, or was there some confusion? Is the image presented informative, businesslike, and objective, or is it sloppy and trivial? The image conveyed to the viewer will invariably reflect back on the source despite the accuracy of the message.

CONCLUSION

Adherence to the lessons learned from the older, well-tested audiovisual technologies can carry the new ones to an exciting and effective instructional level. The innovations are so appealing, in fact, that it is all too easy to lose sight of the two most important factors in library instruction: the people we need to teach and the information we want to teach them. We must see to it that technological innovations themselves, however new and exciting, are not the focus of our efforts.

> A bicycle becomes transparent for a cyclist when his mind is filled not with the physics of balance and momentum but with winning the race, getting to the store, or enjoying the scenery. To a competent reader, the words on a page are transparent; he looks through the ink patterns and letter shapes to the meaning being conveyed. Pictures are most effective in classroom communication when teachers and learners focus on the meaning created from them. When any communication medium is used effectively, the audience becomes absorbed in the message it carries rather than the medium itself. And so far as the video technologies are concerned, our most effective use of each new device will have to wait until we can look beyond the gleaming, glittering hardware. Information is more important than the technologies which store and transmit it. (Hutton, 23)

List of Works Cited

Batista, Emily J. "Putting on a Show: Using Computer Graphics to Train End-Users." *Online* 11 (May 1987): 88-92.

Crowell, Peter. *Authoring Systems: A Guide for Interactive Videodisc Authors.* Westport, Conn.: Meckler, 1988.

Cubbage, Charlotte. "Slide-Tape Orientation Programs: Still an Option for the Eighties." *Research Strategies* 4 (Spring 1986): 75-80.

Deeney, Kay. "Teaching Search Strategies without Going Online: An Example Using Medline." *Online* 12 (July 1988): 116-19.

Elliott, Geoff. *Video Production in Education and Training.* Dover, N.H.: Croom Helm, 1984.

French, Nancy. "Quiet on the Set! Library Instruction Goes Video." *Wilson Library Bulletin* 63 (December 1988): 42-44.

Hutton, Dean. "Video Technology in Higher Education: State of the Art?" In *Video in Higher Education*, edited by Ortrun Zuber-Skerritt. New York: Nichols, 1984.

Phillips, Brian. "Projecting Real-Time Video Output." *Database* 11 (August 1988): 71-73.

Planton, Stanley. "Videotaping Your Computer's Output." *Database* 11 (August 1988): 66-70.

Smith, Jean. "Teaching Research Skills Using Video: an Undergraduate Library Approach." *Reference Services Review* 16, no. 1-2 (1988): 109-14.

For Further Reading

Cameron, David, et al. "Tutored Videotape Instruction (TVI) in Library User Education." *British Journal of Academic Librarianship* 2 (Spring 1987): 37-43.

Davis, Scott, and Marsha Miller. "New Projection Technology for Online Instruction." *Technicalities* 8 (February 1988): 3-6.

Kautz, Barbara A., et al. "The Evolution of a New Library Instruction Concept: Interactive Video." *Research Strategies* 6 (Summer 1988): 109-17.

Miller, Charles R. *Essential Guide to Interactive Videodisc Hardware and Applications*. Westport, Conn.: Meckler, 1987.

7

Why Use CAI?

Margaret W. Gordon

HOW IT WORKS

As part of her training to use the online search services offered by her library, a patron is required to complete a computer-assisted instruction CAI module. She obtains the floppy disk from the reference desk and returns to her office to view the program at her leisure. When she boots up the disk on her PC, she is greeted with an introductory screen that summarizes the purpose of the program. At the bottom of the screen is the message, "Press space bar to continue."

The lesson, which takes about 20 minutes to complete, begins by explaining such terms as *vendor*, *database*, and *record*. Short, progressive segments instruct the patron in the steps necessary to prepare a computer search: define the topic, choose the database, use logical operators. Information is presented in both text and graphics, and a variety of interesting techniques, such as highlights and animated figures, are used to illustrate the material.

Toward the end of the lesson, the patron participates in the simulation of an actual online search. She is prompted to enter the search terms and commands, and the CAI responds with the search results. Occasionally the simulation pauses, and a dialogue box appears to explain a concept or command. The simulation continues when the space bar is pressed.

When the demonstration is over, the patron has the opportunity to review the material or to take a short quiz on what she has learned. She opts for the quiz, which consists of several multiple-choice questions. Too many incorrect answers would automatically send her back to review the material, but a passing score allows her to move on to the final screen, which prints a record. This sheet is returned to the reference desk, along with the CAI disc, as proof that the instruction has been completed.

A CAI lesson like the one described above can be compared to a flip book that shows an animated scene when the pages are viewed in rapid succession. A lesson is a series of frames or slides that are created separately and strung together with a computer program that orchestrates the entire effect. A single frame can be programmed to pause for 2 seconds or for 20 before proceeding to the next one. It can likewise be programmed to pause indefinitely until a specific key, such as the space bar, or a sequence of keys is pressed. Branching occurs when the frame proceeds to one of several others, depending on the input received. For example, the patron is given the option to continue to the next lesson or to review the preceding material. If C is pressed, the program proceeds to the next frame in the sequence. If R is pressed, the program branches to a previous frame. The program can branch to error messages, help screens, or to any other frame in the lesson.

INTRODUCTION TO CAI

Computer-assisted instruction is the presentation and testing of learning material using a microcomputer. There have developed many areas of focus for this type of programming, from computer-assisted counseling to computer-managed testing. Despite the amount of material that has been written in each area, the distinctions between them remain blurred. Here, greatly simplified, are the three major areas:

1. Computer-assisted instruction (CAI) or learning (CAL) is the use of a computer to present, test, and certify learning material. It enables the student to participate in an interactive, one-on-one relationship with the computer.

2. Computer-managed instruction (CMI) or learning (CML) encompasses the entire learning program by means of testing, test analysis, record keeping, and assessment. CMI can, but does not necessarily, include CAI in the overall program.

3. Computer-based training (CBT) or computer-assisted training (CAT) makes a distinction between educational instruction and training. Since both training and instruction involve learning, it seems logical that both can equally take advantage of the computer as a teaching tool.

For the purposes of this chapter, the term CAI will be broadened to include all applications that use a computer to assist learning.

CAI IN EDUCATION

Educators have designed, used, and evaluated CAI for almost three decades: the amount of material that has been written on the subject is overwhelming. It is used as a teaching tool in a variety of ways, from simple drill and practice exercises to elaborate interactive simulations. There is, appropriately, a programming language or authoring system available for almost every level.

CAI IN LIBRARY INSTRUCTION

CAI is used successfully in libraries in a variety of applications. Programs have been designed to teach users to use a card catalog, to use call numbers to locate books, and to use a simple magazine index (Zsiray). CAI can provide an interactive "tour" of a library complete with diagrams of call-number ranges, questions and answers on library procedures, and simulations of library activities (Nipp). Custom-designed packages demonstrate research strategy that focuses on a library's special resources.

CAISSON, computer-assisted instruction for searching online, is used in library schools to train online searchers (Howden). Dialtwig, Trainer, and Medlearn are examples of this type of training. CAI trains catalogers to use automated systems and can help to prepare reference librarians who have no online searching experience (Glogoff).

As online catalogs replace card drawers, libraries are faced with a training problem: no library can afford the staff necessary to offer individual training to patrons, and group training sessions put an immense strain on staff time. CAI offers a refreshing alternative. Training can be accomplished individually, taking the burden of training off the shoulders of overworked bibliographic instructors.

End-user searching is an excellent area for CAI programming skills. Although end-user search services, such as BRS/After Dark or Knowledge Index, ideally require no training preparation, libraries that offer them are aware that some sort of user training is vital to ensure more efficient searching, both to save money and to minimize user frustration. The ability to create simulated searches provides the trainee with experience, perhaps the single most important asset for an online searcher.

ADVANTAGES OF CAI

The primary advantage of CAI in teaching computer technologies is that it makes optimum use of the computer as the training medium. One obvious objective for instruction in computer technologies is that the trainee become familiar with the system at hand. CAI makes the adjustment from training mode to system use as smooth as possible for the trainee.

CAI allows for individual instruction with the computer. The CAI package stands in for, but does not replace, the instructor. (It has been said that any teacher who can be replaced by a computer ought to be.) It provides for self-paced learning among trainees that is seldom achieved in a classroom setting. For trainees unsure of their computer skills, it also grants anonymity; privacy in which to make mistakes is a luxury that library users should be afforded at every opportunity. The interactive nature of the instruction gives immediate feedback from the "instructor," and the trainee doesn't have to wait while exercises are corrected. Positive reinforcement for each correct response encourages the trainee toward further levels of achievement. Training is consistent, because all trainees using the same package are able to learn the same material.

Periodic testing throughout the program ensures that the material is learned before the trainee advances to the next lesson. Testing can involve simple multiple-choice questions, fill-in-the-blank sentences, or a more involved interactive session. Through this testing the trainee's progress can be evaluated. In the long run, the effectiveness of the CAI lesson in teaching the material is also evaluated.

CAI is a versatile tool, and designing an in-house package provides limitless possibilities. It can be customized to fit the needs of the project at hand. The goal may be to teach specific search service commands, how to formulate search strategy, or both. A CAI package can be adapted to various environments. The projected audience, for example, might be high school students, public library patrons, or university faculty. Mastery of a specific system, such as the BRS/After Dark search service, the library's online catalog, or a serials check-in system that new staff members must learn, may be the goal. Or a CAI package may focus on searching in a specific subject area. It might describe the different databases available in a subject area, such as business or the sciences, and teach their use. A lesson might introduce faculty and business students to the business services offered by the library, with segments on Dow Jones News Retrieval, ABI/Inform, and so on. In addition to explaining the type of material covered by each service, the lesson could demonstrate a sample search in each. CAI can be designed to complement other training methods: lecture, classroom practice, workbook, or individual search sessions. Each method has its strengths, and the strengths of each can be emphasized to teach the trainee in the most effective way possible.

CAI is cost effective when there are many patrons and few librarians. Its use can maximize librarians' time in other areas. If desired, it can be portable. Give trainees a disk, or directions to access the mainframe, and send them to their home or office. Library computer stations need not be burdened, and trainees can work at their convenience. A CAI package will also make up for inconsistencies among librarians' teaching styles, because training is standardized.

There is an often overlooked benefit to using CAI as a teaching method. Working with a computer is more fun for the trainee than other, more traditional teaching methods. Manypeople prefer to sit down at a computer than to attend a class or read through instructional materials. This additional asset should be kept in mind when it finally comes time to write the CAI.

DISADVANTAGES OF CAI

CAI is a less-than-practical option for many libraries. Two reasons for this are, predictably, time and money. CAI is time consuming to design, to write, and to update should changes become necessary. Robert L. Burke estimates that it takes approximately two hundred hours to produce a one-hour lesson (Burke, 25). An author who is learning to write CAI for the first time will need even more time. If it is written in-house, there will be a serious commitment of time; if it is hired out to a professional, there will be a comparable commitment of money. A library must be confident in its decision that CAI is the appropriate training solution.

The cost of the software for the authoring language or system ranges from inexpensive shareware programs to sophisticated, customized software that runs into the thousands of dollars. A versatile, relatively easy-to-learn authoring language that enables the author to write a perfectly respectable lesson will cost from $250 to $450.

Computer costs must be added to the initial calculations. If the CAI is to be written in-house, then there must be a microcomputer (or mainframe terminal) to write it on. It should be dedicated to that use for the duration of the project. A computer must also be available for those who need to view the CAI, unless it is to be portable only. Ideally there should be more than one computer available; otherwise, the number of patrons who can be trained at one time is limited.

CAI is also time consuming for trainees, and that is a significant factor in their attitude toward training. CAI lessons can be of any length, or in as many segments as desired. A segment of an hour, however, can cover only a handful of topics in anything more than a cursory fashion. Training objectives should be reasonable. A trainee's desire to complete the training must outweigh its inconvenience, or the balance might otherwise shift toward boredom and resentment. This problem is compounded if the training is optional, since few patrons opt for inconvenience.

The style and skill with which the program is written also affect its success with the trainee. Too many questions, or questions for which the trainee has been inadequately prepared, are frustrating. Wordy explanations might just as well be presented on paper. A poorly designed package with frames that lead nowhere is inexcusable. The author must be willing to spend a great deal of time and effort to produce a smooth, creative, and intelligent instruction program. Half-hearted attempts waste time and money and lose the respect of the trainees.

The information to be covered by the CAI should remain fairly stable. Updating a program is far too time consuming to be undertaken with any frequency. Anticipated changes should be planned for well in advance, so that there is time to adapt the CAI. Changes can be unpredictable. If BRS/After Dark updates its menu system, for example, the CAI author must consequently spend hours updating the simulation in the training lesson.

If the situation is appropriate, and if the time and money can be afforded, the advantages of CAI undoubtedly outweigh its disadvantages. The attractions of CAI can also be seductive, and it is far too easy to be lured into a vast commitment of time. Before committing itself, a library must be certain that the number of trainees justifies the expense of training them. The cost in staff time and materials must be balanced against the staff time that will be saved from training each patron individually.

APPLICATIONS FOR CAI PROGRAMS

The possibilities for CAI increase with each new technological service a library adopts. The possibilities for using CAI to train library patrons are limited only by the practical considerations of time, both for the CAI author and the trainee, and of money. End-user database searching, online catalogs, and systems used by library staff all offer the opportunity for CAI to make optimum use of the computer as a training tool.

End-User Searching

A CAI package can be designed to introduce an absolute beginner to the basics of online searching. As an example, the lesson begins with a sample record as an illustration of database construction. The lesson explains that many such records compose a database and demonstrates how a database is searched by matching character strings to retrieve records. With a little creativity, successful search strategy can be illustrated by isolating key concepts in a topic, expanding those concepts with synonyms, and combining the terms into search statements using logical operators. The graphic possibilities for illustrating each of these topics should excite anyone who has taught them in a classroom using traditional methods.

Search commands, as well as techniques such as truncation and proximity searching, can be taught through drill and practice or by demonstration. Commands may be generic, in order to teach general concepts, or they may be specific to a search service. Illustrating the results of costly blunders that can be made online, such as inappropriate use of the wild card, misspellings, and the use of vague terminology, is particularly effective.

The ability to create simulations is perhaps the finest asset of CAI in these applications. For beginning online searchers, taking part in a simulated search is the next best thing to being online. Simulation can require varying degrees of interaction. In its simplest form it reproduces a search, perhaps with highlights or dialogue boxes to explain commands. The program assumes the role of the user by "typing in" commands while the trainee watches. After the print command is "typed" on the screen, for example, a dialogue box might appear to explain what each element in the command phrase represents. The trainee is a passive onlooker at this level, needing only to strike a key to continue the simulation.

A more demanding level of simulation requires the trainee to type in the appropriate commands and phrases. If an incorrect phrase is typed, the trainee is prompted again for the correct one, perhaps with a hint, or perhaps given a choice to return to the previous instructional segment. The simulation continues when the correct phrase is entered. The most elaborate type of simulation involves the creation of an actual database, with a small number of records, in which the trainee can perform searches. The trainee searches these records freely using the commands previously learned; there is no predefined structure that must be followed. It should be noted that this method requires advanced programming skills and a great deal of computer memory.

The Online Catalog

Any of these techniques can be used to train users of an online catalog. One difficulty in writing such a training package is deciding what type of audience to focus on. Patrons of any but the most specialized libraries have a wide variety of skills and experience, and some patrons will need more guidance than others. Should CAI be required for all online catalog patrons? If this isn't feasible, then the program must be as attractive as possible to potential users. This argues for a short demonstration that demands little or no work from the trainee.

The applications are broadened for online public access catalogs (OPACs). The important advantage of a CAI package in training remote users is its transportability. If the program fits on a single disc, the range is unlimited. The audience, however, may be diverse and the package should be designed with this in mind. See chapter 3 for a more complete discussion of online help for remote OPAC users.

Other Applications

Many laserdisk and CD-ROM search products include their own online tutorials, the quality and consistency of which vary considerably. An in-house CAI training package can help users find common ground between different databases, vendors, and search software. For example, a CAI package that focuses on general database construction, search strategy, and choosing an appropriate database is a perfect introduction to an end-user service area that offers a variety of search services.

An in-house package can supplement vendor-provided tutorials. It might be useful to focus on advanced techniques for a specialized group of users, to emphasize particular points, or to make up for shortcomings in the tutorials. Users of SilverPlatter's PsycLIT or ERIC databases, for example, might need additional training in the use of the thesaurus. Wilsondisc users will find useful a CAI program that demonstrates advanced techniques, or that focuses on a single search mode, such as Wilsonline.

Training Library Staff

In any situation where many patrons must be trained in a particular skill, chances are that library staff must be trained first. If the number of staff members warrants it, then CAI is an option for training them as well.

Retrospective conversion projects, creating machine-readable cataloging (MARC) records for online catalogs, and automated serials check-in all require a concentrated, costly training period both for the supervisor and the trainee. A CAI program at the Pennsylvania State University Libraries successfully trains cataloging staff in the use of automated systems. The program, consisting of seven courses that provide hands-on experience in creating online records, relieves supervisors of the burden of repetitive training (Glogoff). Again, it is important to balance the cost of training one-on-one against the cost of designing and writing a CAI program.

A CAI package that introduces online searching to beginning reference staff saves the cost of sending new searchers to the introductory sessions offered by BRS, Dialog, and other vendors. Costly mistakes made by beginning searchers can be reduced or avoided altogether, and the money saved might be better spent sending searchers to the advanced training sessions (Grotophorst).

Training Student Assistants

As student assistants take on more automated chores in the library–at the circulation desk, the reserve desk, and the technical services department–their training may need to be automated as well. One-on-one training is both costly and time consuming for the staff members involved. The cost of training student assistants is compounded by the turnover at the beginning of each semester. A CAI training program would ensure that assistants are trained competently and consistently, sparing supervisors large blocks of time previously spent in repetitive training sessions.

TYPES OF AUTHORING SYSTEMS

There are three general categories of authoring capability: programming languages, authoring languages, and authoring systems. It is becoming increasingly difficult to distinguish between them, and choosing one over another calls for compromise. The more flexible a system, the more difficult it is to learn. Programs that are easiest to learn are also more rigid and allow for little creativity. The range of programs within each category also varies widely. Below is a description of what programs in each category can generally be expected to do.

Programming Languages

Any general-purpose programming language such as BASIC can be used to write CAI. Authors who are skilled at this level of of programming often prefer its versatility and unstructured approach. The lack of structure might be daunting, however, to someone with little or no programming experience. Learning a complex programming language may be far beyond the scope of a beginning CAI author; it takes years to achieve competency in even the simplest languages. Unless there is an in-house programmer who can turn your lesson plan into a functioning program, it might be best to look at some of the CAI authoring languages available.

Authoring Languages

An authoring language is almost as powerful as a programming language, but is more structured in its approach. The command language is geared toward the techniques used in CAI: presenting information, receiving input, and branching in different directions. In most authoring languages the command language is mnemonic, and therefore easier to learn. PC/PILOT is one example of a programming language. Sample PILOT commands are A (to accept answer), J (to jump to another frame) and M (to match student answer.) It is also less time consuming to write in these languages: it would take up to 20 lines of assembly code to recreate a single PILOT command. Some of the more advanced languages, such as PILOT or LOGO, allow the author to create slides that incorporate graphics with sound and text. Once mastered, these authoring languages allow for enormous creativity. Less complex than programming languages, they are nevertheless time consuming to learn. An authoring language will take weeks or months to master compared to the years it may take to master an advanced programming language.

Authoring Systems

Authoring systems permit an instructor to sit down at a computer and almost immediately begin to create a CAI lesson. No programming skills are required, as the system translates the instructor's input to a language the computer can understand. Systems use prompts, windows, or menus, and do not require the mastery of a command language. Many have a predesigned format and offer automatic branching in response to student input. Some systems, such as Dan Bricklin's Demo Program (Sage Software, 3200 Tower Oaks Blvd., Rockville, MD 20853) or Instant Replay Professional (Nostradamus, Inc., 4525 S. Wasatch Blvd. Suite 335, Salt Lake City, UT 84124) create elaborate, timed slideshows that respond to input and permit branching. Other systems can be rigidly inflexible and permit little creativity in lesson design. The author with little or no experience can create a CAI lesson quickly, but with severe limitations due to the predefined lesson structure.

The ease of writing CAI invites another potential drawback: it is now easier than ever to write bad CAI. The educational market is flooded with it, and library applications will undoubtedly generate more. Screens loaded with animated blips and flashing lights do not compensate for a poorly designed lesson plan. Without well-defined objectives and exhaustive planning, a great deal of time and money will be wasted.

CREATING CAI

Four useful steps in creating a CAI lesson are:

1. stating objectives

2. designing the program

3. writing the program

4. testing and revising the program

The first two steps involve planning, while the last two call for hands-on computer work. The purpose in planning is to state the objectives based on the needs of the project, then design the presentation to satisfy those objectives. When the planning and designing are completed, the actual writing should go smoothly. The final step is to test, revise, and prepare the finished program for general use. The success of a CAI lesson depends on the thoroughness of the planning process, before the computer has been turned on. Having completed this work, sitting down at the computer to write the program will be a pleasure.

1. Stating Objectives

Clearly stated objectives help to determine exactly what material is to be learned and at what depth. Several factors need to be taken into consideration in the initial planning. These include:

- audience
- subject material
- level of training
- technical details
- program length
- staff time
- certification
- training methods

Audience

Who is the intended audience? The presentation of the material will be be determined by it. Are trainees undergraduates or faculty members? Are they absolute beginners, or will they have had some experience on computers? Have they had experience using a database or system similar to the one being demonstrated?

Subject Material

Material to be covered in the CAI lesson should be stated in detail. In the field of online searching, possible material includes search strategy, Boolean logic, proximity searching, truncation, specific commands, specific databases, choosing a database, use of thesauri, and so on. Focusing on a specific system, such as the online catalog, produces a similar list of topics: contents of the database, commands, searching by author, by title, by subject, or by keyword.

Level of Training

What level of training is required? Expectations should be realistic. It may not be possible to cover all the material that you would like in a one-hour lesson. It may be necessary to divide the CAI into two or more modules. Sections can be graded: introductory, advanced, or specialized by subject. The CAI may be intended as a general introduction that will be supplemented by other, more advanced, materials when necessary. Or if some prior knowledge or skill is assumed, the CAI can concentrate on advanced techniques.

Technical Details

Physical considerations and technical details quickly moderate unreal expectations. What equipment is available for the project, and where will it be kept? A computer station must be available for the long hours during which the author writes the CAI. Depending on the projected audience, one or more stations should be available for trainees to view the lesson. Are the facilities well lit and free from distraction? An advantage of CAI is that trainees can learn at their own pace and convenience. Will the facilities be open at reasonable times to take advantage of this?

What microcomputer will be used? The CAI should be written on the same machine, or a compatible one, that will be used to view it. It would be very embarrassing if all the flashy highlights and diagrams that look great on one monitor don't show up at all on another one that recognizes a different character set. If the CAI is to be used outside the library, will it work on the computers the trainees will eventually use? Will it be able to emulate the system it is intended to teach? System requirements for the authoring software may have already determined many of these questions. There's no point in paying for a utility such as screen capture if the system can't take advantage of it.

Program Length

Determining the length of the program is an integral part of the planning. Nevertheless, it is difficult to estimate the time needed to cover a given amount of material before beginning to write. Viewing other CAI lessons is the best way to get a feel for the material-to-length ratio. When determining the length, consider the amount of time the trainee can be expected to spend. A lesson that is required for certification is obviously more likely to be completed than one that is not. On the other hand, users will think twice about a requirement that is unreasonably demanding of their time. That consideration may outweigh their desire to learn.

A demonstration program that is placed in a public area should run no longer than five minutes, and even less, if possible. The longer the demo, the more likely it is that people will walk away from it. Programs that are designed as part of a certification process, or that are required viewing before search privileges are granted, can run anywhere from 20 to 40 minutes before most users have second thoughts. Only programs that are an integral part of a library instruction or training course should be designed to run longer than 40 minutes. Often, it is easier on the trainee to divide the course into shorter segments rather than try to fit all the material into one long computer session.

Staff Time

Staff time must be considered along with lesson length in planning the instruction. How much time can one or more librarians be spared from other duties and projects? Burke estimates that 200 hours are required to produce a one-hour lesson, depending on the experience of the author and the complexity of the lesson. A library must also commit itself to a certain level of support after the instruction has been written. The author(s) will need to test, revise, and continually evaluate the program. It may eventually need to be updated, as systems or objectives change.

Who will author the CAI? One or more librarians can take part in the planning and design process, as well as the writing, testing, and evaluation. Advice from colleagues should certainly be solicited at each stage. If future lessons are planned, there is definitely an advantage to having an in-house author, or at least one person who is competent in putting together a simple slide show. If a library decides to use the services of a professional programmer, librarians will still need to become involved in the design of the CAI and the writing of the text narrative.

Certification

Will the training be required or optional? This may depend on the skills that need to be learned. A CAI can be offered as an optional training method for patrons. A brief demonstration of the online catalog, for example, could be one of several choices available to new patrons. To make it attractive it should be fun, brief, and interactive, but not demanding. A demo that is long, boring, or difficult will be passed by. The result is an expensive, unused experiment.

A CAI lesson that is required as part of a training package must also be planned thoughtfully in advance. If it is required for certification, then the CAI must fulfill the objectives necessary for patrons to use a certain system. The length of the program must be appropriate to the training level required. How long can potential end users be expected to spend in training before they are qualified to search? At what point will end users judge the training too inconvenient or time consuming? The author may need to compromise with the training objectives in order not to lose trainees. The required CAI lesson must also integrate record keeping, certification, or both in order to verify that the training has been completed. This can be done through an online record keeping program, a utility offered by many authoring systems. An easier solution requires the trainee to print the final screen of the program, ensuring that the program has been successfully completed.

2. Designing the Program

The design segment of the planning process can be divided into four steps:

- choosing presentation methods
- designing a flowchart
- writing a program narrative
- creating a storyboard

Choosing Presentation Methods

CAI may work best combined with other training methods: classroom lecture, online practice, or written materials, including workbooks or worksheets. Combining several methods is an excellent way to take advantage of the strengths of each. The author should be aware of the advantages of computerized learning in order to reap the greatest benefit from them. Among these assets is the variety of ways in which information can be presented, including text, graphics, and animation. As you review the subject material, consider which presentation method would best suit the material to be learned. If the lesson is interactive, decide which tasks would teach the material most effectively. Drill and practice techniques are appropriate for learning rote material, such as database commands, but not for learning strategies such as proximity searching and truncation.

Designing Flowchart

A flowchart is a graphic representation of the sequence of operations through which the CAI program proceeds. This is where the lesson actually begins to take shape. Properly charted, the program will move smoothly from start to finish with no frustrating dead-ends. Designing a flowchart, a basic step in computer programming, is absolutely essential to the structure of a CAI lesson. Each choice offered to the trainee in a program necessitates branching. Without a flowchart, the author will become lost in programming loops and will fail to maintain the systematic structure of the lesson design. The unavoidable result is bad CAI.

There are standardized shapes and symbols for decision boxes, input and output, processing, and so on. Instructions on how to design flowcharts can be found in general encyclopedias, subject encyclopedias, and books on programming. A flowchart need not be so detailed that it is pages in length. The basic steps, however, should be laid out in a logical, systematic lesson plan.

Writing a Program Narrative

The program narrative is the script for the CAI program and should be completed before the author sits down at the computer. At this point it is possible to accurately judge the amount of material that can be reasonably covered within a given amount of time. Here the lesson takes shape, and the soundness of the lesson plan becomes apparent as it unfolds, step by step. Is new information presented to the trainee in a logical sequence? Is material explained clearly, in a positive tone? Is the vocabulary consistent? Although everything is subject to change later at the computer, it is best to have the writing polished and ready to go beforehand. The author shouldn't have to balance a thesaurus and dictionary along with a keyboard and mouse when it comes time to transfer the narrative to the computer screen.

Creating a Storyboard

Created in conjunction with the program narrative, the storyboard is the CAI program on paper; with it, the author proceeds confidently through the actual writing of the program. Its purpose is to draft the lesson plan on paper, which is easier to revise at this stage, and to give the CAI author a prototype to follow during the writing. Consider the CAI lesson as a series of slides, following one after another on the computer screen. The storyboard is a first draft of those slides on 8½-by-11-inch sheets of paper. They need not be more than rough sketches, but they should give an accurate representation of the size and placement of graphics and text on each slide. Text can even be indicated by blocks that refer to the program narrative.

3. Writing the Program

Most of the technical details involved in writing a CAI program depend on the authoring language or system chosen by the CAI author. The following options may not be possible with every authoring system on the market. Some systems offer more programming options than others, and this should be kept in mind when choosing a system to work with.

General Concerns

A few general concerns about writing apply to CAI lessons in every field. An important point to keep in mind is that the lesson should be designed to stand alone, without the instructor. Instructions must therefore be absolutely clear, and explanations unambiguous. There is no second chance to clarify information once it has been presented. Technical terms must be defined before they are used. A beginner can help the author early in the process by reading through the narrative and pointing out unfamiliar words or concepts.

It is important for the trainee that the author be consistent in the smallest details. Interchangeable terms can be confusing to someone who is unfamiliar with the jargon: *subject heading, subject term*, and *descriptor* all sound fine to a librarian, but will confuse a trainee. Decide on a simple term, easily explained, and use it throughout the lesson. User responses should likewise be consistent. If the *Esc* key is used to return to the main menu, it should be used for that purpose throughout the program. Requiring other keys at different points is unnecessarily confusing.

The writing style should be clear and concise. Keep the audience in mind; an amusing or "cute" tone will seem patronizing to all but the youngest trainees. Most audiences prefer to be addressed as intelligent adults. Sentences should be short and simple: as with most good writing, less is more. A single, precise phrase has a greater effect than several rambling paragraphs. Longer blocks of text do not create visual interest, and the reader's attention is likely to wander. Brevity and emphasis are strengths that should be used to advantage.

The final, onscreen narrative must be scrupulously edited. Inaccuracies reflect on the thoroughness, commitment, and qualifications of the CAI author as a teacher. Misspellings, mistakes in grammar, and typographical errors are inexcusable, and will cause the trainee to question the accuracy of the remaining material in the lesson.

The "less is more" approach applies to screen layout as well as to writing style. A screen crowded with too much information and too many graphic frills has far less impact than an uncrowded screen with one short message. Emphasize one point at a time, rather than trying to fit it all in at once. Creative use of white space will improve readability. The reader will overlook information on a cluttered screen, whereas a single phrase or event on an empty screen will draw the reader's attention.

Variety and repetition are techniques that can also be used to advantage in writing CAI. Repetition should be used for emphasis. Saying the same thing in different ways often helps to clarify a point. In explaining the use of the wild card, for example, it may be useful to explain it first in text, then demonstrate its use with a few examples, then rephrase the explanation again in text. Similarly, repeating key points at different times throughout a lesson helps to underscore their importance. A CAI package designed to teach users "five steps in planning an online search" should repeat those five steps at each stage throughout the lesson.

A variety of presentation techniques is more interesting than a single format used over and over again. Varying the placement of text on a screen adds visual interest, as does the judicious use of colors, highlights, inverse letters, and flashing text. Take advantage of the unexpected; the occasional visual surprise catches the trainee's attention, and can rescue a lesson from monotony. The variety of ways in which information can be presented is one of the advantages of CAI. It must be used with caution, however, or the lesson will appear choppy and unsophisticated. There must be a certain amount of continuity that holds the lesson together as it proceeds from frame to frame.

Designs

Drill and Practice. The simplest form of CAI, drill and practice is often unfavorably described as the electronic version of flashcards. The trainee is presented with a series of questions on material that has already been learned. In situations where repetitious exercises aid learning, the computer offers obvious advantages: an endless number of questions can be programmed, increasing in skill level if desired; a tally of correct or incorrect answers is kept for each trainee; most important, people prefer using a computer to completing page after page of written exercises.

As the sole means of instruction, the usefulness of drill and practice is limited. More likely, it might be combined with other methods to enforce rote learning. Memorizing commands is one example of the type of material that might benefit from drill and practice.

Tutorial. The tutorial design represents a more balanced dialogue between the instructor and the trainee. The CAI package presents the information to be learned, tests the trainee to ensure retention, then branches to new, or increasingly complex material. At its best, the branching in a tutorial resembles the feedback that a human tutor might give.

Consider, for example, a CAI lesson to teach end-user searching that displays information on the use of the wildcard in online searching. A text description introduces the concept, followed by a few examples to demonstrate how the technique works online. The program then gives sample exercises for practice and tests the trainee's knowledge with one or more questions. If the questions are answered correctly, the program then branches to the next section. If the response is incorrect, the trainee is offered a choice: review the material and try again, or branch to more practice exercises before testing again. Questions can be designed to increase in complexity, offering a greater challenge to the trainee as the lesson progresses.

The resemblance of the tutorial design to a human tutor blurs the distinction between the best CAI and its artificially intelligent counterpart, the expert system. Both CAI and expert systems provide an electronic instructor. The former proceeds step by step through the material, testing periodically to ensure that the material is learned. The latter proceeds through the same steps in order to provide an answer for the user. In CAI, the author-as-instructor provides guidance and direction for the patron, and determines what material will be covered in the lesson. Using an expert system, it is the user who decides which route to take with a particular inquiry, and it is the responsibility of the author to ensure that the appropriate material has been included in the knowledge base.

Simulation. Due to the nature of the medium, simulations offer the most practical training option for instructors of library computer skills. What better way to learn a new automated system than to take part in a simulation of it? Trainees learn by doing without incurring the expense of online time. They benefit both from the practice and from the instruction, since the simulation incorporates the experience and advice of veteran online searchers – except that the simulation, of course, saves both the time and the expense of one-on-one training.

A simulation may require varying degrees of interaction. At the most passive level it resembles an automated slide show, moving from frame to frame in imitation of an actual online event. A practical example of this design is a passive demonstration of an online library catalog. New catalog users are drawn by signs and arrows to a demonstration program running on a PC located near the public catalog terminals. The trainee sits down, presses the enter key, and watches: the demo shows sample searches, interjects a few handy tips, and, after two or three minutes, returns to the introductory screen. Our new user has now seen the library online catalog in action, and confidently sits down at a terminal to put this new found knowledge to work. The demo is ready for the next user to sit down and press the enter key.

This type of demonstration is one of the simplest for an author to create. A screen capture utility, available with many authoring programs, makes it possible to "capture" and save a screen from whatever program is being demonstrated, guaranteeing an accurate simulation. For a passive demonstration, the author causes the cursor to move from left to right, with letters appearing as if someone were actually typing to the screen. The effect is certainly adequate for the purpose of a demonstration.

The program can be as demanding as necessary in order to claim the trainee's attention. The more difficult the system to be learned, the more demanding the interaction should be. It need be no more difficult than requiring the trainee to press a key in order to continue the slide show

("Press any key to continue"). This is useful when it's necessary to pause on a given slide in order to give the trainee time to read the material.

More demanding interaction requires the trainee to type a given word or phrase in order to continue. This type of design does guarantee trainee involvement, although it can be annoyingly inflexible. The trainee is locked in to the author's predesigned format and will be beeped at for making a typing error. The design does, however, allow the trainee to "participate" in an online search. Using the commands and seeing how the system responds is valuable for a beginner, even though the simulation is preprogrammed to accept only one search statement. It remains a far more realistic alternative to one-on-one training.

A gamelike design may appeal to a younger audience, and good examples can be found in educational CAI. Word games, war games, mazes, and adventures are all used successfully to teach a variety of skills. It is even possible to imagine computer games appropriate for teaching library skills. The author should be hesitant, however, about incorporating games into a CAI program geared toward adults. It can be fun if done well, but a patronizing tone will invariably offend trainees.

Choosing a CAI design most appropriate to the material takes common sense, knowledge of the audience, and experience with bibliographic instruction. It will come naturally if the CAI author has already had experience teaching the topic to the projected audience. The author can then answer the logical questions: What is the most successful way I have found to explain this concept? In what order is the material best taught? How much information is enough to prepare the trainee? It is likely that a combination of forms, rather than strict adherence to a single format, will serve the purpose best.

Questions, Branching, and Sequence

Branching and sequence provide power and flexibility within a CAI lesson. In response to input from the keyboard the program skips sections to move ahead or jumps back to review an earlier section. The program calls up subroutines or programs from outside the lesson and controls peripheral equipment such as slides or videotape. The interaction between the trainee, who views the lesson, and the author, who has anticipated correct and incorrect answers, brings the CAI to life. With most authoring systems, there are essentially two parts to every CAI lesson: the frames, which are seen by the trainee, and the program, which is not. The frames, or slides, contain the information that is shown on the computer screen, and may be identified by numbers. Like a flip book, the different scenes on each frame, when viewed in rapid succession, produce the effect of smooth motion. The program determines which frames will be seen in what order. The individual frames are programmed to pause for a given amount of time, to accept certain input from the keyboard or to call another frame. The program sets the conditions necessary for frame #34 to proceed to frame #35: the user must press the enter key, for example, or type in a preset string of characters.

To branch, the following conditions would be set: frame #34 poses a question, then pauses until one of two conditions are met. For example, "A database is a collection of records in a subject area, yes/no." If the correct answer, "yes," is typed in, then the program proceeds to slide #42 (the frame that says, "That's right!"). If any other character is typed in, the program moves to frame #35 ("Incorrect. The correct answer is . . ."). Instead of using separate frames that progress in strict sequence, the program branches by referring to, or calling, other frames out of sequence. The structure resembles that of most programming languages. For example: IF INPUT = "N" THEN GOTO #42.

Branching can become incredibly complex and time consuming whether you use an authoring system or language. Each frame must have a set of conditions to be met before it moves to the next frame, as well as another frame to move to. There must be a right and wrong programming loop for each question; that is, an escape route for the trainee no matter what is typed into the keyboard. The more questions there are, the more frames must be programmed for each response. Internally, the program can become a maze of trails that even a flowchart is unable to keep up with. For new authors, questions, and the subsequent branching they require, should be kept to a minimum.

Most programs can accept any string of letters or numbers in response to a question. Thus the question may prompt for a "yes" or "no" answer, a single-word string, or a phrase, which can accommodate multiple-choice, fill-in-the-blank, and even short-answer questions. Long answers can be frustrating for the trainee, who may have to retype the entire phrase because of a single typographical error. The author should be as flexible as possible when programming to accept answers: most systems allow the use of wild cards or "n" values to accommodate misspellings, typographical errors, and synonyms.

A good CAI author (and a good teacher) will anticipate wrong answers, and the program will accordingly branch to help screens, or backtrack to review material when incorrect answers are typed in. A CAI that takes full advantage of branching and sequence capabilities offers immediate feedback to the trainee and reflects the expertise of the instruction librarian.

Extras

There are a variety of showy frills with which to dress up a CAI lesson, depending on the authoring program used. The most commonly used attributes include inverse video, blinking characters, and colors or shading, depending on the type of monitor and graphics card used. Taking advantage of color graphics can be especially effective, although it's tempting to overdo to the point of gaudiness. Other attributes include special characters that can be used for drawing lines and boxes. A screen capture utility is especially useful for reproducing another program, such as a search service. Such a utility can "capture" and save a screen from another program. Sound capabilities also vary; some programs offer only a beep on demand, while others can be programmed for both timbre and pitch.

4. Testing and Revising the Program

The time set aside for testing and revision, before the CAI program is made available for public use, should be equal to the amount of time that goes into writing it. Colleagues should critique the lesson for content, consistency, and typographical errors. The test group should be trainees from the target audience. They will help to evaluate the lesson for length, clarity, comprehension, and deadends or hang-ups. Several test sessions should be adequate to provide the author with a list of possible improvements. These may range from simple corrections in the text to lengthy, time consuming alterations. The author, or a colleague, should have some means of measuring the trainee's grasp of the subject material both before and after viewing the CAI lesson. This might be a written exercise, a practice search, or simply a discussion with the librarian. The final question is: Has the trainee learned the material that the CAI is designed to teach?

The author should sit alongside the "test" trainees in order to see how smoothly the session goes and to make note of any glitches. The author should *not* give assistance or make comments. In the future, the lesson must be able to stand on its own without the trainee having to ask a librarian for help. Any comments or problems the trainee has during the session should be written down and discussed later. Did the software perform correctly, or were there awkward pauses or hang-ups? Was the material presented in a logical sequence, or were some things left unexplained? Was the session too brief to adequately cover the material, or was it so long that it tried the patience of the trainee? Finally, did the trainee finish the session with a reasonable understanding of the material?

Documentation

The author writes down in the documentation exactly what the user needs to know in order to use the CAI. This information is necessary even if the CAI is intended only to be used in-house. For future reference, all pertinent details should be written down. This information, outlined below, is all the more necessary if the lesson will be distributed to remote users.

Be painstakingly specific about hardware requirements; it is most frustrating to have wrong or inadequate information. Many of these requirements will mirror those of the authoring system or language that was used to write the lesson. What computer was the CAI written on? List only the compatible systems that you know for certain can be used successfully. Is a CGA or VGA card required, along with a color monitor? Special effects designed in color may not show up at all on a monochrome monitor. Are any peripherals necessary, such as a printer or CD-ROM drive? How much memory is required? What version of the operating system is acceptable? If you don't know, call the software company. Don't write it down unless you're certain that it works. If the program can fit on a single disk, it will be self-booting if you add the DOS program command.com, as well as an autoexec.bat file. Operating instructions should be typed clearly on the disk label. If the lesson has been installed on a hard disk, instructions should be self-evident for the user either through a menu system or an introductory screen.

If the program will be distributed to remote users, give it a descriptive label: "Demo Program for first-time users of the online catalog" or "Instructional diskette for Knowledge Index searchers." Note down the average viewing time of the program, so users know what to expect. If the lesson is divided into several segments, users should know how many and whether they must all be done at once. A statement about the objectives of the CAI lesson, and specifically the material covered, is useful. It should also be noted if the CAI is a training requirement for some sort of certification.

TRAINING OPTIONS FOR CAI

The classroom teacher or faculty member responsible for grading students wants a testing sequence in CAI in order to determine whether the student has learned the material. The librarian, on the other hand, is seldom in a position to give grades or to establish certification requirements. Instituting a training requirement for the purpose of using publicly available services will not sit well with most patrons. Special situations, however, may call for more careful management.

A library may determine that the additional cost of a search system classifies it as a special privilege, rather than a basic service. The library can then require that a certain level of training be achieved before allowing a patron free access. Library instruction classes, especially those integrated into the standard curriculum, offer the opportunity of instituting a CAI lesson as part of a training requirement. CAI lessons are also perfectly acceptable as a part of job training, either for library staff or for student assistants.

A CAI lesson may be the sole means of certifying that training has been completed, or it may be used in conjunction with other training methods. A performance record embedded in the lesson can serve as a record of completion, as well as pinpoint a user's weak areas. If CAI is to be used in a supporting role, other methods can share the burden of certification. Possibilities include a classroom lecture followed by a quiz, completion of a workbook, or a practice search with a librarian.

Testing does not necessarily have to play a role in computer-assisted instruction for libraries. The option to create an educational package without the burden of testing and evaluation gives librarians a refreshing perspective on a traditional educational teaching method. A competent lesson that takes advantage of the advanced authoring systems now available will be welcomed by library users.

Works Cited

Burke, Robert L. *CAI Sourcebook*. Englewood Cliffs, N.J.: Prentice-Hall, 1982.

Glogoff, Louise, et al. "Computer-Based Training Program for Cataloging Department Staff." *Journal of Academic Librarianship* 10 (1984): 23-28.

Grotophorst, Clyde W. "Training University Faculty as End-Use Searchers: A CAI Approach." In *National Online Meeting Proceedings 1984*, Compiled by Martha E. Williams and Thomas H. Hogan, 77-82. Medford, N.J.: Learned Information, 1984.

Howden, Norman, and Bert R. Boyce. "The Use of CAI in the Education of Online Searchers." *Journal of Education for Library and Information Science* 28 (1988): 201-6.

Nipp, Deanna, and Ron Straub. "The Design and Implementation of a Microcomputer Program for Library Orientation." *Research Strategies* 4 (1986): 60-67.

Zsiray, Stephen W. "A Comparison of Three Instructional Approaches in Teaching the Use of the Abridged Reader's Guide to Periodical Literature." *Journal of Educational Technology Systems* 12 (1983-84): 241-47.

For Further Reading

Armstrong, C. J., and J. A. Large. "OST (Online Search Tutor): A Training Package for End-Users of Online Systems." *Program* 21 (1987): 333-49.

Deeney, Kay, and Beryl Glitz. "Teaching Search Strategies Without Going Online: An Example Using Medline." *Online* 12 (1988): 116-19.

Fitzgerald, Patricia A., et al. "Computer-Assisted Instruction in Libraries: Guidelines for Effective Lesson Design." *Library High Tech* 4 (1986): 29-37.

Foster, Jocelyn. "Computer Assisted Instruction: Putting It to the Test." *Canadian Library Journal* 44 (1987): 161-68.

Keller, Arnold. *When Machines Teach: Designing Computer Courseware*. New York: Harper & Row, 1987.

Richards, Thomas C., and Jeannette Fukuzawa. "A Checklist for Evaluation of Courseware Authoring Systems." *Educational Technology* 29 (1989): 24-29.

8

Expert Systems and Hypertext

Craig A. Robertson

We adopt technology in order to save labor or to make work more productive. It has been said of the service sectors of the economy – us information providers, for example – that we are less amenable to the introduction of labor-saving technologies than, say, manufacturing. If that premise is true, it is so because the judgment and problem-solving skills that characterize most professional work are more difficult to automate than widget-welding. Still, the "teaching technologies" that we speak of in this book can help address the scarcity and expense of skilled service personnel. As we saw in the last chapter, for instance, computer-assisted instruction (CAI) makes a tireless electronic tutor available on disk and on demand when human trainers would prove too expensive or on those rare occasions when we have too many commitments.

In a similar way the emerging software technologies of expert systems and hypertext can extend our professional labor. They do so by making available to others in the form of microcomputer software the diagnostic skills or procedural knowledge of experienced library staff. They imitate some of our problem-solving skills and work habits. Such programs mimic what are admittedly simplistic models of how professionals operate. Expert systems, for example, assume that we work by applying either rules of thumb that we have discovered or developed over time, or knowledge that we have turned into stereotypes, or *frames*, such as "monograph," "teacher," "record," and the like. Hypertext technology, on the other hand, assumes that both we and our public find information most efficiently (despite of the encumbrance of traditional printed materials) by a kind of free association of words and ideas, by browsing. Even such rough paradigms of professional work as these can lead us to useful library applications on microcomputers.

Both expert systems and hypertext appeared first on mainframes and minicomputers more than a decade ago and are still used in industrial settings on special-purpose computers and high-powered workstations. Each of these technologies, however, has migrated recently to personal computers, where it has become available at moderate cost to librarians. Both expert systems and hypertext offer us interesting new service opportunities.

EXPERT SYSTEMS

Let us explore expert systems first. We can gain a quick insight into how these programs function by considering the plight of a student database searcher who has learned the basics of computerized literature searching (by any of the methods discussed in previous chapters) and has conducted a successful search. On a second attempt, however, she runs into trouble. She expects to find perhaps a few dozen periodical references for a topic she is investigating, but her online search yields only two useful "hits," or citations. When she approaches a busy reference librarian for help, he suggests that she gather her search strategy and results together and use them while she consults a microcomputer program called *SearchDoctor*, which resides on the hard disk of the same machine she has just used. This program contains the collected wisdom of several experienced professional searchers, which is compiled in the form of *heuristics*, or rules of thumb. To find out in detail how these experts analyze search problems and use the feedback of their results to revise their strategies, the author of *SearchDoctor* has interviewed them in detail. From what the experts have told him, he has inferred a set of general rules about how users should modify search strategies when they find the online results disappointing.

SearchDoctor asks our neophyte user a series of questions about her strategy. How many sets (or *concepts*) did she combine using the *and* logic in her final search statement? What was the smallest number of references she found for any single concept? Did she use more than one synonym or phrase for that concept? Did she include subject index terms from the appropriate thesaurus in that least productive query? When she responds no to the last question *SearchDoctor* identifies the omission of subject index terms (or "controlled vocabulary," to use library jargon) in that last concept as a probable flaw in her strategy. It asks her to identify the database she is searching and recommends the correct thesaurus in which to find subject terms for a revised search strategy. As *SearchDoctor* tries to solve her problem, it also exposes the searcher to some of the paradigms by which one can solve such problems. It teaches, so to speak, by example.

SearchDoctor is a hypothetical microcomputer expert system. Such programs are the first commercially successful products of artificial intelligence (AI). The rather mystifying term *artificial intelligence* was coined in 1956 by John McCarthy, then of Dartmouth (who later developed computer time sharing and LISP, an important programming language for AI), to describe attempts to make computers simulate such tasks of human intelligence as recognition, decision making, and learning, or to model human intelligence with computers. AI has come to include such diverse fields as natural language processing, speech recognition, robotics, expert systems, computer learning, and automated game playing (for example, backgammon and chess). Expert systems are AI computer programs that aid decision making. They attempt to solve problems and make recommendations to human users based on knowledge that comes from professional experience and can be assumed to be authentic. This knowledge is put into the program in the form of prescriptive rules or sets of observations. Expert systems help to solve the types of problems that involve professional judgment, often with some degree of uncertainty, rather than those that require numerical computation or manipulation of strings of data. For our purposes here, let us avoid any further AI jargon or mystification and turn our attention to the value of these products for librarians. We treat them simply as a new class of *applications software* that takes its place alongside database managers, spreadsheets, word processors, and the like. Let us look at their practical value.

Although manufacturing and financial industries already make widespread use of working expert systems, they are just now beginning to find small niches in the operations of libraries. We find them applied mostly in the small-scale, local types of projects that typify microcomputer use in libraries. They help to solve service or procedural bottlenecks caused by the cost and scarcity of skilled workers. A few specific examples from the literature will help us to get a better understanding of their potential.

Reference work in libraries offers an obvious setting for their use. Reference librarians are discovering that expert systems can help not only in answering users' questions but also in the evaluation and development of reference collections. They are a "teaching technology" in the special sense that they force their developers to confront their resources very attentively. While looking so closely at collections and services a librarian sometimes discovers, for example, that an impressive-looking multivolume treatise really has little practical value, that she or he has overlooked the latest edition of some useful handbook, or that a new CD-ROM product has great potential. The process of authoring an expert system also augments the writer's own command of the reference materials and services, because he or she is immersed in the subject for weeks or even months.

Some real applications in reference work include, for example, *AQUAREF*, a program of the Aquaculture Information Center of the National Agricultural Library, which is a guide to reference materials and databases for aquaculture (Hanfman). In "ABLE: A Business Reference Expert System," Maurice Fortin of the University of North Texas has produced a similar kind of guide to business reference sources (Fortin). Jeff Fadell, Judy Myers, Charles Bailey and their colleagues at the University of Houston have devoted themselves to "The Intelligent Reference Systems Project," a tangible product of which is a program to help users select periodical indexes (Fadell and Myers). The present writer has authored *CHEMREF* (see figure 8-1), a reference expert system to help professional chemists locate literature and data in online or printed sources (Robertson).

Figure 8-1. Introductory Screen of the Writer's CHEMREF, on Expert System Written with 1ST-CLASS

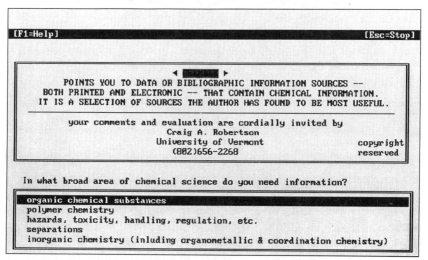

Courtesy of AI Corp./1ST-CLASS.

Librarians have applied expert systems directly to large collection development and management problems. The National Library of Medicine developed *JES* (Journal Expert Selector) to aid in the selection of journals for indexing (Rada et al.). Steven L. Sowell developed an expert system, *Monograph Selection Advisor*, to help in collection of monographs (Sowell). Much of the work of cataloging and classification involves the application of rules, and so this field has also seen the emergence of expert systems. A project in the state of Wisconsin to help local libraries create machine-readable cataloging (MARC) for their own materials led to the development of *MITNET/MARC*. This software helps novice catalogers in school, public, and academic libraries develop their own MARC records on floppy or hard disks (Epstein). Dozens of other library uses, many of them probably unreported and undocumented, have been made of expert systems.

How can we judge which of our own services are appropriate for the development of expert systems? Among the felicitous conditions for their development let us list five factors. First, the problem that such a program addresses should be one that needs professional skill or a significant amount of procedural detail to solve. In other words, the application should not be trivial. Many applications founder on this simple point. Secondly the implementation should be cost effective. It should solve a problem that arises from relative scarcity of skilled personnel, or one that results from a specialization of skills among staff members. For instance, a program might permit substitution of nonprofessional staff in a function that professionals usually perform. The routing of document delivery requests might serve as an example. Third, the project should cover a small "problem domain." It should deal with limited, well-defined concerns rather than global ones. For example, one would not devise an expert system for answering *all* reference queries, because the problem area is unlimited, but one might design a useful product to choose among, say, information sources on prescription and over-the-counter drugs.

Fourth, one should be able to solve most problems in this domain by applying routine procedures, which usually are the implicit or ad hoc rules that the experts have found or have devised from their experience. A great part of the work of all professions consists of such informal heuristics. In response to a patient's presentation of a certain symptom, for example, the physician has learned to order a specific clinical test; in response to certain circumstances in a civil suit, the attorney files for a temporary injunction. A librarian might routinely consult *American Statistics Index* whenever a documents collection is available and the patron needs detailed statistical data by demographic category. Finally, if the work setting already employs microcomputers, implementation of an expert system will fit into users' habits more naturally and require less orientation.

Notice that our hypothetical *SearchDoctor* meets these criteria. It addresses a problem that would usually require active intervention by a professional librarian who has database-searching experience. With the growth in popularity of end-user searching, librarians often get requests from new users for help in the correction and modification of search strategies. The librarian in this case delegates the job to his silicon assistant. The problem to be solved is finite: broadening or narrowing the retrieval in an online search in response to observed results. Librarians habitually approach problems of this sort by applying the rules of thumb that they have learned through years of trial and error. The program resides on the very microcomputer that the end-user has already operated.

Expert Systems Shells

Writing your own expert systems requires only a modest familiarity with microcomputers and the enthusiasm to spend a few hours learning your way around a new piece of software called an *expert system shell*. It may take as little as one day to learn the basics of such a program. Although it is possible to write an expert system with a standard programming language such as Pascal or with a special AI language such as Prolog, no one really needs to learn programming, because expert systems shells make the job much easier. The distinction between shells and programming, however, is not an absolute one, because some shells require the user to write rules or procedures in a strict syntax.

A shell is a type of applications software that helps you write specific expert systems. It facilitates this task in much the same way that a spreadsheet management program such as *Lotus 1-2-3* enables you to create specific spreadsheets. Shells let authors develop expert systems with little or no programming skill. The term *shells* is entirely fitting because these products are themselves empty expert systems that provide forms to hold knowledge but lack any specific intelligent contents until you supply them. The shell provides several functions. It has an "inference engine" (the logical paradigm or algorithm that it uses to find answers with your knowledge); a simple editor of some sort to enter knowledge rules and text; a user interface for carrying on dialogues with end users; documentation that explains expert systems applications; and added features, such as graphics, mathematical functions, or gateways to other programs.

Because they are so easy to learn and to use, shells are growing quickly in popularity. Several dozen for IBM-compatible computers are currently on the commercial market. Others are available as shareware or public domain products. This writer knows of less than a dozen for the Apple Macintosh. Altogether, we might be able to compile a list of almost 100 such products. These numbers tell us that the market for such software is still in its infancy or early adolescence. At some time in the near future the market will crowd out the weaker products, or those with thin capital or business skills behind them.

Shells vary greatly in both cost and features – two factors that are not always closely correlated. Most vendors of expert system shells offer a demonstration version of their software for a modest price, say $20 or $30, which usually can apply toward the purchase of the product. Be sure to test drive software before you buy it.

There are many possible criteria that you can weigh in choosing among the large number of shells available. Let us consider four factors that stand out: the cost (including a tricky issue of the runtime license); the likely commercial viability or survival of the product; the scheme that it uses to represent your knowledge; and its calls (read/write capabilities) to external files, programs, spreadsheets, or databases.

Consider the tricky issues of cost. By *cost* I mean more than the advertised price. One usually buys expert systems software directly from the publisher. When you talk with a salesperson, ask whether an educational discount applies, because most vendors do offer one. Mail order retailers sell *VP Expert*, which has the largest market share, at a deep discount (40 percent or more). Always ask about a *runtime license*, a serious cost consideration that you must not overlook. Unlike a document that you compose with a word processor, an expert system is itself a computer program. In order to run, it must contain not only your knowledge, properly arranged, but also some of the publisher's programming code. On a simple level the problem is that if you want to make and distribute runtime (that is, stand-alone) copies that contain that copyrighted programming, you may need to pay the publisher a royalty. What looks like a bargain-priced shell may not be if you add in royalties for copies that you may want to install at different sites or give to colleagues. For example, *VP Expert* costs less initially than most shells, but charges $100 per product for a "noncommercial" distribution license.[1] On the other hand, *1ST-CLASS*, *KnowledgePro* and *MacSmarts*, which include an unrestricted runtime license, spare you that expense.

A more serious issue of concern to us also lurks here. The arrival of expert systems as advisory tools for our services creates exciting opportunities for librarians to cooperate. This unusual new technology lets each of us share some of his or her own know-how with other members of the profession by the exchange of runtime copies of expert systems on a floppy disk. The intrinsic value of this technology, as we have seen, is its ability to organize and distribute problem-solving skills. To do this in a practical way, however, we must start with development software that does not burden impecunious librarians with costly license fees that are designed to extract revenue from business users.

We spoke above about the fragmented state of the market for this genre of software. Before you buy a shell it is only practical to ask whether, given this Darwinian state of affairs, its producer will be around next year to offer you product enhancements and over-the-phone support. In the case of a shareware product that you buy for $25, the answer is probably no. Remember that you are investing far more than the price of the software. You are also spending quite a few hours of your professional life, so pick software that looks likely to survive in the commercial market. I describe several good bets below.

You enter your knowledge into an expert system in a *knowledge base*, where it takes one of several stereotyped forms. The specific shell determines which of these forms you can use. The most common methods of knowledge representation are rules, examples, and frames. There are, of course, other schemes. One of these probably fits your own expert knowledge. Rules (also called production rules) are the most common pattern and the easiest to understand. Rules take the form of sets of "if...then" statements. For example, a simple rule from an expert system for interlibrary loan protocols might take the form represented in figure 8-2.

Figure 8-2. A Typical Rule from a Hypothetical Knowledge Base for Interlibrary Loan Procedures

```
IF   OCLC ▪ NO       AND
     RLIN ▪ NO       AND
     PUBLISHER ▪ NON-U.S.
THEN  SOURCE ▪ BRITISH LENDING
               LIBRARY
DISPLAY: "SEND THE REQUEST TO THE
          BRITISH LENDING LIBRARY
          OR TO AN APPPROPRIATE INSTI-
          TUTION FROM THE WORLD OF
          LEARNING. WARN THE PATRON
          ABOUT A DELAY."
```

Examples (or "induction") use sets of empirical observations, from which the program "induces" or infers rules. This approach proves especially useful when the problem is so large that its rules are not obvious. Frames are a third scheme for representing knowledge in a stereotyped form, using built-in "slots," which are much like the records and fields in a database. Each entry in a frame, however, can in turn be a frame, and frames can be linked in hierarchical ways, so that one inherits attributes of another. In a hypothetical advisor for periodical indexes, for example, *Reader's Guide*, *Humanities Index*, *Art Index*, and *Social Sciences Index* might each have its individual slots as well as attributes that it inherits from a *Wilson Indexes* parent frame.

Most shells provide you with some ability to call external programs from within your expert system. There are, broadly speaking, two ways to do this.

The simpler means is for the shell to provide a window to the disk operating system software (DOS), and thus to batch files and executable external programs. A more polished method is for the program to make invisible calls to database management systems (typically, *dBase* and its clones) or spreadsheets (*Lotus 1-2-3* and its clones) that allow your expert system to import or alter data in the latter. Some shells allow you only to read data into your expert system but not to write to the external file. Others provide both read and write capabilities. If your application is sophisticated enough to need these powers, be certain that the shell that you buy can provide the appropriate kind of external access.

Specific Products

Among the dozens of shells available, let us take a quick look (in alphabetical order) at eight, but with an admonition that other products not listed here may be as good or better for your particular applications. These eight, however, do all have a following and seem likely to survive in the marketplace.

EXSYS 3.2 and EXSYS Professional
EXSYS Inc., Products Division
P.O. Box 11247
Albuquerque, NM 87192-0247
(505) 256-8356.

$395 (*EXSYS*) and $795 (*EXSYS Professional*). The vendor offers a 30 percent prepaid discount to academic accounts. The demo costs $15. A noncommercial runtime license is $600 (*EXSYS*) or $1000 (*EXSYS Professional*).

Both versions of *EXSYS* support color graphics adapters and make good use of the color. Their knowledge representation scheme is rule-based. *EXSYS* can explain its reasoning by displaying applicable rules. It can support a large expert system and has good external calls and built-in math functions. *EXSYS PROFESSIONAL* adds chaining together of knowledge bases, screen utilities, and a command language.

1ST-CLASS and 1ST-CLASS Fusion
1ST-CLASS Systems, Inc. (Formerly, Programs-in-Motion)
One Longfellow Ctr.
286 Boston Post Road – 150 East
Wayland, MA 01778.
(800) 872-8812.

1ST-CLASS costs $495 ($395 to academic accounts). *1ST-CLASS Fusion* costs $1495. Prices include an unrestricted runtime license.

1ST-CLASS has been taken off the market, but the producers still support it and still sell it to schools and libraries. These programs, personal favorites of this writer, are easy to learn and have excellent documentation and free phone support. *1ST-CLASS* lets you build large applications by "chaining" smaller knowledge bases together, supports CGA and EGA, and can use *PC Paintbrush* screens. Its pricey sibling, *1ST-CLASS Fusion*, adds support for Hercules graphics. *Fusion* also offers more powerful calls to external programs. These products can represent knowledge either as rules or examples.

INSTANT-EXPERT PLUS
Human Intellect Systems
1670 S. Amphlett Blvd. Suite 316
San Mateo, CA 94402.
(415) 571-5939

The list price is $498.

This is the successor to an early shell called *INSTANT-EXPERT*. It is one of the more popular shells for the Macintosh and makes good use of the Mac's graphics capabilities.

KNOWLEDGEPRO
Knowledge Garden, Inc.
473A Malden Bridge Road
Nassau, NY 12123
(518) 766-3000

The basic program sells for $495. This price includes a runtime license. Optional add-ons include a Graphics Toolkit ($89); a Knowledge Maker Toolkit ($99), which offers example-to-rule conversion; and a Database Toolkit ($99), which provides hooks to *dBase*, *Lotus 1-2-3*, and other software. A demo with a manual costs $30, which can be applied toward purchase. The current version uses only EGA for graphics. A new and faster version is expected.

KNOWLEDGEPRO uses a unique kind of knowledge representation based on "topics," which are the "objects" in object-oriented programming languages. In fact, *KNOWLEDGEPRO* is not an expert system shell. It is a high-level, restricted-purpose programming language that is capable of producing both expert systems and hypertext, and combining them in appealing products. When the toolkits are added in the expense grows. It requires more work to master *KNOWLEDGEPRO* than it does to learn a typical shell. This language, however, is an almost ideal development tool for certain applications, such as browseable online manuals and end-user guides to new library technologies.

LEVEL-5
Information Builders, Inc.
1250 Broadway
New York, NY 10001
(800) 444-4303

List price is $695, but it is only $200 to academic accounts. A demo costs $20.

There are versions of this established product (formerly called *Insight 2+*) for IBM compatibles, the Apple Macintosh, and Digital Equipment's VAX. The IBM version provides good access to *dBase*, Pascal programs, and *PC Paintbrush* graphics screens. The knowledge representation here is strictly rule-based. *Level-5* may, however, be a good choice for intelligent *dBase* applications.

MacSMARTS
Cognition Technology Corporation
55 Wheeler Street
Cambridge, MA 02138
(800) 622-2829

The price for version 3.0 is $150. A more advanced *MacSMARTS Professional* sells for $495. An academic discount is offered, but the amount was not specified in my conversations with Cognition Tech. No demo is yet available.

As the name suggests, this is a product for the Apple Macintosh. The producers claim to have the largest installed retail base for Macintosh expert systems. *MacSMARTS* offers links to both Apple's *HyperCard* and Silicon Beach's *SuperCard* hypertext programs (see below). It uses either rules or examples to represent knowledge.

Personal Consultant Easy 2.01
Texas Instruments
M/S 7722
P.O.Box 1444
Houston, TX 77251
(800)527-3500

The list price is $495.

PC EASY is a very capable, easy-to-use, rule-based shell written in Texas Instruments' proprietary version of the LISP language. With the support of a large corporation that was a pioneer in AI, it is likely to survive the rigors of the marketplace. This shell can read and write to *dBase* and *Lotus 1-2-3* files. It supports graphics on computers with EGA and VGA monitors. A major drawback is the fact that T.I. allows only one free runtime copy of any expert system. The company charges a $95 royalty for every additional runtime copy.

VP Expert 2.02
Paperback Software International
2830 Ninth Street
Berkeley, CA 94710
(415) 644-2117

The list price of $249 is reduced to about $145 by mail order discounters.

This powerful shell is an excellent buy. One fly in the ointment, however, is the runtime license of $300 per year. The charge may be reduced for noncommercial users. I recommend calling the company for details. Sharing of ASCII (standard text) files of rules among owners of the program is possible, because these cannot be subject to licensing. Knowledge representation is both rule-based or derived from an induction table. The new version 2.02 has some hypertext capabilities, although they are not well integrated with the expert systems. *VP Expert* has good "hooks" to external programs. The user interface is not as attractive as some others, but third-party extensions are available to deal with this problem.

HYPERTEXT

Although the two are sometimes used for similar ends and both can make library staff more productive, hypertext technology differs from expert systems. Because hypertext lacks the heuristics of real human experts, it does not belong to the field of artificial intelligence. It contains knowledge, but it does not try to mimic human reasoning. In fact, the term *hypertext* lacks a single, agreed-upon meaning, just as *artificial intelligence* does. Some writers argue that Apple Computer's *HyperCard* program, the very software that springs first to mind at mention of the word, is not true hypertext. As with artificial intelligence, we gain nothing practical here by digging further into the semantics. For our purposes, the common characteristic of hypertext, as the last syllable of the name implies, is its organization into "documents," or alternatively, "stacks" of note cards, which an end user can browse at will in a variety of paths.

Let our novice user of teaching technologies once again blaze a path for our understanding. By now she has collected a bibliography of periodical articles on the topic she is researching. She discovers that many of these periodicals are owned by a large public library in a neighboring city, which she decides to visit. When she reaches the Megalopolis Public Library and enters, she finds herself in a cavernous and unfamiliar lobby. She approaches an information desk at one end of the lobby and explains to the librarian that she is a first-time visitor and needs to use periodicals and microforms, and to make photocopies from both. The librarian suggests that she start with *TourGuide*, a self-directed, computer-assisted orientation to the library and its services, which is available on a Macintosh computer at the counter. Attached to the microcomputer by a cable is a *mouse*, a pointing gadget that moves an arrow-shaped cursor on the computer screen as the user rolls the device itself on the surface of the counter. The *TourGuide* program is rather like a self-paced slide show in which the user controls the sequence of screens. It contains series of "cards," or images, which provide information about the library's physical plan, services, and policies. An introductory screen bears the logo and photographic image of the library. The mouse allows our user to move from a forward (right) arrow on the first card to a "home card," a diagram that shows the 20 or so departments and functional areas of the library (see figure 8-3).

She points the cursor to a box labelled "periodicals reading room," clicks a mouse button, and sees a plan of the entire second floor, which includes that room. When she clicks the mouse button on the reading room, the computer produces a blueprint quality enlargement of that area. This sketch contains highlighted "buttons," or hot spots, that respond to the mouse click by displaying specific information. For example, when she clicks on the photocopiers a window appears in the computer screen that explains their use (with coins or smart cards) and also mentions an alternative drop-off photocopy service on the ground floor. Next, when she presses the mouse button on a back (left) arrow in the upper left corner, the program returns our researcher to the home card: the diagram of the library's departments. She selects the microforms area and begins to learn about its location, policies, services, and so on.

Figure 8-3. Display Screen Illustrating Information Application for Higher Education

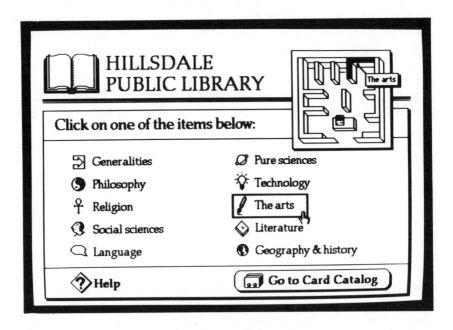

Courtesy of Apple Computer, Inc.

TourGuide, like *SearchDoctor,* is a hypothetical program. It illustrates some characteristics of hypertext, such as its user-controlled browseability, its division of information into page-sized units, and its extensive use of graphics. The notion of an interconnection of information through nodes that allow the reader to determine the sequence of browsing dates back to the World War II era. The name *hypertext* was coined by Theodor H. Nelson in the 1960s. Nelson envisions a kind of global database, or "world library" to use his term, in which information published anywhere, in any form, is so connected electronically that users at any point in the world can browse it. This grand vision inspired him to start a project he calls *Xanadu.* The essence of hypertext (or *hypermedia,* because the technology can also incorporate modern audio, animation, and video technologies) is a system of dynamic links between concepts that lets a user browse in a variety of directions. He or she can jump from a text to definitions, diagrams, or related issues. The user is thus freed from the tyranny of "sequential reading," which printed books or periodical articles impose. The proponents of hypertext believe that this kind of "associative" information gathering is both more natural and more creative. On the other hand, with existing products, the browsing is not exactly random, but is constrained by the links and possible pathways defined by the author of the program.

How can we judge which, if any, of our own services might be suitable hypertext or hypermedia systems? What are some guiding principles? First, consider that a hypertext or hypermedia document or stack divides information into small and discrete concepts, which the writer usually must confine to one computer screen each. Implied here is a certain simplification of thought, so subtle reasoning does not belong in most pure hypermedia. Text must always be clear and concise. Second, remember that graphics and media often communicate better than text – especially for younger users. So if images and sounds can convey much of the content of an application, it is probably a good bet for hypertext/hypermedia. Third, because the program actually restricts browsing to pathways defined by the author, its quality depends not only on content but also in large measure on the insight that goes into the scripting of these possible routes. In other words, any candidate application for a hypertext program should be capable of being outlined on a storyboard, as if it were a daytime television serial with concurrent plots.

Notice that our hypothetical *TourGuide* meets these criteria. The information need is rather shallow. Basic information about the library can be divided into small, interwoven units. Because the physical plan of the library provides an organizing theme, the program can make good use of graphic diagrams for the floor plans. Finally, the experience of greeting new users of the library at the information desk provides a basis for the multiple scripts to meet their most common needs.

In contrast to expert systems, hypertext has caught on quickly with librarians. One cannot attend a national conference in the library and information trade without hearing papers about and seeing demonstrations of such computer applications. An obvious and practical use of hypermedia in libraries is to provide automated tours of services and facilities, along the lines of our hypothetical *TourGuide*. A number of libraries have done this. For example, Larry B. Hlavsa wrote a *HyperCard* introduction to the services of the St. Paul Public Library system (Vaccaro, part 1). Wayne State University uses a *HyperCard* application to help patrons locate books by call numbers in the WSU libraries and those of several neighbor schools (Kane). Participants in the second National LITA Conference in Boston (October 1988) got oriented to the program, the exhibits, and the Boston area by means of a clever *HyperCard* stack written by Ann F. Bevilacqua and Daniel W. Lewis (Vaccaro, part 2). The Library of Science and Medicine at Rutgers University uses *HyperCard* for its *LSM Infomaster*, a networked program that it modestly calls a tour, but which is really basic user education

(Kesselman). Kitty J. Mackay of Converse College in South Carolina has exploited *HyperCard*'s unheralded character as a relational database manager for a rather novel circulation use. Her *Overdue Writer* automates the production of overdue notices in a college library that does not yet have an online circulation system (Mackay).

Bill Coons and his colleagues in the Mann Library at Cornell University have created a *HyperCard* interface to the online public access catalog (OPAC). Their program, called *MacPac*, combines *HyperCard* stacks with communications programming to make searching, saving to disk, and printing of bibliographic records more intuitive and attractive for new users. Coons points out quite properly that the vendors of such OPAC software as NOTIS, GEAC, and CLSI have done a good job of writing powerful search software, but have left us with clumsy user interfaces (Coons).

Specific Products

As with expert systems, one might use many criteria to select the right hypertext authoring program. In the interest of clarity, let us once again consider four important factors: the method that the software uses to develop applications; the issue of the runtime license (again); the graphics capabilities of the program; and the likely commercial survival of the product.

Two standard approaches to the development of hypermedia applications are used. The more common method is to create individual screens, graphics, or blocks of text, variously called "cards," "nodes," or "pads," and then to tie them together by means of a "script," which one writes in a special-purpose language that creates such links. These scripts, used by products like *HyperCard*, *SuperCard*, or *KnowledgePro*, are programming, although in a very restricted language. The other common method uses a special sort of text editor to embed the links in text files to connect other blocks of text and graphics. This approach, which is more transparent to the developer, is available in products such as *Black Magic* and *Architext*.

Because graphics often convey information more clearly and concisely than text, they form an integral part of most hypertext and hypermedia. You must consider two possibilities: bit-mapped or character-based graphics. These standards are not as arcane as they may sound. *Bit-mapped* refers to images generated from a map of the monitor's screen in the computer's memory in which the color and intensity of each pixel, or tiny area of the screen, is represented by a discrete bit of random access memory (RAM). This method permits a fine resolution of images. Often this capability is available because the product "runs under" (that is, operates with) graphics-based operating systems software, such as Apple's *MultiFinder*, or so-called environments, such as *Microsoft Windows*. *Character-based* or ASCII

(American Standard Code for Information Interchange) graphics, on the other hand, are limited to mosaics of the 256 standard characters that can be generated from the computer's keyboard. To see some examples of these, hold down the *Alt* (alternate) key on an IBM or IBM-compatible keyboard while you type, say, 177 or 206 on the numeric keypad. If you expect to use detailed diagrams or scanned digital images in an application, choose a program that offers bit-mapped graphics.

The runtime issue that we spoke of earlier in connection with expert systems is also a major concern when you choose hypertext authoring software. Some products include a runtime program; those that do not either expect any recipients of your application to own their own copies of the entire program or require you to pay a license fee to distribute copies.

Finally, as we have said, the success of any software product in the market is an important assurance of continuing support from its vendor and any third-party or add-in software producers. In your own interest stick with the winners. With these four yardsticks in hand, let us take a brief look at eight products for hypertext on IBM-compatible and Macintosh personal computers. These products all have a following and seem likely to survive, thought other products may work as well or better for your particular applications.

HyperCard
Apple Computer, Inc.
1025 Mariana Ave.
Cupertino, CA 95014.
(408)996-1010

Hypercard has a nominal price of $49, but in reality Apple gives every buyer of a Macintosh a free copy.

HyperCard has this market largely to itself; other products must find niches to fill. Apple considers this program to be a key product for marketing of the Macintosh line and promotes it heavily. Because *HyperCard* is without doubt the dominant product in the field of microcomputer hypertext, many "stacks" have been written for it. Many of these are available on bulletin board services, such as Compuserve, or through shareware distribution channels. The program uses a scripting language called HyperTalk. No separate runtime program is available, but this is a less serious difficulty than it seems because, as mentioned above, a copy of the program comes with every new machine. Because *HyperCard* uses Apple's proprietary graphics user interface, it supports high-quality (monochrome) images.

ArchiText
BrainPower, Inc.
24009 Ventura Blvd. Suite 250
Calabasas, CA 91302
(818) 884-6911

The list price of $350 includes a free runtime program.

This is another product for the Macintosh world. As the name hints, what distinguishes this program from rivals is its ability to provide hypertext indexing or links in large text files. It does this better than its various "card" rivals. *ArchiText* is not meant for cute slide shows or control of external media devices, but rather for text-intensive applications.

Black Magic
NTERGAID Inc.
2490 Black Rock Turnpike
Fairfield, CT 06430
(203)368-0632

Sold as shareware and also directly by its publisher. Like most shareware products, the price depends on how much support you need. The program with full documentation and support costs $80. A runtime utility, MAGREAD, is available free on bulletin board services, such as Compuserve, or from the company for a $7 handling fee.

Black Magic is a product for the IBM/MS-DOS market, which needs a color graphics adapter (CGA or EGA) and a hard disk. The kernel of this program is a special text editor, or "hypertext word processor," as the producers call it. An author creates links to other parts of a document, or to explanatory text or graphics, by imbedding special color-coded characters in the text. *Black Magic* has its own screen capture utility, *Grabit.com*, which allows it to import bit-mapped images from a variety of other programs. In part because of its attractive price, this program is developing a following.

Guide 2
Owl International
1428 N.E. 21st Street
Bellevue, Washington 98000
(206)747-3202

The list price is $275 (IBM version) or $295 (Macintosh version). You can buy the IBM version from mail order discounters for under $150.

Guide, the original microcomputer-based hypertext program, was written first for the Macintosh, but because Apple's free distribution of its own *HyperCard* hurt this product in the marketplace, Owl rewrote the program for IBM compatibles. The IBM version runs only under the *Microsoft Windows* environment of Bellevue, Washington, neighbor Microsoft, Inc., and uses graphics only from programs, such as *Micrografx* and *Windows Paint,* that use the same environment. These are high-quality, bit-mapped images. A runtime version of *Windows* is included in the price.

HyperPad
Brightbill-Roberts
120 E. Washington Street Suite 421
Syracuse, NY 13203
(315)474-3400.

This is an inexpensive product for the IBM/MS-DOS market that is similar to *HyperCard* in its use of cards (here called "pads"). The mail order price is about $100. Mail order availability is a good sign of its popularity.

HyperPad uses a scripting language called PadTalk that has many features akin to HyperTalk. It has a plain vanilla appearance and uses only text (or ASCII) graphics characters, which a companion screen capture utility can import. *HyperPad* does not offer the detail of bit-mapped graphics. The program has some rough edges, but is a good value at the price. Nevertheless, the price does not include a runtime license, so some librarians have spurned this product.

KNOWLEDGEPRO

KnowledgePro is a high-level programming language that lets an author combine hypertext and expert systems in unique ways. For details, see the description above, under expert systems.

LINKWAY
IBM Educational Systems
P. O. Box 2150
Atlanta, GA 30055
(404) 238-3245

The price is $110 for a single copy, or $495 for a "school" package that includes a site license for 12 copies.

This product, unsurprisingly, is intended for the IBM and compatibles. It is a mouse-driven and bit-mapped graphics-oriented program plainly designed to make IBM competitive with the Macintosh in the school market. It allows an educator to tie together in a single application text, graphics, video (for example, laser disks), and sound. IBM's products do not invariably succeed, but this one no doubt will.

SuperCard
Silicon Beach Software
9770 Carroll Center Road, Suite J
San Diego, CA 92126
(619) 695-6956

It sells for a modest $199. The price includes a royalty-free runtime license.

SuperCard is a more powerful and flexible rival for *HyperCard* in the Macintosh market. It requires greater effort to learn in return for the added features. *SuperCard* can create and use either color or monochrome (gray-scale) bit-mapped graphics. *Hypercard*, on the other hand, does not support color. Silicon Beach had third-party software developers climbing on its *SuperCard* wagon before the product was even released. That is a positive sign for its survival.

A PATCH OF BLUE SKY

At the moment, expert systems and hypertext offer different avenues for the development of automated library services. Both have become affordable microcomputer software, and libraries are using them almost exclusively to solve local service problems and augment the work of their staff. In many situations, either of these technologies can be applied to a particular problem. Happily, in the next few years librarians may not need to chose one class of software over the other, because the producers of expert systems are moving quickly toward incorporating hypertext into hybrid products that combine features of both expert systems and hypertext. *1STCLASS-HT, KnowledgePro, VP Expert, Intelligent Developer* (from Hyperpress Publishing), and *HyperX* (from Millenium Software) all provide examples of various stages in the integration of hypertext features into expert systems.

Hypertext itself may have less importance in years to come as a stand-alone technology than as a part of many other things. As I write, for example, a computerized thesaurus in my word processor provides a hypertext function. If a word in my text lacks the right sonority, I can summon up a list of synonyms and antonyms and choose any of these to see other lists, or return home to my document. You understand, of course, that I never actually need to do this. But the technology of hypertext is becoming part of many other software products. If you purchase a third-generation (80386) IBM-compatible computer, there is a good chance that it will come supplied with hypertext-like diagnostic software already copied onto the hard disk. *Enable O/A*, a popular integrated software package from Enable Software, comes with all of its documentation online in hypertext form. A new category of free-form databases, such as *askSam* (from AskSam Systems) and MemoryMate (from Broderbund Software) use hypertext techniques to manage large amounts of text information. Bill Coons of Cornell suggest that in the future vendors of library online catalogs will probably supply hypertext user interfaces for OPACs (Coons).

Artificial intelligence and hypertext technologies, whether they are incorporated into other applications or used for stand-alone applications, will grow in importance to information professionals in the coming years as we struggle to cope with the flood of information published in electronic forms.

Note

1. I have been told, but have not confirmed, that the producers of *VP Expert* will allow schools and other nonprofit organizations to use the runtime version without paying royalties.

Works Cited

Coons, Bill. "Providing Macintosh Access to Cornell Library's Online Catalog." *THE Journal*, Special Macintosh Issue (September 1989): 52-55.

Epstein, Hank. "An Expert System for Novice MARC Catalogers." *Wilson Library Bulletin* 62, no. 3 (November 1987): 33-36.

Fadell, Jeff, and Judy E. Myers. "The Information Machine: A Microcomputer-Based Reference Service." In *Expert Systems in Reference Service*, edited by Christine Roysdon and Howard D. White, 75-112. New York: Haworth, 1989.

Fortin, Maurice. "ABLE: A Business Reference Expert System." Paper presented at the Machine Assisted Reference Section of the annual meeting of the American Library Association, Dallas, 24 June 1989.

Hanfman, Deborah. "AquaRef: An Expert Advisory System for Reference Support." In *Expert Systems in Reference Service*, edited by Christine Roysdon and Howard D. White, 113-33. New York: Haworth, 1989.

Kane, William P. "A HyperCard Call Number Directory: Using Stacks to Find Stacks." *College and Research Libraries News* 50, no. 7 (July/August 1989): 576-77.

Kesselman, Martin. "LSM Infomaster: A Hypercard CAI Program on a Macintosh Network" *College and Research Libraries News* 49, no. 7 (July/August 1988): 437-40.

Mackay, Kitty J. "Automating Overdues in a Non-Automated Library: the Hypercard Solution." *College and Research Libraries News* 50, no. 1 (January 1989): 23-27.

Rada, Joyce Backus, Thomas Giampa, Christina Gibbs, and Subash Goel. "Computerized Guides to Journal Selection." *Information Technology and Libraries* 6, no. 3 (September 1986): 173-84.

Robertson, Cray. "CHEMREF: An expert System for Chemical Literature in a Special Library Setting," *RASD Occasional Papers*, forthcoming.

Sowell, Steven L. "Expanding Horizons in Collection Development with Expert Systems: Development and Testing of a Prototype." *Special Libraries* 80, no. 4 (Winter 1989): 45-50.

Vaccaro, Bill. "HyperTours!" Parts 1 & 2. *Computers in Libraries* 9, no. 1 (January 1989): 28-31, no. 2 (February 1989): 23-26.

9

Special Training for Special Users

Teaching Technologies in Libraries is intended to be a basic guide for librarians working with automated resources in all types of libraries. Since the principal authors are academic librarians, however, we did not feel confident that we had the experience to address the special issues involved in teaching the use of technology in public, school, medical, and business libraries. Librarians working in these settings, we felt could speak with much more authority and insight. We also wanted to include the viewpoints of an academic librarian from another college or university.

The five essays in this chapter reflect a rich variety of interests and experiences related to instruction and technology. We contacted librarians working in each of the types of libraries we wanted analyzed and asked them to discuss the issues involved in teaching their users about technology. We greatly appreciate their contributions of time, thought, and talent.

Teaching Public Library Users How to Use Technology

Blaine Victor Morrow
Coordinator of Automated Services
Grosse Pointe Libraries
Grosse Pointe, Michigan

What makes training in the use of technology a special problem in the public library? Three areas strike me as being especially complex in public library settings: (1) the library's public (that is, its users); (2) the library's staff; and (3) the training process itself.

THE LIBRARY'S PUBLIC

In public libraries, many users don't know and don't care about new technologies in the library that have no direct relevance to their needs or reasons for visiting the library. In the Grosse Pointe Libraries, for example, we've added public access microcomputers, several CD-ROM reference tools, and online catalog terminals, yet many of our users simply ignore these rather conspicuous exhibitions of computer technology and continue to carry out their library visits in the same "business as usual" manner month after month and year after year. As long as the mystery books remain in the same room and occupy the same shelf space, mystery lovers can walk by the computers and whatever other novelties we introduce and fulfill the object of their quest untroubled by the need to learn more about the technological enigmas they pass. The videophile needs only to know where the videos are stored and how they can be accessed, and does not necessarily care to know that the library has added a new online catalog or a business reference CD-ROM tool. There is no reason to assume that the preschooler, teenager, businesswoman, housewife, or retired senior citizen will take an interest in the library's newfangled contraptions.

On the other hand, some of our patrons in the public library – particularly those who frequent other types of libraries or institutions where computer tools are commonplace or those who are otherwise familiar with the implementation of computer-based information equipment – are automatically drawn to whatever computer terminals we install for public use. With this type of patron we often recognize a kind of opening faith in the computer-based tool over and above its printed counterpart, even without experience with the particular computer application. These folks are much more likely to believe implicitly that the computer application will be easy to use and to learn, and will provide more useful information than would traditional print media. Would that this were always so!

Given these realities, where we in the public library place our computer-based reference tools, how we array our staff with respect to this placement, and the amount of assistance we sanction will have profound effects on the degree to which public library patrons learn to use these tools. The videophile who has to walk around a computer en route to the video shelves can't help noticing its presence. The mystery lover in search of a particular title will be impressed by the library staff member who can locate the book at another library agency by means of the online computer terminal. And the computer-literate patron who happens to notice the presence of computer terminals while standing at the circulation desk will be drawn to them out of natural curiosity and the aforementioned implicit faith in their usefulness. If we decide to tuck computers away in remote, sequestered regions of the library, we automatically enforce a need to alert our patrons to their availability through unnatural means (such as, publicity and signs) and make them virtually inaccessible to the casual public library user.

I refer to signs and publicity efforts as "unnatural" because they deviate from the general manner in which public library patrons use their libraries. By and large, folks who come into a public library don't come in to read signs or brochures: they come on a particular information- or material- or activity-related mission and are oblivious to such extraneous concerns. Weekend and evening visitors often have no idea that public libraries offer preschool story hour programs during daytime hours; people tend to follow patterns of library use, and to think that what they see when they visit the public library is all there is to see and use. If you spend hundreds or thousands of dollars on a computer-based information service and entrust its fate to publicity efforts alone, without allowing the service to become a manifest and easily recognized "fact of life" in the library environment, chances are you'll be disappointed in the public's response to the service.

THE LIBRARY'S STAFF

The bulk of professional staff in public libraries have some measure of appreciation for the role of computers in the profession and have received at least introductory training (if nowhere else than in library school) in the use of information-related computer tools. In recent years, some have even been attracted to the profession by the promise of "high-tech" involvement in the information industry. These latter are likely to be disappointed and confused if the reality of the public library does not reflect their expectations of an environment teeming with computer-related chores and activities. Meanwhile, more seasoned public library staff recognize the need to devote time and energy to learning the use of new tools, but cannot help wondering how all of this new technology will affect the patrons, the staffing patterns, and the ambiance of the organization they've been serving for some time.

Public librarians perpetually complain about being understaffed, making efforts to use staff in training programs all the more complex. A staff that perceives itself as already overburdened is not likely to welcome the addition of a new job or duty. Not only is it difficult to acquire free staff time for implementing patron training, but it is an even more demanding task to locate the type of worker who would best undertake the job of teaching others in the use of computer tools. The "How may I help you?" service orientation of the public librarian does not necessarily translate into technical expertise, reliable computer skills, or familiarity with technological developments. And the inability to add this proficiency to the packed agendas of most public library staffs—whose primary focus is on person-to-person (rather than person-to-machine) dialogue – is a pervasive administrative problem.

What may be more important is the perspective of public library workers toward patron training. Unlike librarians in school or academic environments, public library staff members do not always perceive obvious benefits from participating in structured user-training programs. Indeed, there is often a rift among the staff concerning this issue. The suggestion that we in public libraries can – and should – educate our users to find their own information may actually be threatening to public librarians, whose job-related gratification is in large part derived from their own ability to find the information the patron normally is at a loss to uncover. Public library staff members are traditionally the "experts" with regard to even the most elementary details of library use, and in many public libraries a tradition of leading patrons to expect answers from staff, rather than from the tools available to staff and patron alike, has been encouraged in the pursuit of a generalized service orientation.

THE TRAINING PROCESS

Given that public library patrons may have no interest in or knowledge of computer-related information tools, and that the public library staff may not have time to, want to, or know how to offer instruction in their use, how do we offer technology-related training to those for whom such training is indispensable? In the Grosse Pointe Libraries, we've addressed the training issue from two main fronts.

One front has involved training staff members themselves. As part of a generalized staff development program in our libraries, workshops for library staff have been offered regularly to cover the use of any new computer-related tools. Attendance at these workshops is not mandatory, but is conscientiously offered to all staff members in an effort to familiarize and instruct them in the use of new tools. In-service and in-house workshops are the preferred modes for these ventures; equipment and software variables are kept to a minimum when you train people with the same tools they'll be using later. The choice of instructors has varied according to the degree of in-house expertise and the availability of qualified and creditable outside authorities. A general outline for such a training effort would include these steps: (1) develop a plan for staff orientation and training to new tools; (2) prepare a calendar for staff orientation and training; (3) obtain training documentation from vendors and other reliable sources; (4) identify a qualified and creditable trainer; (5) conduct specific application workshops; and (6) provide follow-up training as requested or needed.

The second front has been the use of volunteers from among the community of public library users to serve as a "training corps." I have already mentioned that users vary considerably in their enthusiasm for and interest in new technology in the public library. The patron who greets new terminals or computer services with excitement and curiosity is a plausible candidate for training efforts. Who can better tell you what your patrons need to know than they themselves? So long as your staff does not perceive this as a usurpation of authority, you should be able to enlist a solid crew of willing and spirited computer volunteers from among your community who will serve well as trainers in your technology education efforts. Admittedly, the use of volunteers is fraught with its own issues and anxieties, but one noteworthy side effect is that it provides a forum from which the public can encourage library staff members to assimilate new tools themselves and to see the benefits of such tools.

It's a mistake to assume that an isolated course or workshop will invoke incentive for attendance on the part of either patrons or staff. Because of the nature of the public's divergent use patterns and interests, a "one-shot" training effort will be doomed to failure or, at best, disappointment. The training should be offered at various times of day and days of the week, so as to accommodate various schedules and also to identify the public's interest in the subject matter. Where possible, the training program should create training opportunities that speak to various aspects of that technology, since the far-reaching implications of computer technology are also diverse. A series of programs can inspire curiosity and use and should be monitored by administrators to determine further directions and goals for the training effort. A general outline would include these steps: (1) develop a general publicity program; (2) develop and implement user education classes; (3) recruit interested trainees for further training; (4) develop and implement volunteer training classes; (5) design, prepare, and distribute "how to use" brochures for each tool and course; (6) monitor progress; and (7) make adjustments as necessary.

Teaching Technologies in School Libraries

Cynthia LaPier
Director
Schuyler-Chemung-Tioga BOCES School Library System
Elmira, New York

School systems are embracing computer technology and especially networking with overwhelming enthusiasm. Although the school library is usually the last place to benefit from the computer fervor of administrators, there have been rapid and significant changes in library automation. Two recent developments have had significant impact on the school library: the growth of CD-ROM technology and the increase in storage capacity of the microcomputer. By taking advantage of the availability of databases on CD-ROM, school librarians are able to bring online searching, which has previously been limited to the rich and the few, into a school setting at any level. Microcomputers have become so sophisticated and have been brought up to such high levels of computing power that it is now possible to install an integrated library system in a school library at a fraction of the cost of a mini-based system.

School librarians have the responsibility to prepare students for the most effective use of CD-ROM, for integrated library systems, and for the use of public and academic library systems. School librarians are also responsible for taking advantage of networking systems to bring into the school more and more resources that have never before been available. Regardless of the grade level of the student being introduced to the new technologies, and regardless of the type of technology being used, student success will depend upon a keen understanding of the terms *keyword* and *Boolean*. The student today does not have to be taught how to use a computer; most students even have keyboarding skills. The librarian may be anxious about using several different types of search engines for the CD-ROM databases and the online catalog, but it is most likely that students will not be intimidated by a variety of methods of access. Once they understand the basic concepts, transfer follows in all programs.

But because school districts are resistant to change and libraries are a low priority on most school administrators' lists, it will be necessary for the school librarian to approach the online or CD-ROM technologies in a two-stage (or -level) process. Public school librarians are not able to argue that the school will become more attractive to potential tuition-paying students, or that the patron population is demanding better services to match the capabilities many are experiencing in the workplace. School students as patrons do not have a strong voice requesting the latest in technology and the most effective means of obtaining resources. The school librarian, therefore, should develop a plan to prepare the administration for implementation and a plan to teach students and teachers how to use the technology.

PREPARING THE ADMINISTRATION

One possible argument might be that if it is a goal of the library media center to support lifelong learning and if that goal is supported by the board of education, then it is imperative to include the online lesson in the library skills program for the following reasons:

- It will demonstrate that information comes to the seeker in a variety of ways.

- It will demonstrate that the student not only should rely on the sources of the library of occupation but should also locate and use resources in other libraries.

- It will illustrate that the most effective research techniques zoom in on the specific rather than the general and that this is an acquired, not an intuitive technique.

- It will give the student experiences in using higher-level thinking and decision making skills in a relatively safe and successful environment.

- It will prepare the student to use other libraries (public and academic) that are also going through the automation process, so that the student will not be denied access to any resource.

TEACHING STUDENTS AND FACULTY

The following is a skeleton lesson plan that can be adapted for any grade level and student interests to introduce a student to a CD-ROM union catalog, specifically Brodart's LePac.

Lesson objective. The student will locate materials using CD-ROM or online catalog.

Title. "Finding It Fast."

Overview. The student will experience the online search procedure through the use of CD-ROM. Included in the lesson will be the use of keyword searching, Boolean logic, and an evaluation of the CD-ROM versus the card catalog.

Length of project. Two to three class sessions.

Goal. The student will be able to locate resources effectively and independently.

Library media skills objectives. The student will learn to locate materials in the library using the online catalog or the CD-ROM union catalog.

Performance objective. Given a demonstration and an introductory lesson on the use of an online search system, the student will use the online catalog to locate resources for class project and for reading pleasure.

Subject area. Adaptable to all areas.

Learning strategy. Cooperative groups of two or three.

Resources. Card catalog, online catalog.

Methods. The librarian will give overview of technology. Each student will receive a hand-held guide explaining the functions of the program, the various roles of the major keys, and some sample searches. The librarian will, with whole class, select keywords appropriate for a research topic, for example:

Topic. Space technology in the United States.

Things to consider. Is the topic too broad? How might it be narrowed? What are the keywords?

Keywords (narrowed topic). Development of satellites, past, present, future.

Background data. Checking Grolier's Electronic   Encyclopedia for historical data.

Practice session. Search for satellite development in the card catalog; note steps taken to locate a book. Search for satellite development using the CD-ROM catalog:

1. Use the browse mode, *F2*, subject.

2. Use the express mode, *F3*, subject.

3. Use the express mode, *F3*, anyword.

Discussion questions. Which method is easiest to use? Which is the fastest? Which method is the most aesthetically appealing; that is, which is the most comfortable for the patron? Which method helps the patron locate the most appropriate sources? On a scale of 1 to 10, 10 being the highest, rate each method for the previous questions.

Group practice. Randomly divide the class into groups of three or four. The objective of each group is to teach each other how to do browse searches and express searches. The evaluation will be that the librarian or teacher will call on a member of the group to explain how to complete a search for a particular topic. If the student is unsuccessful in the explanation, then the group must reteach itself until all members are independently capable.

Real-life test. Give each of the small groups the task of teaching several teachers or administrators how to use the system. Limit the time available to 15-30 minutes, depending on the cooperation of the adults. This accomplishes many obvious benefits, a simple one being that it brings the school community closer together. A really enthusiastic librarian might even consider establishing races or contests: How much time does it take for each group to locate a source on the computer and then actually retrieve the item?

SUMMARY

Technology is a readily available tool that can help lead students to success. All components of schools are developing accountability through measurable educational outcomes. The school librarian can provide a support service to achieve these goals through the use of technology as the path to information.

Public Access Computer Technology in the Academic Library: Toaster, Type, or Transformation?

Terry Plum
Coordinator for Computer-Based Information Services
University of Connecticut Library
Storrs, Connecticut

Among academic librarians there seem to be three prevalent constructs for teaching students and faculty about public access computer technologies. These constructs are influenced, and even created, by how the vendors present their databases, by what students and faculty expect from the equipment, by the librarian's imagination, and by the purpose of the library. In the academic library we must choose the construct or model that best reflects the educational goals of the college or library. Instruction guided by the library's mission differs radically from some other possibilities and determines which construct or model we should choose to frame the presentation of the CD-ROM or PAC.

One possible construct for teaching technology is a consumer model. In this view, justified by its defenders on patron expectations, CD-ROMs or online public access catalogs (OPACs) are pieces of equipment designed for consumers. The equipment may be as simple as a toaster or as complex as a VCR, but to the naive patron it is clearly a machine that produces something when operated correctly. It is a means to an end, and the end is a consumed product, such as toasted rye, *Death Wish VIII*, or a printed bibliography on a topic.

Producers and librarians who see library technology in the toaster role opt for CD-ROMs and OPACs that are as simple as possible for users to operate. The searching options are limited, the help screens short, and ease of use is the foremost criterion for displays, searching controls, and printouts. No assumptions are made about the patrons, other than they are consumers, and thus there is no attempt to build upon any academic framework. InfoTrac, with color-coded keys and only the simplest search mode, is a good example of CD-ROM as toaster.

The VCR simile is a more complex example, but one that is still within the consumer construct. The VCR can have onscreen programming, index and address search, four heads, and super-VHS capability with 400-plus lines of resolution. Librarians and producers who see CD-ROMs and OPACs as VCRs look for as many options as are possible. The manual or online help screens become longer and much more complex. The full range of logical operators, adjacency, limiting, searching by fields, and downloading are all offered. These options are explained in the style of a technical manual, and reviewers of CD-ROMs for whom the VCR example is operative are impressed by the number of indexes, even if they will never be searched.

The patron, of course, recognizes when he or she is being treated like a consumer, and then, reacting to expectations, acts like one. Consumers learn only what is necessary to use, to consume, to solve the immediate problem. Thus, each PAC or CD-ROM becomes a separate hurdle, unrelated to other online technologies, and the lessons of searching one database are not easily transferred to other databases or other searches. Learning how to use a product is not pedagogical learning. The difference between the toaster and VCR examples is not pedagogical; it is the complexity of the equipment that produces the consumable item. SilverPlatter or WILSONDISC are good examples of CD-ROM as VCR, which is not to say that their elegantly complex indexes, limits, and search modes are bad, only that they should not be the focus of the instructional efforts of academic librarians.

Products based on the consumer model are highly promoted, used, and popular. Academic libraries have, however, an obligation to resist such attitudes and CDs because they engender the greatest passivity. Demands for such products, especially the toaster examples, should be handled in the same way beleaguered parents handle children's demands for more television. For example, WILSONDISC CDs should default to the WILSONLINE mode, since BROWSE is for making toast.

A second model for teaching computer technology in the library is based upon taxonomic type. Here the librarian explaining the CD-ROM or PAC is concerned with the underlying complexities and the patron's ability to transfer the understanding of those complexities to other online products of the same type or class. Unlike the toaster model of teaching, where mastery of the single piece of equipment is the object, the taxonomic model of instruction examines the similarities between the computer technologies. In the bibliographic instruction class the librarian describes the particular product in such a way that it becomes an exemplar of a type or class of online finding aids. CD-ROMs are presented in a simple manner so that learning appears possible and so that the patron will attempt to learn. But it is not so simple that the presentation belies the underlying complexities.

Under the taxonomic model, the particular CD-ROM or OPAC example leads to talking about the shared characteristics of all public access computer technologies, such as the nature of databases, effective searching, search strategy formation, logical operators (both implicit and explicit), keyword and subject searching, limiting, truncation, and creative fruitful interaction with the databases. The online technology under discussion in the bibliographic instruction class is a member of a set, and the other members of the set share the same traits. It is the traits that are of interest, not the members.

The type model attempts to teach the neophyte searcher the concepts by applying the model to real-world phenomena, essentially by telling a story. The story draws the patron from the outwardly simple and fair presentation of the model to its inner complexities, and then shows either implicitly or explicitly how one's understanding of the complexities will help solve other information problems in the online environment. The story may be the evolution of the database from print to online; it may be examples of researchers' successes or failures in the field; it may be examples of fraud in the literature; it may be any of the ideas described in the various "conceptual framework" approaches to bibliographic instruction, regardless of whether they assumed a print or online environment.

For example, talking about the structure of the literature in the discipline is a story that can draw in the online complexities. The thesauri for *Psychological Abstracts* or the *ERIC* system clearly are discipline-determined, and such a discussion is a good way to approach how the online environment treats descriptors. Conversely, using the WILSONDISC demonstration CD with its six-month swath of 16 databases explodes the boundaries of disciplines and is a story about the nature of a database, perhaps even leading to a discussion of networked databases through OPACs. The question of discipline approach versus a nondiscipline approach is unimportant. What is important is the veracity of the story to the inner complexities of online searching.

To teach online technology as an example of a type or a member of a set requires considerably more intervention by the librarian than that required in the consumer model. Classes, handouts, online aids, help screens, computer-assisted instruction (CAI), expert systems, hypertext – all are possible and none is precluded. In the academic library, we have an obligation to assume the pedagogical approach and we can make assumptions about our audience that allow us to say it is the best approach. Our patrons must be approached as learners, not consumers.

The third model for teaching library technology sees the technology as a transformation, a new metaphor, a new idea that influences how we view the process of finding information. Online searching as transformation is distinct from the various concepts (such as logical operators, truncation, and so on) involved with teaching or using online products. In this view library online technology affects the traditional patterns of research and writing in strikingly new ways, some of which are parallel to the transformation the microcomputer has had upon the teaching of writing.

For example, because both writing and the literature search can take place through a microcomputer, the chronological and spatial distinctions between the two processes are muddied, and the circular and interpenetrating nature of writing and research can be reinforced by the librarian. Imagine a student writing a paper in the Writing Center or a dormitory room. At some point in the writing process, the student saves the file, logs into the library's online catalog, searches for books, downloads the results, signs off, and then logs into an online vendor or networked CD-ROM chain that has remote access, downloads the journal article citations, or perhaps the text of the articles themselves, and then continues writing the paper, with the intention of looking at the sources later. The physical bounds of the library are eroded, and the information in the library becomes inextricably mixed with the writing process. The linear model of research, read, write, and rewrite is no longer true, if it ever was.

The microcomputer has also promoted collaborative cooperation among student writers through networking, file transfer, and free writing. Similarly, online technologies foster collaborative strategies among student researchers as well. Again, from the Writing Center imagine a group of students and their writing teacher logging into the online catalog or searching CD-ROMs cooperatively, making suggestions for subject headings, exploring cross-references, examining the full record for subject terms, comparing keyword and controlled vocabulary searches, trying out new ideas, creatively interacting with the database, and exposing to the writing teacher a cognitive process in the students that previously was closed.

Cooperative, creative online searching reveals the inexactness of two library metaphors, the "solitary heroic quest" and "narrowing the topic." In the heroic quest information must be wrested away from the library, like Hercules wresting the golden apples of Hesperides the from Atlas. Finding information in the library is daunting, solitary, accompanied by sacred talismans (the three-by-five cards, the sharpened pencil, the magical place to sit), taken at some personal risk, and not always successful. With online technologies the quest can take place with your colleagues by your side, peering at the screen and helping with the match of resources to topic, in a cooperative, noncompetitive environment that mirrors the teaching of writing.

The idea of topic definition is also transformed in the online environment. It is possible to be much more creative online, trying out new ideas, slipping smoothly from database to database, exercising maximum choice over the retrieved citations and not limiting oneself to what is easily available. Librarians teaching technology should emphasize the creative aspects. What we are actually trying to do is to engage the student with the topic, and narrowing is not the right metaphor for this process. Narrowing and broadening are at best inaccurate metaphors for the process the student undergoes. The image of narrowing leads the student away from the truly exciting, more important topics that have global implications, and that therefore affect the student's life, to topics that replicate the worst of academic research, that is, termite scholarship. Students are not excited by tiny topics, and a research process that forces them to fasten on "researchable," confined subjects, seemingly divorced from their large and messy experiences in life, will only convince them of the irrelevance of the entire exercise. Topics should grow organically as the student learns more and becomes more engaged with the topic. "Growing" rather than "narrowing" is a far more fruitful way to look at this process. Yet, without a clear sense of engagement and organization (but not "narrowing"), the garden can turn into a jungle. Growing is an organizing metaphor, and does not mean expansion. It means engagement with what the student finds controversial about the topic he or she has chosen, and is based upon reading, learning, and thinking about the topic.

Perhaps the most important transformation that technologies bring to patron and librarian alike is the vision of library resources as infinite. Just as human memory was assumed to be finite, but has been found to be infinite by A. R. Luria (*The Mind of the Mnemonist*) and other psychologists, so the library is an infinite resource to the creative and noncompetitive inquirer searching in the technological environment. For example, if all the books on bulimia are checked out, CD-ROM databases will quickly identify noncirculating journal articles. They lead the student to other databases, to new ideas, to available resources, and to a new and creative way of approaching the topic that is uniquely the student's and that transforms the mundane topic of bulimia into something important for the student and new for her audience, the teacher.

If, with online technologies, the image of the library is transformed from a limited resource with a finite number of books to a virtually infinite universe of information where data is always available to the searching mind, then cooperation is a more powerful method of inquiry than competition. It does not matter that all the books are charged out; the information is still available in noncirculating journals and magazines identified through CD-ROMs that can be discussed with colleagues, teachers, and librarians.

In the academic library, because our mission has to do with education and learning, we should reject the consumer attitudes toward our technology, and encourage teaching of a specific online source as an example of a type. We should further think about the transformation that technologies have brought to libraries and look for links between our technological transformation and the revolutions that are occurring simultaneously all over the campus. The stories we tell patrons when we teach library technologies should illustrate the underlying ideas behind the technology, or should grow out of our understanding of the transformation that technology has created, for it is this understanding that the patron will remember.

Medical Libraries

Patricia C. Buchan
Medical Librarian
All Children's Hospital, St. Petersburg, Florida
(Formerly MEDLARS Training Coordinator
National Library of Medicine, Bethesda, Maryland)

The computerized counterpart to *Index Medicus*, the primary index for biomedical literature, is MEDLINE. Produced by the National Library of Medicine (NLM) in Bethesda, Maryland, the database contains approximately 2,800 *Index Medicus* titles and about 700 journals from the *Index to Dental Literature* and the *International Nursing Index*. MEDLINE's coverage dates back to 1966 and contains nearly 6 million biomedical citations. MEDLINE is available online from the NLM, for many years its sole vendor, as well as from several commercial database systems and in CD-ROM format from an ever-increasing list of companies.

During the 1970s and early 1980s the primary user of MEDLINE was the medical librarian. The NLM consequently instituted a detailed course to prepare librarians adequately for their roles as searchers in hospitals, medical school libraries, health science centers, pharmaceutical companies, and so on. The first level of training, originally known as the Initial Online Services Training class, is now called "Fundamentals of MEDLARS [Medical Literature Analysis and Retrieval System] Searching." With the development of more sophisticated hardware, software, and telecommunications, the course has been condensed into three days of MEDLINE training and one and a half days of specialized database training. A sequel to this course is "Follow-Up to the Fundamentals of MEDLARS Searching" (formerly the Advanced Online Services Training); it is designed to provide in-depth training on a number of the more than 25 MEDLARS databases.

The hallmarks of both of these training classes are extensive video demonstration of online search interactions and hands-on practice by attendees. After almost every lecture, searchers are able to log into the system via nonbilled codes and try out the techniques most recently discussed. Generally, two trainees share a computer terminal during these sessions. This design enables participants to gain from one another's experience and to be able to explore together possibilities that emerge from their brainstorming. Instructors are constantly available to monitor their progress, assist with telecommunications problems, answer technical questions, and provide strategy suggestions.

Classes are usually no larger than 20 attendees. Class size is important so that the trainer/trainee ratio is manageable. In-class video demonstrations are especially useful as trainees are able to see how the program "should" work. They also allow the trainees to take a more passive role where they can observe the strategies without feeling pressure to produce the same results. A primary benefit is that the instructor can be asked to pause at any time to illustrate or explain a particular point. Online demonstration also provides the flexibility to give on-the-spot troubleshooting tips when real-life problems occur.

In the late 1970s a computer-assisted instructional (CAI) program was developed to complement the classroom training. *MEDLEARN* was designed to give searchers practice at their own computer terminals in their own offices. It covered access procedures, searching some of the key data elements, and practice using MEDLINE's controlled vocabulary, Medical Subject Headings (MeSH). *MEDLEARN* is a mainframe-based tutorial that incurs online charges when used. The entire lesson requires about four to six hours of online time, which are charged at the prevailing system hourly rate. The major benefit of *MEDLEARN* is that it duplicates an actual online search session supplemented by narrative instructional information.

In the past year, *MEDLEARN* has given way to its successor, MEDTUTOR, a software package that can be installed on any IBM or IBM-compatible microcomputer. MEDTUTOR, one of a series of self-instructional tools for selected MEDLARS databases, can be used not only by librarians and information professionals but also by medical and health professionals who want to take advantage of its menu-driven structure to select various aspects of MEDLINE searching.

MEDTUTOR is an example of using today's high-tech products to be able to master other high-tech systems. The program is designed to anticipate the response of the user and give very specific feedback based on that response. When the correct answer is entered, the program reinforces or summarizes the concepts essential to the problem. When an incorrect answer is entered, the program displays diagnostic feedback and prompts the user to try again. The user can also choose to have the correct answer displayed automatically. Anticipated responses were collected over the years based upon observed learning behaviors in the classroom setting.

If the users do not complete their training in one session, MEDTUTOR's tracking mechanism allows them to enter their names in order to resume the program at the point where they last exited. A glossary of technical terms used in the program is accessible by hitting a special function key. Optional Help screens are available at numerous points throughout to give user assistance in structuring search statements. Summaries are also programmed into each chapter to give bottom-line information about that topic. As MEDTUTOR has just been released, its possibilities have yet to be explored for all the types of training needs it can serve. Similar microcomputer CAI programs are available for NLM's CHEMLINE and TOXLINE databases.

User-friendly programs are another development of the 1980s for learning the intricacies of online systems. Every vendor of MEDLINE has developed its own version of menu-driven search software, and the NLM is no exception. GRATEFUL MED was originally introduced for IBM personal computer users in 1986. In August 1989 a version became available for Macintosh owners. Both versions provide an alternative to direct command-language searching and are especially intended for use by health professionals and other end users.

GRATEFUL MED operates in four basic steps: (1) it provides an Input Form screen where it assists in constructing one search at a time; (2) its built-in telecommunications calls the NLM computer and automatically logs in; (3) the search is executed by translating information entered on the Input Form screen to the command language known to the MEDLARS computer; and (4) the results of the search are displayed and downloaded simultaneously and, if requested, can be printed out immediately. Perhaps the best "teaching" function of GRATEFUL MED occurs when the user is reviewing the results of the search. An opportunity to indicate if the article retrieved was relevant to the topic searched is displayed after each reference. Upon reviewing the entire set of retrieval, GRATEFUL MED suggests *MeSH* headings that can be used if the search is rerun, based upon the articles that were deemed relevant. These suggested *MeSH* headings provide a basic level of initiating the new user into the complexities of *MeSH's* controlled vocabulary and make way for future searches to take advantage of that understanding. In addition, by observing the search strategy and the online interaction, the user can assimilate information about the way to construct similar searches.

In January 1987 another type of new technology was used to introduce online searching to a new audience. A live video teleconference was broadcast by the Hospital Satellite Network to 22 Veterans' Administration medical centers, where over 600 physicians in the Midwest and West were gathered to hear about GRATEFUL MED. A panel of four NLM training staff members presented video demonstrations of how GRATEFUL MED works, provided access information, and answered phone-in questions from the audience. Although this was a costly venture and no real "skills" were taught, it was a novel way to reach so many physicians and administrators at one time and to make them aware of existing technology.

The final technology to be discussed, CD-ROM, is used for database searching and teaching. One such product is CD-Plus, by the company of the same name (formerly Online Research Systems). This system offers great flexibility in searching in that it allows the use of natural language in constructing searches and then maps to MeSH headings. It comes with an easy-to-use tutorial and numerous online help screens. CD-Plus permits a novice to use MEDLINE in the menu mode with little problem and also provides a "professional" command level of searching for those familiar with the MEDLINE structure. Cost is a determining factor, as libraries may save thousands of dollars yearly by using CD-ROM products versus online search time, depending on the volume of searching.

Many companies are currently competing to build the most powerful, most sophisticated, yet easiest-to-use system. The librarian can only stand to gain from this competitive market, where every vendor is trying to win over clients by developing the perfect system with the most capabilities at the most cost-effective rates. The downside? With any luck, the system of choice at your institution won't become obsolete too quickly!

Information Technology Learning and Business

Paul P. Philbin
Business Reference Librarian, Bailey/Howe Library, University of Vermont
Burlington, Vermont

An electronic storm is upon us. It is raining information technology, and libraries are opening the flood gates. Computerized information retrieval, long the province of librarians, is seeping into the populace in the form of end-user systems. The flow has reached nearly every discipline, and business is no exception.

End-user information systems for the business student and professional are numerous, perhaps surpassing other disciplines in their number and sophistication. Some systems are available online, others on CD-ROM, and still others on floppy disk. But before looking at these systems and their potential for learning, an understanding of the typical business student and professional is required.

PROFILE OF A BUSINESS USER

The mythical profile of the business person, an individual on a treadmill, going nowhere fast, always needing something yesterday, is exactly that – a myth. There are business people who are breathlessly demanding, abrasive, and impatient, but these traits certainly do not describe the typical business person. Business people have no monopoly on these personality traits. The business world is, however, a competitive environment in which computers and information play significant roles. And, says William G. McGowan, Chairman of MCI Communications, "individuals who possess both business and information technology skills could become invaluable to their companies, and highly prized candidates in the job market" (Wurman, 296).

Today's business person is computer literate. She has a knowledge of programming languages and spreadsheet and database management concepts. The education of future business people reflects this situation, since a typical business student is required to purchase a microcomputer for course use. Many business schools also support management information systems (MIS) laboratories.   The business person is also results oriented. Business students and professionals using an information retrieval system want more than just a reference to a result. They want to retrieve the result per se, be it an article, annual report, beta value, market share, or stock quote.

The type of database a business person needs to consult can be radically different from what the average library user requires. This means going beyond bibliographic systems. Their need for and reliance on numeric data is strong, and libraries have been slow in acquiring and providing access to numeric databases.

Business students are frequent users of libraries, and librarians at academic and public library reference desks can substantiate their presence. Gerald Gill, business reference librarian at James Madison University's Carrier Library, estimates that 60 percent of reference questions are business related (Gill, 173). At the University of Vermont, business majors and MBA students are second only to education students when it comes to using end-user systems (Crane). This suggests that business students are frequent users of academic libraries. Can the same be said of the business professional? Yes, but with a qualification.

There are two methods business professionals use to acquire information: one is through "personal" sources, the other is through "impersonal" ones. Personal sources imply direct contact with people such as customers, competitors, colleagues, peers, librarians, and faculty for information. Impersonal sources pertain to printed documents such as trade and industry publications, research and investment reports, and output from internal and external databases. Internal databases refer to a company's in-house computerized information system, whereas external ones are those available through dial-up services such as DIALOG and BRS.

The small business person is a good example of a user relying on personal information sources. This person uses such sources to obtain immediate feedback, thus minimizing the risk of misinterpretation, which can occur from summarized printed sources. Small business persons can be characterized as those who "tend to trust their own judgement and centralize" (Hammers, 29). Therefore, self-employed and entrepreneurial types are less likely to use a library's impersonal printed sources because when they do they are not likely to receive the immediate gratification that personal sources provide.

On the other hand, the business person employed in a large company tends to rely more on impersonal sources (Hammers, 29). In general, this type of individual is more likely to use a library and is probably more comfortable in a library environment where the emphasis is on impersonal sources of information. There is no doubt that the business student and professional need information to complete a case study or implement a strategic plan. But they need more than just information, they need the "right" information to maintain a competitive edge. Richard Wurman, author of *Information Anxiety*, writes, "Who among us can argue with Daniel Bell, John Kenneth Galbraith, Bertrand de Jouvenel, and others who have defined our 'post-technological' period as one in which only those who have the right information, the strategic knowledge, and the handy facts can 'make it' in the last quarter of this century?" (Wurman, 205). Robert Waterman, author of *In Search of Excellence*, stresses that "information is the differential" (Wurman, 298) when planning and executing business strategies. The future business professional can obtain the "information differential" by using the information technology available today in most academic libraries.

INFORMATION SYSTEMS

Business libraries, business schools, and companies are subscribing to numerous business-related end-user information retrieval systems that can provide access to both bibliographic and numeric data. The first generation of these systems introduced the menu-driven dial-up services such as DIALOG Knowledge Index and BRS/After Dark, which targeted business and home microcomputer owners.

Next came DIALOG's Business Connection (DBC) and Dow Jones News Retrieval Service (DJNRS). DBC's approach to data presentation is noteworthy. It features a menu-driven interface with the focus on data rather than database (O'Leary). A typical search on DBC begins when a searcher selects a type of data needed (for example, share of market data) rather than first specifying a database, a trademark of most bibliographic information retrieval systems. Both DBC and DJNRS also provide the searcher with the results they need rather than a reference to a document – the kind of raw data that can be downloaded for later analysis.

For Dow Jones, software is available to collect data for postprocessing purposes. Titles of such software include *Dow Jones Spreadsheet Link* and *Market Analyzer PLUS*. *Spreadsheet Link* is compatible with *Lotus 1-2-3*, *Visicalc*, or *Multiplan* spreadsheet software.

Optical disc products are the relative newcomers to the business information retrieval arena. One of the first optical business information systems was *Lotus One Source*, available from Lotus Development Corporation. *One Source* is a collection of six business and financial databases providing access to text and numerical data. There are several other optical business information products available, including those published by Standard and Poor's and Moody's and the standard bibliographic indexes such as *ABI/INFORM* and *Business Periodicals Index*.

Floppy disk-based systems also exist. A good example is *Business Week's TOP 1000*, a financial tool to help make investment decisions. It provides search and sort capabilities, and data can be converted to Lotus or ASCII formats.

One of the most appealing features of these systems is the currency of information. The Dow Jones News Retrieval Service, for the most part, is updated daily. This is a tremendously important factor in a world that places a premium on acquiring information about late-breaking international economic and political developments. Another noteworthy feature is the "one-stop" approach to information access. Dow Jones, Lotus One Source, and DIALOG's Business Connection are good examples of systems bringing together information from different providers through one workstation. Each of the systems mentioned above offers a mixture of command and menu-driven search modes, and online help and adequate documentation are also available.

LEARNING

Most of the teaching techniques discussed elsewhere in this book have been used successfully at the University of Vermont and elsewhere with business students and will not be discussed here. What will be covered are approaches to attract business students to the library to expose them to information technology and maintain acquired information retrieval skills.

Earlier I mentioned the use of personal sources as a method of information acquisition by the business person. In my mind, the business librarian needs to become a "personal information technology source" to the business faculty and students. The librarian, as an authority on information access, must be prepared to demonstrate how various systems can meet research and instructional needs. The important step in all of this is becoming a "personal" source, which is crucial at institutions where there is no separate business school library. This is achieved by meeting with faculty members by attending their department meetings, and by forging a relationship with students by connecting with business student associations (most institutions of higher education with MBA programs have an MBA student association). In so doing, the librarian develops a forum in which to show the clientele how information technology can fit into course work.

Business faculty members and students are not so much interested in how an information system works as they are in the validity of data retrieved from it. To impart this type of knowledge to the business user, the librarian should be familiar with such guides as *The Dow Jones-Irwin Banker's Guide to Online Databases*, *The Dow Jones-Irwin Investor's Guide to Online Databases*, and *Inc. Magazine's Databasics*. Each of these publications will assist the librarian in formulating answers to users' questions and suggest some concrete applications. They also attend to the issue of information reliability. Reading Marydee Ojala's regular business column, "The Dollar $ign," in *Database* and *Online* magazines is also an excellent way to increase knowledge of business information technology and obtain ideas and strategies to market information retrieval systems to the business student and faculty.

In marketing information technology to business students and faculty, the librarian should focus on system features that appeal to them. Go back to the business user profile and information systems sections discussed earlier and you'll have the makings of a marketing plan. If it's results they need, show them the kinds of data that can be retrieved and highlight the potential of downloading data along with the different formats in which data can be converted. The saving of financial data for later manipulation with spreadsheet software has been reported to be popular among business students at the Wharton School, University of Pennsylvania (Halperin, 16). In short, know your users and give them what they need. Experience has shown that business students have a JIT, or "just in time,"[1] attitude toward information technology instruction – give me what I need now, nothing more, nothing less. Exploit this kind of thinking by approaching the economics faculty and showing them how *ECON/STATS I*[2] can be used to retrieve Consumer/Producer Price Index data for inflation analysis. This should be enough to get a faculty member to include an information technology component into her course.

Including an information retrieval component as part of a course and offering systems that students feel they can "jump on" to retrieve information have no substitutes in attracting business students to information technology. Business students tell us that they learn more effectively from actual hands-on experience than from demonstration and lecture (Garman and Pask, 164). In addition, having a librarian in the "personal" information network of business faculty and students and being available for point-of-service instruction are elements of an environment conducive to information technology learning in business libraries.

Notes

1. JIT is "a production control technique involving synchronized assembly operations, whereby raw materials and component parts arrive as needed (or just-in-time) for production and assembly" (Shaw and Jack Weber). "The basic business vocabulary." *Across the Board* 26, no. 12 (December 1989): 15-16.

2. ECON/STATS I, a CD-ROM product for economists and marketers available from Hopkins Technology, contains unabridged data from eight U.S. government databases. Exported files from ECON/STATS I are input compatible with most spreadsheet and database software.

Works Cited

Crane, Nancy. "Automated Reference Center (ARC) User Survey." Unpublished survey results, University of Vermont, Bailey/Howe Library, Reference Department, 1989.

Garman, Nancy J., and Judith M. Pask. "End User Searching in Business and Management." In *National Online Meeting Proceedings 1985*. Medord, N.J.: Learned Information, 1985.

Gill, Gerald. "Business Reference: Reaching Out for the BRASS Ring." *RQ* 27, no. 2 (Winter 1987): 171-74.

Halperin, Michale. "Company and Industry Information: Online and Ondisk." *Business Information Review* 4, no. 1 (July 1987): 12-17.

Hammers, Pamela Specht. "Information Sources Used for Strategic Planning Decisions in Small Firms." *American Journal of Small Business* 11, no. 4 (Spring 1987): 21-34.

O'Leary, Mick. "DIALOG Business Connection: DIALOG for the End-user." *Online* 10, no. 5 (September 1986): 15-24.

Shaw, Gary, and Jack Weber. "The Basic Business Vocabulary." *Across the Board* 26, no. 12 (December 1989): 15-16.

Wurman, Richard Saul. *Information Anxiety*. New York: Doubleday, 1989.

10

Future Teaching Technologies

Mara R. Saule

When a patron enters the library in 5, 10, or 20 years to find answers to a question, what will she see? Perhaps there will be a kiosk offering an interactive videodisc program to orient her to library collections and services. After approaching the kiosk, the patron will discuss her information need or problem verbally with the kiosk; the videodisc program will intuitively assess the nature of her information need and, using a range of different media from animation to live-action video and sound, will show her how to find what she needs. Maybe the kiosk will emit a life-sized, three-dimensional holographic image of a librarian who will guide her to pertinent information sources. Or, after identifying her information need, the holograph may provide the information to the user directly, downloading text, numeric data, and pictures into the personal computer in her backpack. More likely, the patron won't physically come to the library at all. She will access library collections and other kinds of information from her home and incorporate that information into her personal knowledge base.

It is always interesting yet dangerous to predict the future; crystal balls are notorious for having small but significant cracks. Predicting the future of technological developments is especially risky: promising prototype projects are often unsuccessful in practice; economic and market influences are unpredictable; new development can take surprising turns. What we *can* follow, however, are current trends in new educational and information technologies and their applications in libraries. By following current trends and making future extrapolations from them, librarians can play a strong, proactive role in the directions that instructional technology will take. We can be better poised to serve as advocates for our users' needs, openly welcoming new developments rather than simply reacting to them.

TRENDS IN NEW TECHNOLOGY DEVELOPMENT

We can trace developments not only in new technologies themselves but also in the ways they are combined and presented to the user.

Focus on the User

As new instructional and information technologies evolve, users of these systems, whether they are librarians or others seeking information, will play a greater role in new technology development and use. Information providers, vendors, system software developers and programmers, librarians, educators, and information users will work together to create software and applications for new technologies – software and applications that address individual user-group characteristics and needs. In the development process, the focus will be increasingly on the user of a new system.

Many technologies themselves, such as the hypertext stacks and expert system shells discussed in chapter 8, put the design of the program directly in the user's hands without the need for intermediary special programmers. Future development will continue this trend to give users more control over what a system does and how it is applied to an individual's needs. Karen Frenkel draws an analogy between interactive technology and avant-garde theater: "For centuries, stories have been told linearly. Tales would vary slightly with each retelling, but the story-teller alone determined what listeners heard. Now, audiences of all kinds are beginning to have a say in the matter. The distinctions between playwright and theatergoer, and more recently between producer and television audience, are blurring a little" (Frenkel, 872). Similarly, the lines between database producer, software developer, and database searcher are also blurring.

Users will also be able to communicate with each other more easily through innovative communications links such as electronic mail, electronic bulletin boards, and teleconferencing systems. Librarians are already sharing ideas and approaches to integrating technology into their libraries through networks such as BITNET, INTERNET, and ALANET. A National Research and Education Network (NREN) has been proposed in the U.S. Congress as an outgrowth of the National Science Foundation's NSFNET. If implemented, NREN would link data and research bases with researchers, educators, and users nationwide and internationally. The unprecedented speed of NREN "could move 100,000 typed pages or 1,000 satellite photos every second" (Cisler, 1). In the future, sharing information with other computer system users will become even more important. In addition, the technology will allow not only for transmitting text and data across telecommunications lines, but also graphics, still photos, and even motion video. By taking full advantage of communications technologies, users of electronic information systems will be able to initiate and support more cooperative projects as well as set the agenda for new technology development.

Interactivity

Not only will those involved in system development and system use interact on a more basic level, but the systems themselves will display a higher level of interactivity. In order for instructional programs to be successful, the learner must be engaged in the learning process. She must feel that the educational process has direct relevance to her information needs. Interactive technologies, such as interactive videodisc, CD-I (computer disk interactive), and DV-I (digital videodisc interactive), let the learner progress at her own pace, focusing on the skills she, as an individual searcher, most needs. She can choose how to progress through the interactive program, depending on her level of knowledge and skill at the time of the training session. The use of interactive step-by-step sequences can simulate the research or database-searching process, allowing the learner to be guided through realistic situations that will maximize her overall understanding of system concepts and procedures.

Multimedia Integration

The popularity of a multimedia approach to entertainment can be easily seen by walking through any shopping mall or by chatting with most adolescents: today's video games employ graphics, animation, and sound to attract players to interactive competition in game parlors and homes. New technologies for education and information delivery use the same multimedia approach to enhance learning via microcomputer. "Now, the PC [personal computer] is receiving a major transfusion of video technology. That should lead to a dazzling new hybrid that can display sharp, moving color images on the same screen with spreadsheets and text. Add to that high-fidelity sound and some imaginative software, and the PC may become a 'multimedia' tool that – once again – could change the way people work, learn, and play" (Shao and Brandt, 152).

One of the earliest multimedia interactive technologies that has been used for entertainment, information storage, and training is the interactive laser videodisc, or analog videodisc. Available since the 1970s, videodiscs offer varying degrees of interactivity and incorporate text, audio, video and graphics, depending on the application; because videodisc is an analog technology, it cannot support digital information, such as computer programs. Since it can be used alone or with a microcomputer and because its video capabilities offer a great sense of reality, videodiscs have been extremely popular in business and industry training applications. In fact, 58 percent of the videodisc market is for training uses such as driving simulations and military training (Mascioni, 184). Videodiscs can be controlled by touch screens, traditional keyboards, or by hypertext programs to enhance access to the videodisc sequences.

The two most promising multimedia interactive technologies are CD-I and DV-I. Both are based on the same optical technology as CD-ROM, which can store great amounts of data and text but has limited multimedia capabilities. CD-I, and DV-I in particular, can offer the full range of media: audio, text, graphics, video, animation, still photography. CD-I is less expensive to master and reproduce than DV-I, although DV-I can offer full-motion video, unlike CD-I. Both technologies are directed to the large consumer audience, rather than just to the library or information market.

The same technologies that are giving more power to the user and that are becoming more interactive are also employing a variety of media to support educational applications. Graphics, audio, animation, full-motion video, still photography, and text can all work together for a more effective educational experience. In fact, current market discussions about the future success of new interactive technologies focus on the mix of media that those technologies can support: because DV-I can support full-motion video, it is predicted to become predominant in the entertainment and information markets. More importantly, technologies that offer a range of media give librarians and other educators exciting opportunities to design instructional systems that can attract users, command their attention, and provide solid, dynamic instruction.

Diverse Information Formats

Not only will the media employed by new interactive technologies become increasingly diverse, but the kinds of information conveyed via these and other information technologies will cover a wider range of formats. We are now seeing the emergence of nonbibliographic databases, such as full-text databases and numeric files, as important new factors in information storage and retrieval. Libraries are making available to users nonbibliographic databases along with the traditional indexing and abstracting systems. Prototype projects at the Library of Congress, the National Agricultural Library, and the National Gallery are using innovative technologies to store sound recordings, photographic images, illustrations, and paintings. We can predict that in the near future these media will also become commonly available and accessible through microcomputers and mainframes.

With the increasingly broad definition of the terms *information* and *database* to include visual and audio formats, the instructional challenge for librarians becomes greater. Choosing the appropriate database for a searcher's query and then formulating a workable search strategy that will answer the question is not now an easy matter; when those databases include other media, finding the best answers to a question is more complicated. We can, however, look again to technology to help solve the problems of database selection, search strategy formulation, and the searching process.

Artificial Intelligence

Artificial intelligence, expert systems, and natural language processing will continue to be important forces in the development of user interfaces that are not dependent on knowledge of how a particular system operates. System users will no longer need to be concerned with search strategy formulation or with database selection; the systems themselves will be able to interpret a search statement from the user's natural language patterns and then choose the most appropriate database and format of information. "The ultimate transparent system would enable a user to interact with all retrieval systems as if they were a single system and to engage in a cooperative dialogue with the system in unrestricted natural language" (Warner, 17). Much recent research has centered on the development of standardized "intelligent" front ends to library systems that access a variety of databases using different search software. These front-end interfaces interpret a user's search request, direct the query to the appropriate database, and translate the request into the appropriate search system syntax. With more and different kinds of databases being added to and accessed by library systems, the development of consistent front ends to the systems will become increasingly important.

As Craig Robertson discusses in chapter 8, expert systems, artificial intelligence, and hypertext are all being used to make the user interface more facile. And, with the use of microcomputer input technologies such as touch screens, voice response systems, and point-and-click mice, the user doesn't even need to know how to type (or spell) in order to retrieve the needed information from a system.

Linking Information

Libraries are currently expanding their collections by linking to other libraries' catalogs through telecommunications networks such as INTERNET and other local and regional systems. Of course, access to remote databases such as those offered by DIALOG and BRS has been available since the early 1970s; however, now we are broadening our definition of access. As individual library acquisitions budgets dwindle, and costs of journals and other publications increase, libraries are finding that the way to maintain a satisfactory level of support to library users is to go beyond the library walls for access to information and collections. Librarians are finding that their roles are expanding to include facilitating the use of collections in many libraries, not just their own.

Lawrence E. Murr and James B. Williams take out their crystal ball to look at the future importance of linking people and knowledge: "The library of the future will be much more than a conglomerate of hard copy collections. It will be a dynamic, multimedia switching point–node–in a regional and national information network. It will store information and knowledge bases, and will provide processes through which to retrieve, use, and extend that information and knowledge. It will be a center for electronically managed information, knowledge, and publishing support activities" (Murr and Williams, 19). In order to facilitate these information and knowledge base networks, telecommunications will become increasingly important; in fact, "telecommunications sophistication will, more than any other single element, make or break the prototypical library of the future" (Murr and Williams, 19).

The technologies used to create the interlinked libraries of the future–satellite, cable, and fiber optics communications–are no longer, then, the domain of television and telephone companies alone. In linking information, libraries and the institutions and users that they serve become closely involved with telecommunications technologies and the access issues prompted by linking systems.

In most cases, users will no longer need to come into the library to access information from a variety of sources, including collections of other local, regional, and national libraries. "'Library,' as a place, will give way to 'library' as a transparent knowledge network providing 'intelligent' services to business and education through both specialized librarians and emerging information technologies" (Murr and Williams, 7). As a consequence of the library becoming a "transparent knowledge network," the approaches to instruction that we take with remote users of diverse information sources must differ by necessity from approaches used with in-library searchers. The remote user base itself is more diverse and its anonymity creates difficulties in assessing user needs and searching skill levels.

Personalized Information

At the same time that libraries are "looking out," expanding their grasp beyond library walls to access remote databases and collections, the information user is "looking in," drawing the information that she finds from diverse sources into her microcomputer's personal information base. The concept of the "scholar's workstation" has received some attention in recent years; until recently, however, the technological links and computer storage media have not been available. A true scholar's workstation is a microcomputer-based personal information system, connected via telecommunications networks to remote information sources, that integrates a range of information, using high-density storage media, to be manipulated for the user's own applications.

Several emerging information technologies are facilitating the creation of a true scholar's workstation. Digital transmission systems and telecommunications links are now being established internationally to make scholarly communication and the transmission of text and data possible. Interactive optical technologies that can store large amounts of multimedia information are being designed for use with a personal computer, such as the CD-ROM discs used with the next microcomputer. Furthermore, microcomputer software such as hypertext and fourth-generation database management programs can facilitate access to personal information systems in a dynamic and creative manner.

Personal information systems that access and integrate a variety of information and media, often using hypertext programs to access the information, are already being used by physicians and researchers in medical schools. It is the goal of the National Library of Medicine's Integrated Academic Information Management Systems (IAIMS) project to make information stations that integrate research, clinical, patient care, and management information available to medical researchers and personnel throughout the country.

It is not just the scholar or the professional who will have such personalized information systems. As the cost of sophisticated microcomputer technologies and peripheral devices goes down, computer users at all levels will have systems that integrate a variety of information sources and media. These users will not be library users in the traditional sense, but will be accessing information that may have been historically available only in libraries. Librarians, then, need to redefine their roles in terms of these remote and independent users.

Document and Information Delivery

The ability to find references to books, journal articles, and other types of information engenders the desire to find the actual books, articles, and information themselves. Availability and access to information then become a major concern of librarians, users, and information providers alike. The traditional methods of document and information delivery—interlibrary loans and photocopies sent via mail systems—are slow and cumbersome processes.

Users are demanding quicker means of getting the actual information they need. Telefacsimile transmission of documents and information is already a commonly used mechanism for fast document delivery, although it still has some format limitations. Future developments in the smooth and accurate transmission of text, data, graphics, and photos will enhance the usefulness of telefacsimile. We can also look forward the transmission of other media, such as video and animation, as new telecommunications technologies emerge.

Users will be able to order documents directly, using telefacsimile and computerized ordering systems and networks, without librarian or other intermediaries. Again, the user may not need to come into the library, or any document repository, in order to find identified items. Database selection, the interpretation of retrieved data or citations, and the evaluation of the usefulness of what was retrieved or cited are on the user's shoulders. And, again, the librarian must think about his role, his obligation to this invisible user.

Publishing and Storage Media

Another way to make documents available to a great number of users is to develop high-density information storage media that can be quickly and cost-effectively reproduced for large-scale dissemination. The Library of Congress and other U.S. national libraries are working on storing collections on videodisc as a means of dissemination and preservation. At this point, the market for these prototype videodisc collections is the library; however, optical media such as CD-ROM, CD-I, and DV-I are being used to store information for the general consumer. We can foresee that more dense storage technologies for full-text and other information will be developed for the consumer, largely with impetus from the publishing world. If the consumer can be encouraged to buy and own information directly, dangers of copyright infringement through telefacsimile transmission of documents will be avoided.

Like the Library of Congress, smaller local and regional libraries will also become involved in their own publishing of in-house collections. Greater access to individual library-owned materials, such as manuscripts, letters, state documents, locally constructed indexes and union lists, is made possible by in-house CD-ROM and videodisc mastering. Through the telecommunications systems discussed earlier, remote users will also be able to access these collections.

Independently from the library, some research centers and universities are beginning prototype text digitizing projects through which literary and historical texts, including illustrations and other graphic material, are being stored and made available in a digitized format. In this way, the texts will not only be preserved but also be made available widely to scholars and students. We can expect this movement to preserve and disseminate primary texts to continue and to be driven by scholars outside national or regional libraries. The onus, then, is on librarians to monitor text-digitizing projects and to determine whether they should become involved in their creation.

A Confluence of Technologies

The result of recent trends in new technology development is that, for the user, the lines distinguishing publishing and information technologies will be blurred. From the user's home personal computer, she will not know that, when she dials into the campus computer, the census information she wants is on CD-ROM and the library's catalog is on a mainframe; she may not even know that the way she is entering a request on her PC is being interpreted for her by artificial intelligence programs and directed to individual, separate information sources. In learning how to use information systems, either in the library or from without library walls, the user will also see a mix of instructional technologies: computer-aided instruction (CAI) using a variety of interactive media, videotape and videodisc, artificial intelligence and expert systems, online help and tutorials will all work together to orient the library user to the world of information storage and retrieval.

The lines between instructional technologies are already blurring. CAI includes aspects of hypertext and expert systems; help screens and online tutorials also look forward to artificial intelligence developments to smooth the user interface; the videotaping process can use computer technologies, its natural extension being interactive videodisc. The librarian looking at instructional technologies for use in her library must be aware of the range of technologies and of their natural overlap.

EDUCATIONAL IMPLICATIONS OF NEW TECHNOLOGIES

Who Are Library Users Now?

The nature of the library user is transforming from an in-house patron looking for answers in printed sources to a remote information user looking for answers in a variety of computerized sources offered directly to her by a wide range of information providers, including libraries. Of course, some information seekers still come to the library, in person, to find answers; however, the sources that they use may employ many different information media. In order to teach both remote and in-house library and information users how to ask questions and find answers on their own, librarians must define for themselves who their users are and what the characteristics and needs of the users might be.

Central to developing effective teaching methods is a clear and defined understanding of the learner. Teachers need to be able to identify the student's educational needs and to predict how a student will react to a particular instructional approach. Individual learning styles also need to be understood and to be taken into account when we design applications for new technologies. As we develop interactive technologies for teaching research strategies and skills, we must be able to identify the information needs of searchers and to predict their reactions to each step of an interactive learning encounter. Furthermore, "interactive systems will generally be successful only if the human-computer interface is carefully developed according to principles of graphic design and cognitive psychology, and is thoroughly tested. If cognitive concerns are to be emphasized, an understanding of users and their needs is essential" (Fox, 796). Especially if we are concerned about teaching the concepts behind information retrieval systems rather than just mechanical searching skills, as discussed in chapter 1, then we must understand the cognitive processes of our user groups.

In thinking about the user groups we serve, we must also think about how far our teaching or helping commitment extends. For example, do we spend extensive development time producing a CAI diskette to give to remote users of library systems if we don't know who these users really are? Is our instructional focus, on the other hand, to be on the in-house user? If so, will instruction be limited to institutional affiliates or will we give anyone coming into the library an opportunity to be formally trained in computer system use? Given that users come to systems with different levels of expertise, how do we address different levels of users (such as, novices or experts) through instructional technologies? The answers to these questions will vary from library to library, depending on existing access policies, staffing, and computer systems available.

What Do They Expect and What Do We Want?

What we teach to library users will depend on how we define our user population. Different user populations will demand different forms and levels of instruction. We can teach more to the in-house user, especially the frequent library user; we see the user, can gauge her reactions to instructional approaches, and adjust our teaching programs accordingly. What we teach to remote users will be dependent upon what systems those users will be searching: it may be more difficult to teach remote users concepts and models because we have no control over the pace and success of the instructional program.

Because of the speed and attraction of interactive technologies, all users will be impatient to learn new systems. Furthermore, user expectations of computer search training may drive some of our instructional approaches. If some users will stand only for "quick and dirty" instruction for "quick and dirty" searches, then we must re-examine our instructional goals. Nonetheless, we can look forward to using interactive teaching technologies to provide more knowledge and information about the research process to a greater user base than was previously possible. Albert L. Lorenzo and Kul B. Gauri observe that technology is changing the kind of knowledge we can pass along to learners: "A new mode of education, called the 'industrialization of education' is emerging. Learning on demand by all age groups, without any restriction on place or time, is likely to become the dominant mode of learning in the future. We have always spoken of life-long learning, flexibility in delivering education, and a system that is open-ended. The new technology holds those promises" (Lorenzo and Gauri, 56-57). While "learning on demand" and "life-long learning" may seem to be contradictory, librarians can teach information system users what they need to know in order to search a particular system while, at the same time, imparting to them the knowledge they will need for information literacy. To do this, we need to clearly define our roles as teachers of information-seeking skills.

IMPLICATIONS FOR LIBRARIANS

Who Are We?

With the drive for more user control over system design and applications, librarians must also develop a clear sense of ourselves, of who we are. Can we still fit the traditional model of a librarian facilitating patron use of library collections? If our role has expanded, what direction should librarianship take in view of changing information media and technologies? What is our role in information or computer literacy? What, exactly, are our instructional obligations and mandates in the information age?

The formal instructional role of librarians is being challenged by the very technologies we attempt to teach. The growth of interactive information media will cause us to re-examine how we can help to direct the development of educational technologies. Hugh Gibbons, a columnist for the journal *Computer*, feels that "the educators of the Information Age will be the software designers, the system integrators, and the users of tools, not professional educators. The new educators must see the tools and systems they create as a form of communication with others, as part of an interaction with users who are trying to understand and expand their capacities" (Gibbons, 66). It can be argued, however, that the role of professional educators, such as instruction librarians, is exactly to help users "understand and expand their capacities," especially in the face of the many and diverse new information technologies. In addition to our traditional roles as bibliographers and reference librarians, we will also need to look to other models of information providers to help define our new position.

Consultant, Agent, and Advocate

When we picture exactly how a library patron, or a remote information user, might need to use information technology to find answers, our role with the information seeker becomes more like a consultant to a client than a librarian to a patron. The information seeker needs guidance, she needs help formulating her question and search strategy and, to a lesser extent, she needs help with individual system protocols. The librarian is called upon in an extended advisory role to help analyze the information need, find the best source to fill the need, and give basic support in the mechanics of searching the source. The focus of the librarian-client interaction is the whole information-seeking process rather than the simple question and its answer.

Another model for the new role of the librarian is that of an information agent: "the word *agency* may suffice to describe the future role of librarians and libraries. Growing out of work in artificial intelligence is the concept of a facilitating partner, an agent, that guides the user through complex information gathering and decision making. The librarian will have to become an agent who helps increasingly sophisticated knowledge workers accomplish more complex tasks" (Murr and Williams, 17). In other words, the librarian will "carry" information from the information provider or database vendor to the user, explaining to the user how the information is constructed and how it could be used. The librarian-agent will personalize information and provide knowledge in the context of the recipient's interests and needs.

Another important function that the librarian can play in the face of rapidly emerging new technologies is as an advocate for users' needs to database vendors and software designers. Because of our training and experience in information management and retrieval, librarians are poised to be instrumental in the development of new information and instructional technologies. We can assess our users' needs and advocate for them in the marketplace. We can also work with database producers and vendors to create better products, products that address user needs as well as fill a market niche.

The most important role for librarians remains, however, as teacher, educator, and guide. In the face of emerging new interactive multimedia technologies, our focus is still to show and educate, to teach and encourage.

When looking at other models, it is important to remember that, while information technology may demand new instructional approaches and a re-examination of our instructional goals, we are still concerned with instructing people in how to find answers to questions.

MANAGEMENT IMPLICATIONS

Library instruction is part of the larger complex of library departments and functions. As information technologies develop and instructional approaches for those technologies change, the management structure of the library or library system will need to adapt accordingly. As patrons gain access to more local and remote library collections, and as patrons come to expect fast and direct information retrieval, library organizational structures will need to respond to these expectations quickly and directly. The organization and management of collection development, interlibrary loan, circulation, reference, and systems functions will need to respond to the new needs created by the expansion of the online catalog and other information retrieval systems (Lipow, 865).

The role of strategic and long-range planning is especially important as the roles of libraries and librarians are being redefined. The library's instructional mission must be viewed as essential to the survival of the library and its supporting functions, especially in terms of planning for new technologies that will be used in and out of the library itself. "A refusal to plan for the long haul, however, both dooms libraries to a permanently reactive posture and enhances vendors' ability to manipulate the information environment" (Shill, 438).

As part of the planning process, libraries must also look at a variety of environmental and societal factors that will affect how a library integrates electronic information sources and how it plans for instruction in the use of those sources. Trends such as an aging population, home and school environments that focus on microcomputer competencies, a reduction of federal support for education and libraries, and changes in scholarly communication patterns all affect how searchers will approach information technologies in libraries (Shill, 439-45). Instruction programs will need to take these trends into account.

The library is quickly becoming no longer a library–or, at least, not *only* a library. Interactive multimedia information technologies are changing the way people view personal entertainment and information. Information sources are not found only in libraries; questions are answered through a variety of mixed media sources. When computers first became commonplace, the standard analogy for the computer revolution was to the invention of movable type for the dissemination of previously handwritten texts and the great impact that the printing press has had on the progress of civilization. As Lorenzo and Gauri point out, "unlike these earlier technologies that extended human physical prowess [such as the invention of printing and the steam engine], the new information technology is an extension of the mind. While books and other recorded materials are forms of external memories, the new technology, which can combine audio, video, and data, and can process and transmit information, is an extension of the thinking power of the human brain" (Lorenzo and Gauri, 56).

Although the library may be changing, the librarian's instructional role is no less important. In fact, the very technologies that we use for information retrieval can also be used to teach information retrieval. Librarians are poised to use new technologies to extend the "thinking power of the human brain" in new and dynamic ways. Using different instructional technologies, such as videotape, CAI, expert systems and artificial intelligence, will keep our users in step with the changing face of information retrieval as well as keep our profession alive and challenging.

Works Cited

Cisler, Steve. "NREN: The National Research and Education Network." *LITA Newsletter* 11, no. 2 (Spring 1990): 1-3.

Desmarais, Norman. "CD-I vs. DVI." *CD-ROM Librarian*, March 1989, 24-28.

Fox, Edward A. "The Coming Revolution in Interactive Digital Video." *Communications of the ACM* 32, no. 7 (July 1989): 794-99.

Frenkel, Karen A. "The Next Generation of Interactive Technologies." *Communications of the ACM* 32, no. 7 (July 1989): 872-81.

"The Future of Reference II." Special section. *College and Research Libraries News* 50, no. 9 (October 1989): 780-99.

Gibbons, Hugh. "Computing as Conversation." *Computer* 21, no. 8 (August 1988): 64-66.

Lipow, Anne Grodzins. "The Online Catalog: Exceeding Our Grasp." *American Libraries* 20, no. 9 (October 1989): 862-65.

Lorenzo, Albert L., and Kul B. Gauri. "Educational Implications of Technological Innovations: A Perspective." *Library Hi-Tech* 6, no. 1 (1988): 55-59.

Mascioni, Michael. "Optical Media in Training." *Optical Information Systems*, July/August 1988, 184-89.

Murr, Lawrence E., and James B. Williams. "The Roles of the Future Library." *Library Hi-Tech* 5, no. 3 (Fall 1987): 7-23.

Ripley, G. David. "DVI: A Digital Multimedia Technology." *Communications of the ACM* 32, no. 7 (July 1989): 811-23.

Shao, Maria, and Richard Brandt. "It's a PC, It's a TV – It's Multimedia." *Business Week* October 9, 1989, 152-66.

Shill, Howard B. "Bibliographic Instruction: Planning for the Electronic Information Environment." *College and Research Libraries* 48, no. 5 (September 1987): 433-53.

Warner, Amy J. "Artificial Intelligence and the User Interface." *Bulletin of the American Society for Information Science* 15, no. 4 (April/May 1989): 17-19.

Woodsworth, Anne, et al. "The Model Research Library: Planning for the Future." *Journal of Academic Librarianship* 15, no. 3 (July 1989): 132-38.

Young, Philip H. "Library Research in the Future: A Prognostication." *College and Research Libraries News* 50, no. 1 (January 1989): 7-10.

Index

A

ABI-Inform, handout for, 108
ABLE: A Business Reference
Expert System, 204
Academic libraries, 231-35
consumer model for teaching
technologies, 231-32
taxonomic type model for
teaching technologies, 232-
33
transformation model for
teaching technologies, 233-
35
Adult learners
characteristics of, 32-34
computerized systems and, 7-8
See also Audience; Users
Age and learning, 7-8
AI. *See* Artificial intelligence
ALANET, 50-51
Alberico, Ralph, 125
American Psychological
Association (APA) booklets,
101

Andragogy, 7-8. *See also* Adult
learners
Anthropomorphizing computers,
7, 10, 66
APA (American Psychological
Association) booklets, 101
AQUAREF, 204
ArchiText, 218
Arizona State University, 73
Artificial intelligence (AI), 203
future of, 249
See also Expert systems
ASCII graphics, 216-17
Audience
for audiovisual productions,
168-69
for CAI programs, 187
See also Users
Audiovisual technologies, 157-75
advantages of, 159-61
audience for, 168-69
costs of, 163-64
design process, 167-68
disadvantages of, 161-62
distribution of, 173

W

X

The Authors

Linda Brew MacDonald is database services coordinator at the Bailey/Howe Library, University of Vermont. She is coauthor of *CD-ROM and Other Optical Information Systems: Implementation Issues for Libraries.*

Mara R. Saule is instruction coordinator at the Bailey/Howe Library, University of Vermont. She is also coauthor of *CD-ROM and Other Optical Information Systems: Implementation Issues for Libraries.*

Margaret W. Gordon is reference specialist at the Bailey/Howe Library, University of Vermont. She is author of a computer-assisted instruction program on online searching.

Craig A. Robertson is chemistry/physics librarian at the Cook Chemistry/Physics Library, University of Vermont. He is author of an expert system in chemistry reference.